Introducing Macrobiotic Cooking

D0826061

Aveline Kushi's
Introducing Macrobiotic Cooking

by Wendy Esko

Foreword by Michio Kushi

Japan Publications, Inc.

Note to the reader: It is advisable to seek the guidance of a qualified health professional and macrobiotic counselor before implementing the dietary and other suggestions for specific conditions presented in this book. It is essential that any reader who has any reason to suspect serious illness in themselves or their family members seek appropriate advice promptly. Neither this or any other book should be used as a substitute for qualified care or treatment.

Published by
Japan Publications,Inc.,Tokyo and New York

Distributors:
UNITED STATES: Kodansha America, Inc., through Farrar, Straus & Giroux, 19 Union Square West, New York, N.Y.10003. CANADA: Fitzhenry & Whiteside Ltd., 195 Allstate Parkway, Markham, Ontario L3R 4T8. BRITISH ISLES AND EUROPEAN CONTINENT: Premier Book Marketing Ltd., 1 Gower Street, London WC1E6HA. AUSTRALIA AND NEW ZEALAND: Bookwise International, 54 Crittenden Road, Findon, South Australia 5023. THE FAR EAST AND JAPAN: Japan Publications Trading Co., Ltd., 1-2-1, Sarugaku-cho, Chiyoda-ku, Tokyo 101.

First Edition: October 1987
Fourth printing: February 1995

LCCC No. 86–82994
ISBN 0–87040–690–6

Printed in U.S.A.

Foreword

We, all people on the planet, are confronting a vast current of physical and psychological degeneration. This current, which gathers force everyday, could lead the destiny of modern humanity toward extinction. From allergies to arthritis, from fatigue to cancer, and from depression to AIDS, the modern tidal wave of biological degeneration has swept across the planet, touching the lives of every family and every individual.

Over the past several decades, macrobiotic education has contributed, together with other approaches, to reversing this trend and realizing the biological and spiritual recovery of humanity. Cooking is the beginning of this process of recovery, when it is properly managed in accord with the natural order. Food is the essence of nature which is transformed into human life, and cooking accelerates this transformation toward a higher biological and spiritual quality.

For many years, Aveline Kushi and Wendy Esko have taught the proper way of cooking according to natural harmony with the order of the universe. Daily cooking that harmonizes humanity with nature needs to reflect changes in season, climate, weather, and personal condition. Aveline, Wendy, and their associates around the world have inspired and guided many thousands of people toward health and happiness through their practice, teaching, and example. Everyone on earth must gain the knowledge and ability to cook properly, in order to secure a more healthy, happy, and peaceful destiny. I sincerely hope that this introductory book will guide every family and individual toward health, peace, and the realization of their dreams.

Michio Kushi
Brookline, Massachusetts
January 1987

Preface

Professor Harvey Cox, of the Harvard Divinity School, once mentioned to my husband and I over lunch that students who ate during his field trips were more alert and seemed to remember more than those who attended trips during which no meals were served. It was an interesting observation because food is intimately related to every aspect of our lives. The simple truth is that we create our physical, mental, and spiritual condition by the foods we eat.

Since living in Boston we have always had two or three people staying in our home, for the purpose of studying macrobiotics. At first, not satisfied with other people's cooking, I prepared all the food myself. But as time passed, I came to enjoy the students' cooking. Some students have stayed with us for six months or a year, living just like members of the family. It has been very enjoyable to see the improvement in their way of cooking and in their health. Many have become excellent cooks and now have beautiful families.

One day, our Japanese friend, Mr. Matsui, saw a young lady cooking a macrobiotic meal in our home and asked, "Is she *uchideshi*?" *Uchideshi* is a Japanese word meaning to live and study in the traditional way. Mr. Matsui, who is a *Noh* drama professional, studied in this ancient manner, living in his master's house and training very strictly, for nearly twenty years.

In Japan, many traditional arts and crafts, such as sword smith, carpentry, tea ceremony, and restaurant cooking are learned by living and training in the master's or teacher's home. From a young age, I have heard how strict these teachers are and how difficult it is to study in this manner.

We did not adopt the disciplinarian ways of traditional Japanese teaching in our home. The students living with us are considered family members who are learning to apply the principles of macrobiotics in their daily lives.

Wendy Esko and her husband, Edward, lived with us for almost three years. Wendy was very busy helping to establish the East West Foundation and doing related work, and did not have much time to cook. But after she moved into her own home, she began cooking regularly, teaching cooking classes at the Kushi Institute and helping many people learn and adopt the macrobiotic way of life.

From time to time I meet her shopping. To fill the needs of her family and the students in her home, she buys a wide variety of macrobiotic groceries and I often tease her, saying, "Seems that you are having another party!"

I understand how the energy of the food Wendy has eaten has been changed into this cookbook. I am very happy to see this basic, yet comprehensive guide. The recipes and advice that follow will enable many people to learn the principles

8

of macrobiotic cooking and will help them to establish their own and their family's health and happiness.

Rather than being a fixed or limited regime, eating macrobiotically is as flexible and varied as the natural world itself. Macrobiotic dietary recommendations actually offer more variety than the standard fare and, as will be seen, the preparation and way of eating, when done properly, can become an expression of art in our daily lives.

The study of cooking is endless and we continually need to refine our technique in accordance with the everchanging circumstances of our lives. I encourage everyone to try new recipes and to experiment with different ways of preparation, but please do not forget to study the real principle of macrobiotics.

This book is an excellent guide for those beginning macrobiotic cooking. I hope readers can further their spiritual development through the practice of cooking. As the value of macrobiotics becomes apparent, please encourage and help others.

I would like to thank Wendy once again for her efforts in creating such a practical and informative cookbook.

Aveline Kushi
Brookline, Massachusetts

Acknowledgments

I extend my appreciation to George and Lima Ohsawa for introducing macrobiotics throughout the world, and for dedicating their lives to spreading this timeless teaching. I would like to take this opportunity to thank Michio and Aveline Kushi for their inspiration, guidance, and support. Through their example and teaching, they have given me and all of their other students an understanding of the order of the universe and the key which enables us to create our own health and happiness. I would also like to extend my special thanks to Michio for writing the foreword to this book and to Aveline for her preface.

I would also like to thank Edward and Elizabeth Esko, for their help in making initial publication of the book possible, and for their inspiration, guidance and support.

I thank my ancestors and parents for making it possible for me to be here to write this book, thus helping others find health and happiness.

For his patience, inspiration, encouragement, and love, I give special thanks to my husband, Edward. I express my gratitude to my six children—Eric, Mark, Daniel, Thomas, Julia, and Matthew—for the love, spontaneity, and insights they continually provide.

To Bonnie and Peter Harris, who illustrated and designed the original edition, I am very grateful. I also thank Christian Gautier for providing illustrations for the new edition.

I would like to express my gratitude to Phillip Jannetta for doing the editing and final proofreading of both the original and this revised edition. I also thank him for being the first person to try many of the recipes as he was editing the book, and offering his comments.

I would like to thank Olivia Oredson for typing the original manuscript, and I extend my appreciation to Judy Pingryn and Susi Ostreich for typing the revised edition.

To all the others, too numerous to mention, who I have studied with, talked to, taught, and learned from, thank you.

Finally, I would like to thank Mr. Iwao Yoshizaki and Mr. Yoshiro Fujiwara, respectively president and New York representative of Japan Publications, Inc., for publishing this book, and for their close association with macrobiotic education over the years.

I sincerely hope that, in some small way, this book can help readers establish health and happiness for themselves and their families. Please feel free to share the insights and understanding gained from the practice of macrobiotics, so that one peaceful world will come about in our lifetime.

Wendy Esko

Introduction

Nearly sixteen years ago, I noticed a sign in a natural food store in my hometown in upstate New York. The sign was an announcement for a series of natural food cooking classes.

I had always loved to cook, so I decided to attend the class in order to learn some new recipes. I had no conscious desire to drastically change my diet and no indication of the adventure I was about to set out on. The class was divided into two parts: a discussion of the principles of *yin* and *yang*, and a cooking demonstration. I was so taken with the new terms—yin and yang—and all that they implied, that I really did not hear much of the lecture. What I did hear, however, was interesting enough to keep me there.

After class, everyone had the opportunity to taste the meal which had been prepared. The first thing I noticed about the food was its pure and clean taste, which was unlike anything I had ever tasted before. Of course, the food was different from what I had been eating, and some items, such as sea vegetables and *miso*, were a little strange, but I could not forget how wholesome the food was and how good I felt after eating it. This impression was so strong that I knew then and there that I wanted to change my eating habits.

That evening, after class, I went home and cleaned my cupboards and refrigerator of all canned and packaged foods, sugar, dairy, animal food, and so on. The following day, I went to the natural food store and bought brown rice and other grains, beans, sea vegetables, miso, *tamari* soy sauce, fresh vegetables, and other whole foods. I completely restocked my kitchen. That evening I prepared my first macrobiotic meal. Having no idea how much of this new food to cook, I ended up eating millet soup, *hijiki*, brown rice, and pinto beans for several days.

Of course I did many things wrong in those beginning years, but I learned from my mistakes. I cooked with too much salt and became too yang. Then I would eat too much yin and end up getting sick. But gradually I learned the meaning of balance and how to judge and use yin and yang.

As I had no books about macrobiotics and only one cookbook by George Ohsawa, I knew nothing about the healing properties of the macrobiotic way of eating. However, as I continued to cook and eat in this way, I noticed that I began to feel healthy and strong. As I attended more cooking classes and became good friends with my teacher, I began to understand the infinite applicability of macrobiotics.

As I changed my diet, many of my friends began coming to dinner and asking how I prepared the food. Several nights a week, I would cook for about ten people at my home.

In 1973, I moved into a macrobiotic study house in Philadelphia. It was there that I first heard about Michio and Aveline Kushi. I knew then that I would someday go to Boston to study. I met my husband, Edward, in Philadelphia, and soon moved to Boston and began studying with Michio and Aveline, while working at the East West Foundation. It was at this time that I had the good fortune to live in the "Kushi house." I am deeply grateful for having had this opportunity. It provided me with the chance to experience the cooking of Mrs. Kushi and the other women who assisted her.

It is a great responsibility to cook for twenty people or even for one other person. By cooking for others, we are creating their mental, physical, and spiritual condition, and their biological destiny. A cook needs to be sensitive to each person's individual requirements. In many ways, the kitchen is like a shrine or a temple where the cook, or creator, directs the health and happiness of the family and of society.

The aim of macrobiotic cooking is to achieve balance or harmony, both within ourselves and with our surrounding environment. If our cooking is balanced, those who eat it will achieve a balanced condition through which they are able to work, study, play, or do whatever they desire. As we achieve balance within ourselves, our relationships with family, friends, and society will become harmonious. When we enter the kitchen, we should strive to develop a feeling of love and respect for nature, for the food that we are preparing, for society, and for the people who will eat our cooking.

I have been teaching cooking classes for more than ten years. Teaching is a great challenge and experience, and every time I give a class I learn something new. During each class I am often asked questions which inspire me to think, study, experience, create, and grow.

This simple, introductory book is based on what I have learned from cooking and studying with Aveline and others, from teaching public and private cooking classes at the Kushi Institute and elsewhere, and cooking for my family and friends.

We are very happy to present this new, revised edition. *Introducing Macrobiotic Cooking* was first published in November 1978, and since that time has gone through more than ten printings and has been distributed all over the world. Other cookbooks, inspired by the Kushis, including *Macrobiotic Cooking for Everyone*, which Edward and I wrote in 1980, following our trip to Japan; the *Changing Seasons Macrobiotic Cookbook*, which I wrote with Aveline in 1984; *Aveline Kushi's Complete Guide to Macrobiotic Cooking*, which our friend Alex Jack compiled with Aveline in 1985; the volumes in the *Macrobiotic Food and Cooking Series*; and *Macrobiotic Family Favorites*, a cookbook for children which Aveline and I wrote last year, have enlarged the macrobiotic cooking library, and have contributed to a better understanding of this all-important art. Each of these books is unique; they complement each other and present the art of cooking from a slightly different perspective.

In this new edition, I have added many new recipes, plus updated material on the standard macrobiotic diet, cooking utensils, and other useful information based on Aveline's cooking classes and teachings. It is my hope that this book will help fill the need for a simple, introductory guide to macrobiotic cooking.

Experience has taught me that it is helpful at first to try the recipes learned in class or found in cookbooks, at least until one becomes familiar with the use of a variety of foods as well as the art of balancing the yin and yang factors in meals. As our condition improves, instead of relying upon recipes, we begin to create our own cooking style. At that time, cookbooks or classes can be used as sources of new ideas.

Macrobiotics is not just a way of cooking, but a total way of life. Learning to cook macrobiotically is an endless study. The more we understand, the more we realize that there is no end to the learning process. With health and humility, life can remain an adventure no matter how old we grow. I hope that through studying and using the recipes in this book, readers can gain the ability to achieve their own health and happiness, and begin to create their own style of cooking.

I would like to thank all the people who have attended my cooking classes for providing me with the chance to learn and grow with them. I also thank the readers of this book for giving me the opportunity to write it. Preparing this book has been a learning experience which has influenced my entire life.

Wendy Esko
Becket, Massachusetts
February 1987

Contents

Chapter 1
Selecting Food Wisely

Cooking is the art of creating life itself. From it arises all of our pleasures and sadness, our success and failure, our health or sickness. The quality of our diet determines whether our life is one of continuing health and development, or one of decline and decay. Cooking is so vital that everyone is encouraged to develop a working knowledge of how to select and prepare basic foods. This education can begin at home as soon as children are able to understand, and can continue throughout life, since proper cooking is essential to every aspect of our destiny.

Our modern world is facing many difficulties brought on largely because we have ignored the vital importance of food and cooking. One need only refer to the statistics which record the epidemic increase in cancer, heart disease, stroke, AIDS, and other life-threatening illnesses, as well as social decline and disorder, to confirm just how widespread the challenges are. As large as these problems seem and as illusive as their solutions appear to be, each can be traced back to what takes place in the kitchen. In a very real sense, a healthy and peaceful world begins with our daily food.

Fortunately, in the midst of these modern problems, there can be found another, more positive trend, one that holds the promise of reversing this rapidly accelerating spiral of decline. From the steadily expanding natural foods movement, to the emerging interest in holistic and preventive health care, to the growing number of people seeking knowledge about macrobiotics, we see the development of a more complete understanding of the role of diet in human health and well-being.

Macrobiotic education is at the forefront of this positive trend. More than thirty years ago, Michio and Aveline Kushi began teaching about the direct influence that diet has on cancer, heart disease, diabetes, and other chronic illnesses. They also began to offer a practical approach to food and cooking that could be applied by anyone at home in the kitchen.

In the mid-1960s the Kushis started educational programs in the Boston area, after having moved there from New York. One result of their lectures and cooking classes was the opening of a small store in Boston's Back Bay. Named *Erewhon*, after Samuel Butler's utopian novel about a kingdom of happy and healthy people, the store made macrobiotic staples available to what eventually became known as the "macrobiotic community" and to the public at large. Erewhon eventually became the standard-bearer for the natural foods industry. The term "natural food" had been chosen by the Kushis to distinguish the products offered by Erewhon from other so-called "health" foods, including vitamins and supplements, that were generally available then.

As macrobiotic education began introducing a variety of healthful "new" foods to a wider public, including traditional staples like *miso*, *tamari* soy sauce, sea vegetables, *umeboshi* plums, *azuki* beans, *kuzu*, *tofu*, and others, Erewhon took a pioneering role in making them available and in encouraging farmers to grow organic rice and other essential foods.

As awareness of macrobiotics continued to grow—largely by word of mouth— an increasing number of people, many of them young, came to Boston to study. My husband and I were among those who journeyed to Boston in the early 1970s seeking a deeper understanding of macrobiotics, with the dream of contributing in some way to building a healthy and peaceful world. After arriving in Boston, we helped organize the East West Foundation, a non-profit organization founded by the Kushis, and it was during these years that I had many opportunities to observe and study Aveline's approach to food and cooking.

Of the many projects started in those days, promoting the macrobiotic view of cancer and other chronic diseases continues to have a far-reaching impact. Interestingly, this effort was started at a time when the macrobiotic approach began to receive support from voices in the medical and scientific communities. One by one, leading public health agencies started to announce that diet was a major factor in the cause and prevention of chronic disease, and advocated dietary guidelines paralleling macrobiotics. Of the many reports on diet and health to appear during that period, *Dietary Goals for the United States*, prepared in 1977 by the U.S. Senate Select Committee on Nutrition and Human Needs, stands as a landmark. *Dietary Goals* focused public attention on the link between the modern way of eating and chronic illnesses such as cancer and heart disease, along with the need for everyone to begin making healthful dietary changes. The recommendations to eat less animal fat, sugar, and processed foods, and to eat more whole cereal grains and vegetables are close to those of macrobiotics.

The movement toward healthful eating received further support as a result of publication of another landmark report, *Diet, Nutrition and Cancer*, in 1982. Compiled by the National Academy of Sciences, *Diet, Nutrition and Cancer* promised, as author Alex Jack put it, to "end the second class status of dietary research in this country." As with *Dietary Goals*, the Academy's dietary recommendations for preventing cancer were close to macrobiotics.

Evidence linking diet and cancer continues to accumulate. In December, 1986, the *New England Journal of Medicine* published an article on the link between high-fat diets and colon cancer. In a study quoted in the article, men with high cholesterol levels were found to be about 60 percent more likely than those with normal levels to develop colon cancer. Another study found a relationship between high cholesterol and colon polyps, which frequently become cancerous.

In research conducted more than ten years ago by Harvard Medical School, people eating macrobiotically were found to have cholesterol levels that were substantially below the normally high averages for modern people. These studies led Dr. William Castelli, director of the Framingham Heart Study, to remark: "These are levels at which we rarely, if ever, see heart disease." The value of macrobiotics in preventing heart disease is well established, and as data on cancer and diet continues to come in, macrobiotics may soon gain wide acceptance as the optimum diet for preventing cancer.

More recently, people with AIDS and other immune-deficiency syndromes have begun to apply macrobiotics in hopes of improving their conditions. Since 1984, a group of men in the New York area with AIDS have been practicing macrobiotics under the guidance of the Kushis and macrobiotic doctors such as Martha Cottrell, M.D. Their blood levels are checked periodically by researchers at Boston University, and so far, the results are encouraging. The experience of these men has opened the possibility of offering macrobiotics as an answer to the problem of immune-deficiency syndromes.*

Macrobiotics is also gaining recognition as a possible solution for social problems. In Boston, the Kushi Foundation is now working with leaders in the field of corrections and mental health to introduce macrobiotics in prisons, correctional centers, and mental-health facilities. A summary of these efforts, including reports by people who adopted macrobiotics while in prison, is included in the book, *Crime and Diet: The Macrobiotic Approach*.

The macrobiotic approach offers everyone a complete yet flexible understanding of the way to select, prepare, and eat our daily foods. Its principles are based on the order of nature. The application of these principles allows us to create the optimum diet under any circumstances. It is our hope that everyone seeking a more natural way of living can use these principles as the basis for health and well-being.

---

* For additional information, please refer to *AIDS: Cause and Solution—The Macrobiotic Approach* by Michio Kushi and Martha Cottrell, M.D., Japan Publications, Inc.

MAKING BALANCE

Through food, each of us can achieve balance with the environment. This is the aim of macrobiotic cooking. The innumerable factors that we use to create balance can be understood in terms of two fundamental tendencies, known in macrobiotics as yin and yang.

Yin represents the primary force of expansion in the universe, and *yang*, the force of contraction. Together they create the universe and everything within it. The ceaseless rhythm of change or movement underlying reality is governed by these two forces.

Although the terms yin and yang were first used in China (the Japanese refer to them as *In* and *Yo*), the concept they represent is not particularly Oriental. In his groundbreaking book, *The Way of Life*, Rev. John Ineson cites many passages in the Bible that point to a similar understanding. In Genesis, for example, yin and yang are referred to as "heaven and earth," while many passages in Ecclesiastes talk about life's alternating rhythms.

Yin and yang frequently appear in contemporary writing as well. In a recent essay in *Time* looking at the differences between Massachusetts and Texas, these states were referred to as the "yin and yang" of American life. In his book, *Great Expectations: America and the Baby Boom Generation*, Landon Jones states, "By having fewer children, the baby boomers have left us with a problem that, like its own tumultuous presence, will stay with us for a lifetime. It is the baby bust generation, yin to the baby boom's yang, which is now growing up behind it." (If we speak in terms of the baby boom's powerful impact on modern culture, we can say that it is more yang. However, in terms of size, a larger number of people would be more yin and a smaller number, more yang.)

In macrobiotic cooking, we use yin and yang to create balance. For example, the factors we use in cooking can be separated into yin and yang categories. Fire, pressure, salt, and time (aging) are more yang, while oil, water, lack of pressure, and freshness are more yin. In macrobiotic cooking, we balance these yin and yang factors in our daily preparation of food. Foods themselves are also classified into yin and yang, for example, more yin vegetable foods, and more yang animal foods; more yin tropical vegetation, and more yang products from colder climates; and more yin processed and chemicalized foods and more yang naturally processed and organic products.

Yin and yang are not absolute but are a matter of degree. Strawberries, for example, are yin relative to azuki beans, but are more yang than expanded tropical fruits such as bananas. In macrobiotics, we try to avoid extremes of either yin or yang while selecting foods that are more centrally balanced.

Within each category of foods, there are yin and yang varieties. Among whole grains and their close relatives, for example, buckwheat grows in colder northern climates. It absorbs water rapidly and is well suited to places with short growing seasons. Buckwheat is a more yang plant. Corn, on the other hand, is more yin.

It needs a longer time to grow and was traditionally cultivated in bright, sunny climates such as Central and South America.

Cooking, for the most part, is the process whereby we take more yin vegetable-quality foods and yangize them with fire, pressure, salt, aging, and other factors to varying degrees, in order to balance our natural and social environments. In all but the most extreme polar climates, the ideal primary foods are whole cereal grains and local vegetables, with a variety of supplementary products.

Proceeding along the scale from yang to yin, daily foods can be classified as follows:

- *More yang*—salt, eggs, meat, poultry, hard, salty cheeses, fish and seafood
- *More centrally balanced*—whole cereal grains, beans, temperate vegetables (root, ground, and leafy), seeds and nuts, temperate fruits, grain sweeteners, traditional vinegars such as brown rice and umeboshi, non-aromatic, non-stimulant herbal teas
- *More yin*—tropical fruits, refined grains, milk and butter, concentrated sweeteners such as maple syrup, honey, and refined sugar, alcohol, spices, ice cream, chemical additives, and most drugs and medications

In order to create the ideal condition for continuing health and adaptability, it is necessary to choose foods which are relatively near the center of the yin and yang scale. The ideal ratio between the yin and yang factors in our daily foods is about seven to one (5: 1 to 10: 1), as this ratio produces optimum balance with our planetary environment. Among possible daily food items, whole cereal grains come closest to this ratio and thus comprise the principal food in the human diet.

Locally grown, seasonal vegetables comprise the main secondary food, followed by beans, sea vegetables, some animal food, preferably in the form of low-fat, white-meat fish, locally grown seasonal fruits, seeds and nuts, and other occasional supplements. Foods from either extreme of the scale, such as more yang foods like meat and animal products, and more yin items such as sugar, tropical fruits, and drugs and medications, will produce an excessive or unbalanced condition within the body, leading eventually to illnesses of various types.

We can summarize the principles of macrobiotics as follows:

1) *Eat according to tradition.* Until recently, the majority of the world's population based their diet around whole grains and local vegetables. With very few exceptions, this trend was universal—appearing in the dietary customs of people in both East and West. In fact, we can trace the use of cereal grains as a principal food back to the origins of the human species itself. Animal products, including dairy foods, were used much less frequently than at present, generally under unusual circumstances.

2) *Vary diet according to climate.* The diet of someone living in Brazil obviously differs from that of someone living in Montreal. More yin, northern climates require the selection of slightly more yang food items along with

emphasis on more yang factors in cooking, while balance is maintained in a tropical climate through the selection of more yin food items, with the use of less salt, pressure, and cooking times. We violate the ecological order of eating when we begin to include items in our diet which have come from climates which differ from our own. Therefore, people living in temperate climates are advised to avoid, whenever possible, the use of bananas, pineapples, citrus fruits, coffee, spices, and other products which originate in the tropics. It is possible, however, to maintain our health by importing high-quality food items which have grown in climates similar to those in which we live, for example, sea vegetables from temperate regions in the Far East.

3) *Vary diet with the changing seasons.* Today, most people eat a relatively uniform diet throughout the year. For example, ice cream and cold soft drinks are often consumed throughout the winter, while eggs, meat and other animal products are frequently consumed during the heat of the summer. Naturally, a diet of this type permits very little adaptation to the changing seasons. In macrobiotics, we try to harmonize our condition with these seasonal changes by emphasizing more yang foods and cooking methods during the cold winter months and by serving more yin, fresh and lightly cooked foods during the summer.

As much as possible, one's diet should be based on foods which are naturally available in one's area during a particular season, or which can be stored without the artificial methods of freezing, canning, or chemical preservation. Cereal grains, beans, sea vegetables, fermented foods such as miso, tamari soy sauce and pickles, and other foods that can be naturally stored in a cool, dry place throughout the year, comprise the majority of a diet for health.

4) *Vary diet according to personal need.* Since everyone is unique, no two people should or ever can eat the same diet. Every person has different needs based on such variables as age, sex, season of birth, previous eating habits, physical condition, type of activity, and others. All of these can be taken into account when we select and prepare our daily food.

Through macrobiotics, we can easily maintain our physical, mental, and spiritual health. However, health is not the final goal of macrobiotics, but only a means to the enjoyment of life. Simple, natural, whole foods, when properly prepared and aesthetically served, are actually the most appealing to our taste. Through macrobiotics, our appreciation of tastes expands tremendously. Our food can at all times be delicious and appealing so that we thoroughly enjoy it. If this is not the case, or if we feel we are missing something in our daily meals, our application is incomplete.

As can be seen, the macrobiotic way of eating is not a certain fixed regime, and cannot be called a diet. It is based on flexible adaptation to our ever-changing environment.

In the beginning, the macrobiotic principle—yin and yang—may seem strange or difficult to apply. However, keep in mind that no matter what we are eating, we are always balancing these two complementary and antagonistic factors in our diet as well as in every aspect of life. If, for example, we take too much salt, we will instinctively be drawn to liquid, sugar, or other yin foods. This intuitive capacity develops even before birth and continues throughout life. Macrobiotics is nothing but the refinement of this intuition through the conscious application of the order of the universe, or yin and yang.

Once we are able to use natural and healthful ingredients to create attractive and delicious meals, it will become clear that we are not following any particular diet but instead are simply eating in the way a human being was intended to. At the same time, we will begin to realize that proper food is the key to a healthy, free, and happy life—the secret which has been in front of us all along.

STANDARD MACROBIOTIC DIET

The standard macrobiotic way of eating offers an incredible variety of foods and cooking methods to choose from. The guidelines that follow are broad and flexible. They can be applied when selecting the best foods for oneself and one's family.

The guidelines presented in this chapter are appropriate for people who live in temperate regions such as North America and Europe, and require modification by those living in tropical, subtropical, or polar climates.

Whole Cereal Grains

Whole cereal grains are the staff of life and are an essential part of a healthful way of eating. For people living in temperate climates, whole grains may comprise up to 50 to 60 percent of daily intake. Below is a list of the whole grains and their products that may be included:

Brown Rice
Brown rice—short, medium, and
  long grain
Genuine brown rice cream
Puffed brown rice
Brown rice flakes

Sweet Brown Rice
Sweet brown rice grain
Mochi (pounded sweet rice)
Sweet brown rice flour products

Wild Rice
Wild rice grain

Barley
Barley grain
Pearl barley
Pearled barley
Puffed barley
Barley flour products

Whole Wheat
Whole wheat berries
Whole wheat bread
Whole wheat *chapati*
Whole wheat noodles and pastas
Whole wheat flakes
Whole wheat flour products such
  as crackers, *matzos*, muffins,

The Standard Macrobiotic Diet*

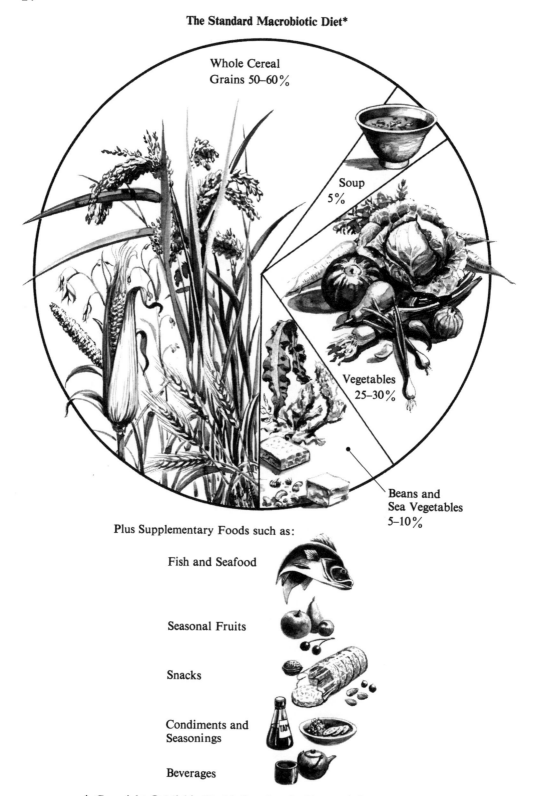

Whole Cereal
Grains 50–60%

Soup
5%

Vegetables
25–30%

Beans and
Sea Vegetables
5–10%

Plus Supplementary Foods such as:

Fish and Seafood

Seasonal Fruits

Snacks

Condiments and
Seasonings

Beverages

* Copyright © Michio Kushi. Reprinted with permission.

and others
Couscous
Bulgur
Fu (baked puffed wheat gluten)
Seitan (wheat gluten)

Millet
Millet grain
Millet flour products
Puffed millet

Oats
Whole oats
Steel-cut oats
Rolled oats
Oatmeal
Oat flakes
Oat flour products

Corn
Corn on the cob
Corn grits

Cornmeal
Arepas
Corn flour products such as bread,
    muffins, and so on
Puffed corn
Popped corn

Rye
Rye grain
Rye bread
Rye flakes
Rye flour products

Buckwheat
Buckwheat groats
Buckwheat noodles and pastas
Buckwheat flour products such as
    pancakes, and so on

Other Traditional Grains
Triticale, and so on

Cooked whole cereal grains are preferable to flour products, or to cracked or rolled grains. In general, we recommend keeping the consumption of flour products, or cracked or rolled grains, to less than 15 to 20 percent of daily grain intake.

Whole grains can be appetizingly prepared in a variety of ways. They can be pressure-cooked, boiled, steamed, baked, fried, sautéed, or roasted. They can be combined with each other or with other foods. Whole grains are delicious when cooked with vegetables, beans, sea vegetables, or fish or seafood. They are wonderful in soups, and make creamy breakfast porridges.

Whole grains are especially good when mildly seasoned with either sea salt, sea vegetables, umeboshi plums, or other natural seasonings. How grains are seasoned depends on the age, condition, and preference of each person being cooked for.

Soups

Soups may comprise about 5 percent of each person's daily intake. For most people, that averages out to one or two cups or bowls of soup per day, depending on individual desires and preferences. Soups can include vegetables, grains, beans, sea vegetables, noodles or other grain products, bean products such as tofu, *tempeh*, or *natto*, or occasionally fish or seafood. Soups can be moderately seasoned with either miso, tamari soy sauce, sea salt, umeboshi plums or paste, or occasionally with ginger. Vegetables may occasionally be sautéed in a little sesame or corn oil for a different flavor. Again, the amount of seasoning can vary for each person.

Soups can be made thick and rich, or as simple clear broths. Vegetable, grain, or bean stews can also be enjoyed. Thick, creamy soups can be made by puréeing the ingredients or by adding whole grains. Prepare hot, warming soups, or cool, room-temperature soups to suit changes in the weather.

Garnishes such as scallions, parsley, *nori* sea vegetable, grated ginger, lemon slices, and croutons can be used in soups. Garnishes enhance the appearance and flavor of soups.

Vegetables

Approximately 25 to 30 percent of each person's daily intake can include vegetables. Nature provides an incredible variety to choose from. Some of those recommended for regular use include:

Acorn squash	*Jinenjo*
Bok choy	Jerusalem artichoke
Broccoli	Kale
Burdock root	Kohlrabi
Buttercup squash	Lamb's-quarters
Butternut squash	Leeks
Cabbage	Lotus root
Carrots	Mushrooms
Carrot tops	Mustard greens
Cauliflower	Onion
Celery	Parsley
Celery root	Parsnips
Chinese cabbage	Patty pan squash
Chives	Pumpkin
Collard greens	Radish
Coltsfoot	Red cabbage
Cucumber	Romaine lettuce
Daikon	Scallions
Daikon greens	*Shiitake* mushrooms
Dandelion greens	Snap beans
Dandelion root	Summer squash
Endive	Turnip
Escarole	Turnip greens
Green beans	Watercress
Green peas	Wax beans
Hokkaido pumpkin	Wild grasses that have been
Hubbard squash	widely used for centuries
Iceberg lettuce	

Vegetables can be served as pressed, boiled, or raw salad; or can be boiled, baked, steamed, broiled, sautéed in oil or water, deep-fried, pickled, or prepared "waterless" style. They can be served in soups, or with grains, beans, or sea vegetables. They can also be used in *sushi*, served with noodles and pasta, cooked with fish or seafood, used in aspics or desserts, or cooked alone. Vegetables may be lightly seasoned with miso, tamari soy sauce, sea salt, *mirin* (fermented sweetener made from sweet brown rice), brown rice vinegar, umeboshi (plums, paste, or vinegar), ginger, or other traditional natural seasonings. Again, the use of seasonings is best adapted to the actual needs of each person.

Beans

About 5 to 10 percent of an individual's daily meals may include beans or bean products. Recommended varieties include any of the following:

Azuki beans
Black-eyed peas
Black soybeans
Black turtle beans
Chick-peas (garbanzo beans)
Great northern beans
Kidney beans
Lentils (green and red)
Lima beans
Mung beans
Navy beans
Pinto beans
Soybeans
Split peas
Whole dried peas

Bean sprouts
Other beans included in traditional diets

Bean Products
Dried tofu (soybean curd which has been frozen and dried)
Fresh tofu
Natto (fermented soybeans)
Okara (pulp or residue left from making tofu)
Yuba (dried soy milk)
Tempeh (fermented soybeans or combination of soybeans and grains)

Beans and their products may be pressure-cooked, boiled, steamed, roasted, baked, or fermented. Fresh tofu can be pickled in miso for several days to make *tofu cheese.*

Beans and bean products are more easily digested when cooked with sea salt, miso, or *kombu.* They may also be cooked with vegetables, chestnuts, dried apples, or raisins, or sweetened with barley malt or rice syrup.

Miso, sea salt, tamari soy sauce, or barley or rice syrup may be used as seasonings. Tofu or tempeh may be fried occasionally in a little sesame or corn oil.

Sea Vegetables

Sea vegetables may be used daily in cooking. Side dishes can be made with *hijiki* or *arame*, and may be eaten every other day. Sea vegetables may be used in soups, with beans, and in other dishes on a daily basis, and may include any of the following:

Arame	*Mekabu*
Agar-agar	*Nekombu*
Dulse	Nori
Hijiki	*Wakame*
Irish moss	Other traditionally used sea
Kombu	vegetables

Sea vegetables may be boiled, steamed, deep-fried, roasted, toasted, pickled, used in waterless cooking, dried, or soaked and eaten in salads. They can be cooked alone, or with beans, grains, noodles, or fish and seafood, and can be included in vegetable dishes, kanten, aspics, sauces, soups, and salads. They make tasty and nutritious condiments. Agar-agar is used in kanten desserts, while nori and dulse are often used as garnishes.

Fish and Seafood

Fish and seafood can be eaten on occasion to supplement the categories of food outlined above. The amounts eaten can vary, depending upon each person's needs and desires. Fish is usually eaten one to three times per week and usually does not exceed 20 percent of the total amount of food eaten in that day. We recommend choosing varieties that are lowest in saturated fat and most easily digested.

Carp	Littleneck clams
Cod	Clams
Dried fish	Crab
Small dried fish (*iriko*)	Octopus
Flounder	Oyster
Haddock	Lobster
Halibut	Shrimp
Herring	
Scrod	*Seafood for infrequent use*
Smelt	(not for regular consumption)
Snapper	Bluefish
Sole	Salmon
Trout	Sardines
Other white-meat fish	Swordfish
	Tuna
Seafood for occasional use	Other blue-skinned and red-meat
Cherrystone clams	fish

Seafood can be eaten as *sashimi* or sushi, or can be marinated, steamed, boiled, broiled, baked, sautéed, pan-fried, deep-fried (*tempura*), and dried and then boiled, steamed, or baked.

Fish flakes or pickled or smoked fish may also be used. Seafood may occasionally be added to soups and stews, cooked as a side dish, or with vegetables, grains (*paella*), or sea vegetables. It may also be used as a seasoning in soups or vegetable dishes.

Garnishes are especially important in balancing fish and seafood. Recommended garnishes include: chopped scallions, chopped parsley, grated daikon, grated ginger, grated radish, grated green Japanese horseradish (*wasabi*), grated horse-radish, shredded daikon, raw fresh vegetable salad, lemon slices, fresh beefsteak plant leaves (green *shiso*), and other natural garnishes.

Fish dishes may be seasoned mildly with sea salt, tamari soy sauce, miso, black peppercorns, red pepper, rice vinegar, sesame, corn, safflower, mustard seed, or olive oil, mirin, or umeboshi vinegar. A variety of delicious sauces for fish or seafood can be made with tofu, kuzu, or oil. As always, the use of seasonings can reflect the needs and desires of each person.

Fruit

In general, fruit can be enjoyed three or four times a week. Locally grown or temperate-climate fruit is best. Tropical fruit is not recommended for regular use for those living in a temperate region. Below are some varieties of fruit that can be eaten in a temperate climate:

Apples	Plums
Apricots	Raisins
Blackberries	Raspberries
Cantaloupe	Strawberries
Grapes	Tangerines
Honeydew melon	Watermelon
Lemons	Wild berries
Mulberries	Other fruit grown in temperate
Persimmon	regions
Peaches	

Fruit may be served fresh, soaked in lightly salted water, or grated. It can also be boiled, baked, or steamed. Fruit juice can be used as a beverage or flavoring, and fruit preserve can be spread on bread, rice cakes, or other whole grain products. It can be used in stuffing or filling, as a dessert, and as a flavoring in kuzu or agar-agar gelatin. It can also be baked in breads or muffins. Dried fruit can be eaten as a snack, garnish, or used in desserts. Again, how much and how often fruit is eaten depends on each person.

Pickles

Pickles can be eaten frequently as a supplement to main dishes. They stimulate appetite and help digestion. Some varieties can be bought pre-packaged in natural food stores, while others can be prepared at home. Certain varieties take just a few hours to prepare, while others require more time—from a few days to a few seasons.

Foods Used Often in Making Pickles

Burdock root	Radishes, red and white
Broccoli	Red cabbage
Cabbage	Scallions
Carrots	Squash
Cauliflower	Turnips
Chinese cabbage	Apricots
Cucumbers	Anchovies
Daikon	Caviar
Leeks	Herring
Lotus root	Salmon
Mustard greens	Sardines
Olives	Other foods traditionally used to
Onions	make pickles
Pumpkin	

A wide range of pickles are fine for regular use, including salt, salt and water, bran, miso, tamari soy sauce, *takuan*, umeboshi, vinegar, and other pickles. Sauerkraut may also be used. Let the needs and desires of each person determine the frequency and types of pickles served.

Nuts

Nuts can be eaten from time to time as snacks and garnishes. They can also be cooked with grains or used in desserts.

Almonds	*Nuts Used Less Often*
Chestnuts	Brazil nuts
Filberts	Cashews
Peanuts	Macadamia nuts
Pecans	Other nuts eaten as a part of
Pinenuts	traditional diets
Small Spanish nuts	
Walnuts	

Nuts can be served in a variety of ways. They can be roasted with or without sea salt, sweetened with barley malt or rice syrup, or seasoned with tamari soy sauce. They can be ground into nut butter, shaved and served as a topping, garnish, or ingredient in various dishes, cooked in breads, cookies, muffins, pastries, pies, and other desserts, or served with dried fruit as a snack.

Seeds

A variety of seeds may also be eaten from time to time, including:

Black sesame seeds
White sesame seeds
Pumpkin seeds
Squash seeds
Sunflower seeds
Poppy seeds

Plum seeds
Umeboshi plum seeds
Alfalfa seeds
Other seeds eaten in traditional
  diets

Seeds may be used in making condiments such as *gomashio*, can be served dried and plain, or can be roasted and served plain or with a little tamari soy sauce as snacks. They can also be baked in cookies, crackers, breads, and cakes, or used in candies and other natural snacks. Seeds also make appetizing garnishes for grains, soups, vegetables, beans, fish and seafood, fruit, and desserts.

Seeds are delicious when seasoned with sea salt, tamari soy sauce, miso, barley malt or rice syrup, or other traditional seasonings.

Snacks

Macrobiotics includes the moderate use of a variety of natural snacks. Please try a wide variety to discover which ones family members like best.

Grain-based Snacks
  Cookies, crackers, wafers, pan-
    cakes, muffins, bread, puffed
    brown rice, barley, oats, millet,
    corn, popcorn
  Mochi
  Noodles and pasta
  Rice balls
  Rice cakes
  Homemade sushi
  Roasted grains
  Other traditionally used and
    commonly consumed natural
    snacks

Bean-based Snacks
  Roasted beans
  Boiled beans

Nut-based Snacks
  Nuts roasted and seasoned with
    sea salt
  Nuts roasted and seasoned with
    tamari soy sauce
  Nuts roasted and seasoned with
    barley malt
  Nuts roasted and seasoned with
    rice syrup
  Nuts used in cookies, crackers,
    and as an ingredient in other
    baked flour products

Condiments

The standard macrobiotic way of eating includes the use of a variety of condiments, some daily and others more occasionally. Small amounts can be sprinkled on foods to adjust their taste and nutritional value or to help stimulate appetite. Condiments are commonly used on grains, soups, vegetable dishes, bean dishes, and sometimes with desserts.

Gomashio (roasted sesame seeds and sea salt)
Sea vegetable powder
Sea vegetable powder with roasted sesame seeds
Tekka (condiment made from soybean miso, sesame oil, burdock, lotus root, carrots, and ginger root)
Umeboshi plum (pickled plum)
Umeboshi plum and raw scallions or onions
Shio kombu (kombu cooked with tamari soy sauce and water)
Chopped shiso leaves (pickled beefsteak plant leaves)
Roasted shiso leaves
Green nori (*aonori*)
Yellow mustard (used mainly for fish and seafood)
Green mustard (used mainly for fish and seafood)
Cooked miso with scallions or onions
Cooked nori condiment
Roasted sesame seeds
Other traditionally used and commonly consumed condiments

Seasonings

A variety of seasonings are used in macrobiotic cooking. Recommended seasonings are those which are naturally processed from vegetable foods, and those which have been traditionally used throughout the world. The use of seasonings should be kept moderate and adequate for personal needs. Seasonings include:

Unrefined sea salt
Soy sauce
Tamari soy sauce (fermented soybean and grain sauce)
Miso* (fermented soybean and grain paste)
  Examples:
    · Rice miso
    · Barley miso
    · Soybean miso
    · Sesame miso
    · Other traditionally processed misos
Rice vinegar
Brown rice vinegar
Umeboshi vinegar
Sauerkraut brine
Barley malt
Rice syrup
Grated ginger root
Grated daikon
Grated radish
Horseradish
Umeboshi paste
Umeboshi plum
Lemon juice
Tangerine juice
Orange juice
Wasabi paste (grated Japanese horseradish)
Yellow mustard paste
Sesame oil

* Dark miso has been fermented for a longer period of time. Light miso has been fermented for a shorter period of time.

Corn oil
Safflower oil
Mustard seed oil
Olive oil
Mirin
Amazaké (fermented sweet brown
    rice beverage)

Freshly ground black pepper
Saké lees (residue in making saké)
Saké (fermented rice wine)
Other natural seasonings which
    have been traditionally used and
    commonly consumed

Garnishes

A variety of garnishes can be used to create balance among dishes, and to create easier digestion. The use of garnishes depends upon individual needs and desires. Garnishes include:

Grated daikon—used mainly as a garnish for the following:
- Fish and seafood
- Mochi
- Buckwheat noodles and pasta
- Natto
- Tempeh

Grated radish—Used mainly as a garnish for the following:
- Same as above

Grated horseradish—used mainly as a garnish for the following:
- Same as above

Chopped scallions—used mainly as a garnish for the following:
- Noodle and pasta dishes
- Fish and seafood
- Natto
- Tempeh

The following:
- Grated ginger
- Wasabi paste
- Freshly ground pepper
- Lemon pieces

may be used mainly as a garnish for:
- Soup
- Noodle and pasta dishes
- Fish and seafood

The following:
- Red pepper
- Freshly ground pepper
- Wasabi paste

may be used mainly as a garnish for:
- Soup
- Noodle and pasta dishes
- Fish and seafood
- Natto
- Tempeh

Desserts

A variety of desserts may be eaten from time to time. Desserts are usually served at the end of the main meal. A variety of ideas for making specific desserts are presented in the chapters that follow. Desserts may include:

Azuki beans sweetened with barley malt or rice syrup
Azuki beans cooked with chestnuts
Azuki beans cooked with squash
Kuzu sweetened with barley malt, rice syrup, fresh fruit, or dried fruit
Agar-agar cooked with barley malt, rice syrup, fresh fruit, or dried fruit

Cooked fruit
Dried fruit
Fruit pies including apple, peach, strawberry, berry, and other temperate climate fruit
Fruit crunch including apple, peach, strawberry, berry, and other temperate climate fruit
Grain desserts sweetened with dried fruit, barley malt, rice syrup,

amazaké, fresh fruit
· Examples of grain desserts: Couscous cake, Indian pudding, rice pudding, and other similar naturally sweetened desserts
Baked flour desserts such as cookies, cakes, pies, muffins, breads, and others prepared with natural sweeteners including fruit and grain sweeteners

Beverages

A variety of beverages may be consumed daily or occasionally. Amounts can vary according to each person's needs and weather conditions. Beverages can be used to comfortably satisfy the desire for liquid. Beverages may include:

Bancha twig tea
Bancha stem tea
Roasted rice with bancha twig tea
Roasted barley with bancha twig tea
Kombu tea
Spring water
100 percent cereal grain coffee
Amazaké
Dandelion tea
Lotus root tea
Soybean milk
Burdock root tea
Mu tea
Other traditionally used and commonly consumed non-stimulating, nonaromatic natural herbal teas (made from seeds, leaves, stems, bark, or roots)

Alcoholic beverages
Saké—more naturally fermented quality

Beer of various kinds—more naturally fermented quality
Wines of various kinds—more naturally fermented quality
Other grain and fruit-based weak alcoholic beverages that have been fermented naturally

Fruit juice
Apple juice
Grape juice
Apricot juice
Cider

Vegetable juice
Carrot juice
Celery juice
Juice from leafy green vegetables
Beet juice
Barley green juice
Other juices made from vegetables that have been traditionally grown in a temperate climate

Additional Foods

In some cases, the standard macrobiotic way of eating can be temporarily modified to include other foods. These modifications can be made according to individual requirements and necessity; though within usual macrobiotic practice, additional foods are usually not necessary to maintain health and well-being.

THE WAY OF EATING

To establish health and well-being, we recommend the following practices:

1) Eat regularly. Adults may eat two to three meals a day, and persons who are very physically active can eat four meals a day. Children may eat more often if desired, but overeating is not recommended.
2) Include whole grains or grain products in every meal. They can represent roughly 50 percent of the daily intake of food. The word "meal" actually means "crushed whole grain."
3) Use plenty of variety when selecting and preparing daily foods. Proper combinations and cooking methods are also important.
4) The best cooking is performed with a peaceful mind, and with love and care. Think always of health and happiness when cooking.
5) Snacks are best eaten in moderate amounts, and not to the extent that they replace regular meals.
6) Beverages can be consumed comfortably, depending on each person's needs and desires.
7) Try not to eat before bedtime, preferably three hours, except in unusual circumstances. Children may eat closer to bedtime if desired.
8) Chew very well, until each mouthful becomes liquid. Eat as calmly and peacefully as possible.
9) Individuals may eat as much food as they need or desire, provided chewing is thorough and proportions are correct.
10) Encourage everyone to eat with the spirit of gratitude and appreciation. Meals can begin with a short prayer or expression of thanks, such as many people practiced until modern times.

LEARNING TO COOK

Macrobiotic cooking is actually very simple once basic techniques are mastered. Before learning the basics, however, it is easy to make mistakes. When starting to cook this way, it is important to learn a wide variety of basic dishes. Recipes and cookbooks are of course helpful, but the best way to learn is to attend classes where one can actually see foods prepared and can taste them. Weekly dinners—which many macrobiotic people and centers sponsor—are also helpful, as they offer the chance to see and taste a balanced meal and to talk and socialize with other people. Most introductory cooking classes run for six to eight weeks and include the basic dishes needed to get started. Introductory cooking classes also include suggestions for setting up a kitchen and locating foods and utensils.

Do not hesitate to seek advice from other people who practice macrobiotics. Every now and then take a dish or two that one has made for them to taste, and ask questions and freely discuss any problems that may have come up.

The following ideas can be kept in mind as one begins to cook macrobiotically:

1) Select materials wisely, from organic products naturally grown, in season, and from the climate or region in which one lives.

2) Try to use whole natural foods that are fresh until the time they are cooked.

3) When cutting vegetables or other foods, do them individually and place each separately so as not to mix their qualities. Try not to mix vegetables until cooking begins. Also, wipe the cutting board clean after cutting each vegetable.

4) Try to cut vegetables as elegantly and gracefully as possible so that each cut is evenly balanced.

5) As much as possible, allow foods to mix themselves during the natural process of cooking.

6) Use seasonings moderately. Unrefined sea salt, cold-pressed vegetable oils, natural grain sweeteners, whole grain vinegar, and other recommended seasonings can be used to enhance the natural flavor of food. It is better if the taste of the seasoning is not so evident.

7) The highest-quality fire for cooking is that produced by wood; next, charcoal; next, coal; followed by gas. Electric and microwave cooking are best avoided for maximum health.

8) The best quality of water for cooking or drinking is clean well, spring, or mountain-stream water. City water can be used for washing foods or utensils. Distilled water is best avoided.

9) Strong spicy seasonings are usually not recommended in temperate climates.

10) Dishes are more appealing when beautifully and elegantly presented. The natural colors of foods can be harmonized through cooking to create colorful and attractive dishes.

11) Keep the kitchen and dining area clean and orderly. Keep the atmosphere of the dining area quiet and calm, and maintain a peaceful, loving, and joyful mind while cooking or eating.

With study and practice, anyone can learn to create beautiful, nutritious, and appetizing meals for themselves and for others. We encourage everyone to study how to cook. The art of cooking is truly the art of creating a healthy and happy life and a peaceful and healthy world.

SUGGESTIONS FOR HEALTHY LIVING

Together with eating well, there are a number of practices that we recommend for a healthier and more natural life. Practices such as keeping physically active and using natural cooking utensils, fabrics, and materials in the home are especially recommended. In the past, people lived more closely to nature and ate a more balanced, natural diet. With each generation, we have gotten further and further from our roots in nature and have experienced a corresponding rise in chronic illnesses. The suggestions presented below complement a balanced, natural diet and can help one enjoy more satisfying and harmonious living.

- Live each day happily without being worried about one's health. Keep active mentally and physically. Sing everyday, and encourage others to sing as well.
- Greet everyone and everything with gratitude, particularly offering thanks before and after each meal. Encourage everyone to give thanks for their food and their natural environment.
- Try to get to bed before midnight and to get up early in the morning.
- Try not to wear synthetic clothing or woolen articles directly against the skin. Wear cotton instead. Keep jewelry and accessories as simple, graceful, and natural as possible.
- If able, go outdoors in simple clothing everyday. When the weather permits, walk barefoot on grass, beach, or soil. Go on regular outings, especially to beautiful natural areas.
- Keep the home clean and orderly. Make the kitchen, bathroom, bedrooms, and living rooms shiny clean. Keep the atmosphere of the home bright and cheerful.
- Maintain an active correspondence. Express love and appreciation to parents, children, brothers and sisters, relatives, teachers, and friends.
- Try not to take long hot baths or showers unless one has been consuming too much salt or animal food.
- Every morning or every night, scrub the whole body with a hot, damp towel until the circulation becomes active. When a complete body rub is not convenient, at least do the hands, feet, fingers, and toes.
- Use natural cosmetics, soaps, shampoos, and other body-care products. Brush the teeth with natural preparations or sea salt.
- Keep as active as possible. Daily activities such as cooking, scrubbing floors, cleaning windows, washing clothes, and others are excellent forms of exercise. If desired, one may also try systematic exercises such as yoga, martial arts, aerobics, and sports.
- Try to minimize time spent in front of the television. Color television es-

pecially emits unnatural radiation that can be physically draining. Turn the television off during meal times. Balance television time with more productive activities.

- Heating pads, electric blankets, portable radios with earphones, and other electric devices can disrupt the body's natural flow of energy. They are not recommended for regular use.
- Put many green plants in the living room, bedroom, and throughout the house to freshen and enrich the air.

Be flexible and creative when preparing food. Remember, each person is different. Please be sensitive and understanding when guiding others toward healthful eating. Along with good food, love, understanding, and patience are prime ingredients for a happy and healthy life.

Chapter 2

Preparation for Cooking

Proper preparation is as important as cooking itself. It offers a good example of the maxim: "the bigger the front, the bigger the back." The more thought, planning, and energy one puts into preparation, the easier the actual cooking will be.

The daily practice of cooking can be visualized as a moving spiral, in which many factors, such as food, fire, water, utensils, and the energy and ability of the cook, converge in the kitchen. Cooking represents the fusion that occurs at the center of that spiral. The coming together of these factors results in a kind of alchemy, in which diverse elements are transformed into nutritious and appetizing meals. Through the process of eating, an opposite, expanding spiral is created, in which food changes into thoughts, emotions, activity, and life itself. Whether or not this process occurs smoothly depends on the skill, understanding, and preparation of the cook.

In this chapter, we discuss the steps leading to the practice of cooking, beginning with the selection of the proper tools.

As one begins cooking macrobiotically, he or she may discover that new utensils are needed or that old ones must be replaced. This can be done gradually, but there are some items which need to be purchased right away. In the following list, utensils are arranged according to their importance. Some items are more expensive while others are relatively inexpensive. High-quality cookware and utensils enable one to cook efficiently and naturally, and create very beautiful and healthful meals.

BASIC EQUIPMENT

Stainless Steel Pressure Cooker—A stainless steel pressure cooker is an essential item in macrobiotic kitchens. It is used mostly for cooking grains, but can occasionally be used to prepare beans, vegetables, soups, and some sea-vegetable dishes. Pressure-cooked grains are superior to boiled grains in texture, taste, and appearance. Pressure cookers can be found in just about any natural food store and are very safe to use. Ask the salesperson for advice on the best-quality pressure cookers. A small five liter cooker is probably the most suitable for the average family. From one to six cups of rice can be prepared in it.

Cookware—High quality stainless steel cookware is essential. One can begin with a large- or medium-sized pot for preparing soups, stews, grains, and beans; two or three smaller saucepans; and one or two skillets for frying and sautéing. These should be sufficient to begin cooking delicious meals.

We do not recommend using aluminum, teflon, or plastic-coated cookware. Aluminum is easily scratched and can be mixed in with foods, and this can cause health problems. Teflon is also easily scratched and has a tendency to chip. These chips of plastic are often unnoticed in food. Plastic-coated cookware has also been chemically treated.

A cast iron skillet may also be needed for sautéing vegetables. To season a new skillet, first roast a small amount of sea salt in it for several minutes. Then brush the skillet with sesame oil and sauté an onion in it. Discard the onion. Bake the oil-coated skillet in a 300° to 350°F oven for several hours. The skillet turns dark or black in color when properly seasoned. Remove the skillet and allow it to cool. When cool, wash the skillet, then place it on a low flame on the stove until it is completely dry. This will prevent the skillet from rusting. Try not to scrub the skillet with metal scrubbers when washing as it may remove the seasoning from it. Also, it is not a good idea to plunge a hot cast iron skillet into cold water. This may cause the metal to become pitted or develop little holes in it. Always allow the skillet to completely cool off before washing it. Treated carefully, a cast iron skillet will last for many years.

A cast iron Dutch oven may also be purchased to use in making tempura.

A small set of stainless steel bakeware can also come in handy.

Earthenware pots are also very nice for making baked beans, vegetables, grains, or casseroles, but are not essential.

We recommend avoiding electrical skillets and cooking pots, as the electrical energy current disturbs or interferes with the natural energy or life-force of food. Foods heated by electricity are not as delicious as those cooked over more natural energy such as gas or wood. They also require more seasoning and are not recommended for optimum health.

Flame Deflector—Flame deflectors are metal pads or discs with wooden handles. They have hundreds of tiny holes in the metal which help to evenly distribute the flame under cooking pots, allowing foods to cook evenly and lessening the chances of burning. We usually place a deflector under a pressure cooker when preparing rice or other grains, or under pots that are simmering on the stove when one wants to keep the food warm but not boiling. These are inexpensive and can be purchased in most natural food or hardware stores.

Wooden Utensils—Wooden cooking utensils help prevent metal cookware from becoming scratched. Bamboo rice paddles can be used to remove grains from pots; cooking chopsticks are helpful for sautéing and stirring; different sized wooden spoons are good for stirring; a roasting paddle can be used when roasting nuts and seeds; and a soup ladle or two also comes in handy. Items such as these are fairly inexpensive and can be purchased in most natural food or kitchenware stores.

Natural Bristle Brush—A natural bristle brush is recommended for scrubbing root or ground vegetables. They are inexpensive and can be purchased at most natural food stores.

Vegetable Knife—A sharp Japanese vegetable knife is very important in a macrobiotic kitchen, allowing one to cut vegetables smoothly and elegantly. There are several types available including those made of stainless steel, carbon steel, and high-grade carbon steel. I prefer a high-grade carbon steel knife as it does not rust easily and holds a sharp edge longer. It will also not chip as easily as other knives, and will last many years when properly cared for.

Sharpening Stone—A sharpening stone can be bought along with a vegetable knife. It is used to periodically sharpen a knife so vegetables can be cut more easily. Sharpening stones can be obtained in most natural food and hardware stores.

Wooden Cutting Board—It is useful to have several wooden cutting boards—one for cutting vegetables and one for fish and seafood—so as not to mix the odors and juices absorbed into the porous surface of the wood. To properly season a cutting board, rub the surface with either corn or sesame oil. Allow the board to sit and absorb the oil for at least several hours. Then wipe the board dry with paper towels to absorb any surface oil. Cutting boards may be oiled once every month or so to keep them from absorbing the juices of the vegetables or other foods cut on them. To clean, simply wipe the boards with a wet sponge after using, instead of plunging them into water. Do not use soap on wooden boards and utensils as it is easily absorbed into the wood and detracts from the taste of foods cut or prepared on them. Oiling cutting boards also helps prevent bending or buckling. A board that is made of high-quality hardwood will last many years if properly cared for.

Colander or Strainer—Colanders and strainers are essential items used for washing grains, beans, and seeds, as well as for draining vegetables and noodles. It is very helpful to have one colander and two strainers: one larger mesh and one smaller or finer mesh for washing small grains such as millet and couscous, or small seeds such as sesame. They are fairly inexpensive and can be purchased in natural food stores with a kitchen section or in department stores.

Flat Grater—Flat metal or porcelain graters from Japan are used for grating, very finely, ginger, daikon, or other root vegetables. They are frequently used in macrobiotic kitchens to prepare vegetables for garnishes or medicinal teas. I recommend purchasing them right away. They are inexpensive and very useful, and can be found in most natural food stores.

Also useful are the regular stainless steel Western-style graters for grating vegetables for salads. These are not used as often as the flat grater.

Tamari Dispenser—These inexpensive, glass dispensers are very useful for pouring small amounts of tamari soy sauce as a garnish on soups and noodles or while cooking. They can be found at most natural food stores. Larger ones which are sealed and prefilled with tamari are also available. Most macrobiotic cooks could not do without them.

Suribachi* and *Surikogi—A suribachi is a grooved, earthenware grinding bowl which is used to hand purée and grind various foods. It is very useful in preparing condiments, dips, and sauces, in puréeing foods, or making soft foods for babies or people who are ill. It is also used in making plasters, compresses, and home remedies. These bowls come in small, medium, and large sizes, and are found in most natural food stores. The small- or medium-sized bowls are suitable for most households. A surikogi is a wooden pestle that is used with a suribachi to grind and purée.

Containers—Glass, ceramic, or wooden containers can be purchased over time to store grains, beans, sea vegetables, noodles, seeds, nuts, condiments, and seasonings. They are fairly inexpensive and are well worth the investment. Proper storage of food prevents spoilage, and makes it easier to find the items needed in cooking. We do not recommend storing food in plastic containers, as the taste of the plastic may be absorbed by food and detract from its delicious natural flavor.

Bamboo Tea Strainer—Although not essential, a bamboo tea strainer is a very practical utensil for straining tea. Strainers come in different sizes, and smaller ones are usually adequate for most families or single persons.

Pickle Press—These special, plastic presses are from Japan and are used to make quick pickles and pressed salads, both frequent items in macrobiotic cooking. The smaller-sized ones are appropriate for the average person or family. They can be found in most natural food stores. If not purchasing one immediately, a temporary press can be created by placing cut vegetables in a ceramic or glass bowl and putting a plate or disc down inside the bowl on top of them. Place a rock or other kind of weight on the plate to create pressure.

Bamboo Sushi Mats (*Sudare*)—These sushi mats are made of thin strips of bamboo that have been tied together. They are used for covering leftovers or keeping food warm. Bamboo mats help prevent food from drying out. They allow air to circulate freely through the thin strips of bamboo, thus reducing spoilage of cooked leftovers. We also use them in making sushi and vegetable rolls. They are inexpensive and it is well worth purchasing several. They can be found at most natural food stores.

Glass Teapot—Although not essential, as tea can be prepared in small saucepans, a glass teapot is useful for preparing and pouring tea. Glass does not influence the flavor of the tea in the way that metal sometimes does.

Steamer Basket—Steamer baskets are available in two varieties: stainless steel, which can be found in most department or natural food stores; or bamboo, which can be purchased in most natural or Oriental food stores. Bamboo steamers need to be seasoned by steaming odds and ends or vegetables in them several times to remove the taste of the wood before using them for everyday cooking.

Stainless Steel Hand Food Mill—Food mills, although not essential, are very useful for puréeing soups, making dips, or preparing baby foods. Mills can be found in most natural food or kitchen supply stores.

Pickle Crocks—After making quick, pressed pickles, one may want to try pickles that require a longer time to age. Heavy earthenware or wooden crocks or kegs are best for producing the highest quality and best tasting pickles. One or two medium-sized crocks are probably sufficient for a steady supply of pickles.

Wooden Bowls—Wooden bowls are used for serving rice and other whole grains. Wood is porous and allows cooked food to breathe. It also absorbs water, resulting in less spoilage. Grains that are kept in a wooden bowl stay fresh much longer than those served in glass or ceramic bowls. At least one medium-sized bowl should be bought right away. Wooden bowls come in various sizes and shapes and are made of different types of wood. Choose one which is appealing and suitable for personal needs. Wooden bowls need to be periodically seasoned with oil in the same manner as a cutting board to ensure long life and attractiveness.

Organic Soap—High-quality, organically made dishwashing soap is helpful in removing oil from skillets after frying, but is often not necessary for most other utensils. A simple washing in hot water is often sufficient.

Electrical Appliances—As mentioned previously, we recommend using electric appliances as little as possible, and converting from electric to gas cooking as soon as it is convenient. It is best to use electric blenders, waffle irons, popcorn poppers, food processors and other appliances only on special occasions, such as parties or for special snacks or treats.

SHOPPING FOR QUALITY INGREDIENTS

Selecting the highest-quality ingredients is a key element in macrobiotic cooking, especially the basic staples which are used frequently. The best possible ingredients are the basis for our health and well-being.

Daily Staples

When buying items that are used regularly—such as grains, beans, sea vegetables, miso, tamari soy sauce, oils, condiments, noodles, flour and flour products, teas, beverages, and others—try to select the highest-quality products, preferably those which are organically grown or naturally processed. They may cost slightly more than non-organic varieties, but they are much better for health. They are a worthwhile investment. For instance, deep-red Japanese azuki beans cost more than other azuki beans, but, because of their nutritional properties, they are more suitable for regular use, especially by persons who are recovering their health. These beans are rich in minerals, as they are grown in the volcanic soil of northern Japan, and help the body discharge toxins. Of course, other varieties are fine for occasional use if one is already in good health, but try to get the higher-quality beans whenever possible.

Vegetables and Fruits

Ideally, fresh produce is bought daily. But if this is not possible, once a week is all right, as long as the items selected are very fresh and vibrant, and the leaves have not turned or wilted.

Whenever possible, select organically grown produce. If organic produce is hard to find, then non-organic will suffice as long as it is properly washed and any sprayed or waxed skins are removed before cooking.

Of course, the best situation is to have a family garden to supply produce several months out of the year, but this is not always possible for many people, especially those living in the city. However, if the practice of food irradiation—including the radiation of vegetables and fruits—becomes widespread, backyard gardening will no longer be a luxury. It will become a necessity for survival.

In any case, make sure to have plenty of variety during each season to ensure a more balanced condition. Try to obtain vegetables in their whole form, including daikon, carrots, and turnips. Use both the root and the green tops, which are rich in vitamins and minerals, in daily cooking.

Oils

The best oils for regular use are dark and light sesame and corn oils. Dark sesame oil is made from roasted sesame seeds, while the light variety is made from raw seeds. The dark variety has a rich, roasted flavor that is delicious for sautéing or deep-frying. It has a slightly stronger flavor than the light sesame oil. Light sesame oil can also be used for sautéing, deep-frying, in salad dressings, or even in baking breads and pastries. It is somewhat lighter and milder than the dark oil.

Corn oil is also nice to use when baking, especially pastries; for making popcorn; or occasionally for sautéing. It has a richer, more buttery flavor. We generally do not use corn oil for deep-frying, since it often foams up and spills out of the pot.

Other oils can also be used on occasion by those in good health, and they are listed in Chapter 1. For those cooking for health recovery, though, we usually recommend limiting the selection of oils to those mentioned above until health is restored.

In most cases, the consumption of raw oil, such as in salad dressings, is not recommended. Oil is best used in small amounts in cooking, or at least heated before use. This is especially important when cooking for someone with a serious illness or with skin problems.

Unlike most commercial oils that are available in supermarkets and variety stores, sesame and corn oil are produced by a method called *cold pressing*. (The seeds are mechanically pressed, which causes heat but not beyond the boiling point.) These oils are not treated with chemical solvents, which are used commercially to extract additional oil from seeds, nor are they bleached or deodorized. By subjecting oils to extremely high temperatures—in some cases up to twice the boiling point of water—we destroy natural vitamin E. Cold-pressed oils retain most of their natural vitamins which prevent them from becoming rancid quickly. Natural vitamin E is also beneficial in maintaining soft skin and smooth, shiny hair.

Cold-pressed oils processed without chemicals do not contain cholesterol and taste very much like the seeds from which they are made, whereas the flavor of commercial oil bears little resemblance to that of the original seeds or grains from which it is extracted. Cold-pressed, naturally processed vegetable oils may cost a bit more, but they are far better for health and have a superior taste to commercial oils.

The amount of oil necessary for building new cells and tissues and maintaining body heat differs from person to person. Generally it is recommended not to take large quantities of oil. A small amount used in cooking daily, or even less frequently, is usually sufficient to maintain healthy bodily functions. Remember that we also obtain fats and oils from grains, beans and bean products, seeds, nuts, and other foods.

In some instances, such as in cases of serious illness, oil intake may need to be temporarily restricted until the condition improves. Also, small children under a year and a half usually do not require oil, as it may be difficult for them to digest, especially since they do not take in the amount of salt necessary to balance it. If children eat too much oil, they can develop skin or digestive problems.

Each persons's activity also influences his or her need or tolerance for oil. For instance, a person who works outdoors doing physical labor may be able to tolerate more oil than a person who works at home or in an office. Also, as people become older, they may require more oil to maintain body flexibility. These and other factors need to be considered when judging how much oil to use in cooking.

THE MACROBIOTIC PANTRY

When storing dried and perishable food items, the key point is to reduce waste and spoilage. The following suggestions can help keep foods fresh longer.

Dried Foods and Liquids

Dried foods such as grains, beans, condiments, sea vegetables, noodles, flours, and products such as fu, seeds, nuts, kuzu, umeboshi, and the like are best stored in glass, ceramic, or wooden containers. Glass containers are often the least expensive and most practical for the average person or family. It is also easier, during cooking, to locate food items stored in glass as the items can readily be seen without uncovering them.

During the hot summer months, it is sometimes common to have a problem with moth infestation. To prevent or at least reduce this problem, store jars in a fairly cool place such as a pantry, and occasionally stir the foods in them to release heat and allow air to circulate.

Sea salt is best stored in a tightly sealed glass jar to prevent it from absorbing moisture from the air and becoming damp, thus making it more difficult to use.

Tamari soy sauce and misos aged for a longer time may be placed in tightly sealed glass containers and stored in a shaded or dark, cool place.

Oils are best stored in tinted glass jars or in a cool dark cupboard to prevent them from going rancid. Naturally processed, cold-pressed vegetable oils do not spoil as quickly as chemically processed varieties.

Quick or mellow misos which have been fermented for a very short time are usually stored in the refrigerator as they may develop mold unless kept cool.

Vegetables and Fruits ——————————————————

The most practical way to store vegetables and fruits is in the refrigerator. If possible, try to obtain fresh produce daily, but if this is not practical, shop once or twice a week and store it in a cool, dark room or in the refrigerator.

For those who have gardens and the space in which to store vegetables for the winter or for long periods, a cool, dark basement or root cellar serves very well.

There are many books available on how to build storage bins for different types of vegetables and fruits. Some of the vegetables which store more easily through the cold winter months are squash, cabbage, pumpkin, carrots, onions, daikon, turnips, and burdock. Squash stores very well on shelves in the pantry, but make sure they do not touch each other as this causes them to spoil rapidly. Also, make sure that squashes still have their stems attached for longer shelf life. Cabbages may be picked and left completely intact with all of the leaves, stem or root still attached. They can be hung upside down from a basement rafter with twine or string. The outer leaves and root become very dry and brown, but the leaves inside remain very green and sweet. Cabbage stored in this manner will keep for the better part of the winter.

Storage bins or baskets filled with dry sand or dry leaves and sawdust are very good for storing onions, carrots, turnips, and daikon. Burdock can also be stored in this manner. If using sand, insert the vegetables so that they are standing upright with only the stem uncovered. When using leaves or sawdust, it is best to layer the vegetables so that they do not touch each other.

The natural environment of lotus root is damp: it grows in the underwater mud of ponds. Lotus root is a member of the water lily family. A student at the Kushi Institute described this method of storing lotus root several years ago. Take several brown paper towels and dampen them with water. Next, squeeze the water out of the towels. Wrap each piece of lotus root in several layers of paper towels and place in a paper bag. Close tightly and place the wrapped lotus root in the bottom vegetable drawer of the refrigerator. The lotus root will remain fresh and moist for about two months when stored in this manner.

Apples are one of the few fresh fruits that store easily in the autumn and winter simply by keeping them in a cool place.

Pickling ——————————————————————

Pickling is another good way of storing vegetables in the cold months. Please refer to our later section on pickle making for specific suggestions.

SALT AND SEASONINGS

The proper use of sea salt, miso, tamari soy sauce, and other seasonings is very important in creating a balanced condition.

The quantity of salt or seasoning needed varies from one person to the next, since factors such as age, condition, constitution, environment or climate, and type of activity all influence our daily requirements. For instance, we do not recommend using salt in food for babies under a year old. Grains and vegetables can be cooked with a small piece of kombu instead, which contains plenty of trace minerals and not as much sodium. As with oil, a person who works hard physically and loses minerals through perspiration may require a little more salt or seasoning than someone who is less active. People in colder climates can generally tolerate more salt than people in warmer climates. Also, if the climate is more humid and wet, a person may need a bit more salt than a person living in a hot, dry climate.

Our bodies need a certain amount of salt in order to keep the intestinal tract and muscles firm, to help digest our food, and to generate body warmth. The amount of salt we usually recommend for most dishes, however, is very small, and the food is best if it has just a mild salty taste. Other side dishes such as condiments, pickles, and some sea vegetable dishes may be a bit more salty, but these are not eaten in such large amounts.

In most cases, we do not add salt, miso, or tamari soy sauce to food after it has been cooked. However, a small amount of tamari soy sauce is sometimes used on noodles or in soups. It is best to do this moderately and not to use tamari soy sauce on daily rice or other grain dishes. Seasonings such as sea salt, miso, and tamari soy sauce are best cooked in food.

Today, salt has become a controversial subject. However, unlike the modern diet which is high in animal foods that contain salt, and prepackaged foods that have a high sodium content, macrobiotics recommends modest consumption of animal foods—most often fish and seafood—and utilizes primarily natural and unprocessed foods. It is very easy to control the intake of salt when eating macrobiotically, and to discover how to use the proper amount.

The type of salt that we use most often in macrobiotic cooking is very different than regular table salt. We recommend using white sea salt, which in most cases contains about 12 percent minerals and about 88 percent sodium chloride. Regular table salt is about 99.9 percent sodium chloride, with little if any natural minerals. Sea salt has a much milder taste than regular table salt. Modern table salt also contains iodine, which aids the function of the thyroid gland. Sea salt does not contain iodine, but this element is available in sea vegetables and various seafoods. Some table salts also contain sugar, to make them pour more easily and to keep the iodine from breaking down. Sodium-bicarbonate is also added to iodized table salt, together with a bleaching agent to keep the salt white. Good sea salt contains no additives, is naturally extracted from the sea, and is simply washed and sun or kiln dried.

In general, we recommend using only enough salt or seasoning to bring out the naturally sweet taste of foods. The proper use of salt in cooking is something that may take time to master, but it is vital to our health and well-being.

WATER QUALITY

The quality of water that we use for cooking and drinking is very important in creating delicious meals and a balanced, healthy condition. The best quality water for daily use is either clean, natural well water or fresh spring water.

It is best to avoid water that has been chemically treated or distilled. Distilled water is lacking in natural minerals and life-force.

VARIETY IN COOKING

Variety is very important in creating a balanced and healthy physical, mental, and spiritual condition. A varied diet allows us to continually change in a harmonious fashion together with our environment. There are many factors that contribute variety to our meals. Some of these include:

Ingredients—Nature endlessly supplies a wide range of grains, beans, vegetables, sea vegetables, fruits, nuts, seeds, and other whole foods. Different sizes, shapes, colors, textures, and energies exist within each category of food. Try to use a wide variety of these ingredients in daily cooking.

Taste—As we all know, we have five primary tastes: sweet, sour, salty, bitter, and pungent or spicy. These tastes are naturally found in the foods that nature provides. It is best to include a wide range of tastes in daily cooking to help create balance in our meals and condition. The naturally sweet taste is abundant in grains, beans, vegetables, and sea vegetables. Simply cooking them properly with a moderate amount of salt helps bring out their natural sweetness. Most of the dishes we prepare have this naturally sweet flavor. The other tastes—salty, bitter, sour, and pungent—can also be used daily, but in smaller amounts in the form of side dishes, garnishes, and condiments. Their function is more to fine-tune or refine our daily condition. If we include all of the tastes daily, we are usually more content and satisfied with our food and have few if any cravings.

Cooking Styles—It is important to use a variety of styles in our cooking. Of course, it may not be possible to use all of the possible cooking methods everyday, but several can be used within the course of a day and almost all of them within several days. The most essential cooking methods include: pressure-cooking, boiling, steaming, sautéing, baking, broiling, roasting, pickling, and deep-frying. Each method allows us to create a wide range of textures, tastes, and appearances in our daily cooking. They also have different effects on our condition.

Another way to create variety is to vary the height or intensity of the flame that we cook with. This also helps create different textures, tastes, and appearances in our food. For instance, if we use a high flame to stir-fry vegetables, the result is a crispier texture. Using a very low flame for *nishime* (see Chapter 5) creates a very soft texture and sweet taste in the vegetables. The height of the flame also influences the energy we receive from food. A high flame creates more quick and active energy, while a low flame results in more peaceful and calm energy. Try to use varying degrees of flame when cooking.

Each of these methods can be varied by changing things such as the amount and type of seasoning, the length of cooking time, and amount of oil.

Colors—Nature provides a wide range of colors to choose from when selecting and preparing our daily food. There are reds, yellows, greens, browns, blacks, and whites as well as varying colors in-between. Color is a very important factor in stimulating appetite as well as creating attractive and balanced meals. Use a wide variety of colors in cooking and remember to use those which combine well and complement each other. Try to use green vegetables everyday, as this color has a very calm and soothing effect on the body. Other colors such as red or black may not be used daily but can be included at least several times per week.

Cutting Methods—In macrobiotic cooking, a wide range of cutting methods are used. We often slice vegetables on an angle to create beautiful cuts and more aesthetically pleasing dishes. But at other times we may cut straight across a vegetable to create a different effect. The way in which we cut our vegetables greatly affects the energy we receive from food, as well as the food's taste, texture, and appearance. Large chunks are often more appropriate when preparing stews, nishime, or other one-pot meals. When cooked over a low flame, large cuts become very soft and sweet, and have a warming effect on the body. More delicately cut vegetables complement a small grain such as millet. They go well together. Smaller cuts such as matchsticks, rectangles, or shavings cook very quickly and are good in *kinpira* or sautéed dishes.

Sometimes, when I make a very fancy and attractive nishime dish, I tie strips of kombu into bows, rather than simply cutting it into squares. At other times, I slice kombu into very thin matchsticks when making a delicate, clear soup or a condiment that includes thin matchsticks of fresh ginger. As can be seen, varying cutting methods offers many possibilities for creating beautiful and appetizing meals.

Seasonings—Although we do not recommend using spices or herbs, there is still a wide range of seasonings to choose from. Macrobiotic seasonings include sea salt, various types of miso, tamari soy sauce and *shoyu*, umeboshi, umeboshi paste, brown rice vinegar, sweet brown rice vinegar, *hato mugi* vinegar, ginger, Japanese wasabi (horseradish), regular horseradish, mustard, mirin, fresh lemon peel and juice, fresh dill, sweeteners such as barley malt, rice syrup, apple juice, and occasionally maple syrup (for those in good health), and very occasionally (also for those in good health) a little red pepper. There are also a variety of oils that affect the taste of food.

Try to use a wide variety of seasonings to stimulate taste and create delicious meals.

Textures—We also recommend preparing foods with different textures. Our foods can be more soft or crunchy, more crisp or watery, smooth and creamy, or firm and chewy. Varying the textures of food allows a fuller range of enjoyment and energy effects. For instance, soft creamy foods such as puréed squash soup are often easier to digest and produce more calming effects. A crisp raw salad requires more chewing and has a rapid cooling effect on the body. Please experiment and discover the various effects of different textures.

Garnishes—Garnishes add an important touch to our meals. They help create balance in our dishes and stimulate appetite. Many items can be used as garnishes. In macrobiotic cooking we use items such as toasted nori squares or strips, chopped scallions, parsley or chives, roasted sesame seeds, whole or chopped roasted nuts, shiitake mushrooms, lemon or tangerine slices, sprigs of watercress and parsley, carrot flowers, cucumber slices, grated ginger, grated daikon or carrot, dry-roasted or deep-fried bread cubes, flowers and leaves, pine needles, and many others. Please try these and other garnishes in daily cooking for taste, appearance, and balance.

Cookware—Cookware influences the flavor and effect of foods. For instance, kinpira or stir-fried vegetables have a very delicious flavor when sautéed in a cast-iron skillet. Although we do not recommend using cast iron exclusively, it is nice to use it once in a while. As another example, a covered earthenware dish imparts a rich and delicious flavor to baked beans.

Use a wide variety of cooking and baking utensils when preparing food in order to experience the full range of tastes and energies.

Serving Dishes—It is very important to serve food in a beautiful and artistic manner. Using a wide variety of serving dishes and trays helps the cook highlight his or her dishes. One can choose from those made of wood, glazed or unglazed ceramics, porcelain, glass, or woven straw or wood. They come in a variety of shapes, sizes, and colors. A serving dish can enhance and beautify the food. For instance, a white tofu dip is more attractive when served in a dark colored bowl, rather than a light colored one. The color of hijiki is better complemented by a light or pastel bowl than a darker one. It is also important to choose an appropriately sized bowl for the amount of food prepared. Small amounts of food do not look as attractive when served in a large bowl as they do in a smaller one. A large bowl filled to the very top is not as attractive as one that is only three-quarters full.

It is best to avoid using plastic serving dishes or containers, as artificial materials detract from the taste of food.

A CLEAN KITCHEN

The old saying, "Cleanliness is next to Godliness" applies as much to our kitchen as to our body. Cleanliness cannot be stressed enough. A clean and orderly kitchen greatly affects the quality of our meals, both in terms of taste and appearance. It also affects the quality of energy we receive from food. Keeping the kitchen clean and orderly reduces the amount of time it takes to prepare meals, as things are easier to find when needed.

Before beginning to cook, wash all dirty dishes and put them away. Clean the counter tops, tabletops, and cutting boards. Sweep the floor and mop, if necessary. Make sure that the stove top is also clean and shiny before cooking. If dishes are cleaned and put away, they can be found more easily when needed.

While cooking it is important to wash dishes or utensils immediately after using them or within a few minutes of use. Dry and put them away. This only takes a few seconds but could save time when a utensil or pot is needed.

The cleanliness of cutting boards and the proper washing of food are both essential. Before beginning to cut, wash the board with a damp sponge, and when one vegetable is finished, remove the cut pieces and place them on a plate so that the juices are not absorbed by the board. Then wipe the board clean and proceed with the next vegetable. This will greatly reduce the chances of the board warping due to the absorption of juices, thus prolonging the life of the board. If a board is not cleaned after cutting each vegetable, the flavor of vegetables will intermingle, and detract from the flavor of the dish being prepared.

Washing vegetables properly greatly affects the flavor of the dishes one prepares. Please refer to the following sections for suggestions.

THE COOK'S ENERGY

Personal cleanliness and orderliness are also important in macrobiotic cooking. Before beginning to cook, make sure that clothing is clean or that a clean apron is worn. If one has long hair, tie it back. Wash hands before handling foods or utensils.

Some people prefer listening to music while cooking. My feeling about this is that quiet is better, but if one feels more relaxed with music playing, it is better if it is not too loud or chaotic. Loud music creates a disruptive vibration and interferes with concentration. It also prevents one from hearing the sounds food makes while cooking, which can sometimes cause dishes to burn. Wearing heavy perfume can interfere with the ability to smell foods as they cook.

Most importantly, enter the kitchen with a calm and peaceful mind. Try to set aside any problems or pressing thoughts and concentrate totally on the task at hand. Cultivate a sense of marvel and thankfulness toward nature for providing food for one's life and health. A peaceful mind, together with love for the people one cooks for, greatly enhances the beneficial effects of the foods one prepares.

If there are small children in the family, at times it may be hard to maintain a peaceful and orderly atmosphere in the kitchen. Try to direct children to play peacefully either in the kitchen or in another room. I do not think that children should be excluded or kept out of the kitchen while their mother is cooking. Children have wonderful energy that, when properly directed, can enhance one's creativity and inspiration. Helping in the kitchen can be a valuable learning experience for children. If children want to cook, find a simple task for them to perform which helps in the overall preparation of the meal. Some of the most delicious macrobiotic meals have been prepared with children either helping or involved in some way. As we all know, children love to eat, and they often eat better when they are involved in preparing their foods. Cooking fosters a sense of accomplishment and allows children to do something for themselves and others.

Entering the kitchen with a calm, peaceful, and happy mind is the best way to begin cooking a meal.

BEGINNER'S MIND

After one has cooked macrobiotically for some time, and has become familiar with the foods and proportions, one starts to gain more confidence. Each meal can then become an exciting challenge. Even as one's cooking improves, there is still much to learn. Always be creative and attempt to go beyond what seems possible with one's cooking. A spirit of beginner's mind is an attribute shared by all good cooks. Taking classes and eating at friends' houses or in restaurants are ways to encounter new ideas. If a particular meal does not turn out the way one would like, it is no cause to be discouraged. Learn from the experience and strive to improve. With time and practice skill naturally increases.

DEVELOPING A PERSONAL STYLE

At first, one may rely solely on recipes from classes or books for guidance in the kitchen. As one becomes familiar with these and feels more confident about cooking, a point may be reached where cookbooks are no longer necessary, except as sources for ideas. The next step is to begin improvising and ultimately create an original cooking style. At this stage, cooking becomes an expression of one's freedom. However, even after reaching this stage, always aim at refining cooking techniques and abilities. Continually strive to broaden and deepen the understanding of food and cooking. When cooking with creativity one's meals become much more satisfying.

WASHING FOOD

Washing food properly can make the difference between a delicious meal and a mediocre one. Below are a few helpful suggestions for proper washing.

Grains—Before washing grains, place a handful or so at a time on a plate and pick out any stones or clumps of soil. Next, place the grain in a bowl and cover it with cold water. Wash the grain quickly but gently, using one hand to stir in one direction. Repeat once more. Pour off the water and place the grain in a strainer or colander. Rinse quickly but thoroughly under cold water to remove dust or other particles which may have settled on the bottom. The grain is now ready to be cooked. Once grains are washed, do not let them a time sit for too long before cooking, as they will absorb the water from washing and expand. If this happens, the proportions of water used in cooking will need to be adjusted or grains may turn out too moist.

Beans—Sort and remove any stones, clumps of soil, or broken and damaged beans before washing. Next, place the beans in a bowl and cover with cold water. Wash by gently stirring as is done with grains. Pour the water off and repeat this process twice. Place the beans in a strainer and rinse under cold water. The beans are now ready to soak or cook, depending on the type of bean being used. Japanese black soybeans are an exception, and are washed differently. Please refer to the chapter on beans for instructions on how to wash them.

Vegetables—We can divide vegetables into three categories: leafy greens, roots, and round or ground vegetables. To wash leafy vegetables—such as turnip and daikon greens, collards, kale, carrot tops, Chinese cabbage, and others—place them in a large bowl or pot and cover with cold water. Swish them around, and pour off the water. Next, wash the leaves, one at a time, under cold water. If some leaves are not fresh, or are yellow or damaged, sort and remove them before washing. Leaves that are tightly curled such as kale may require a little more effort than smoother leaves such as collard greens or Chinese cabbage. Once the leaves are thoroughly washed, they are ready to be cut.

Root, round, and most ground vegetables require the use of a special natural bristle vegetable brush. Place the vegetable under cold running water in the sink, and scrub gently but firmly, trying not to damage or remove the nutrient-rich skin. Onions are first peeled and then washed for a few seconds under cold water until squeaky clean. If vegetables such as rutabaga, cucumbers, or squash have been waxed, wash them first with a vegetable brush and peel the skin with a knife before cooking. Green cabbage can be washed by removing individual leaves or with the leaves still attached to the head, as there is usually not much soil on the inside of the leaves. Fresh mushrooms can usually be cleaned without a vegetable brush, simply by thoroughly rinsing them by hand under cold water.

Fruits—Fruit can usually be washed by hand, without a vegetable brush. Simply rinse each piece thoroughly under cold water before slicing.

We do not recommend cutting vegetables and fruits before washing them, as this causes them to lose vitamins, minerals, and other nutrients as well as flavor. It is also more difficult to wash sliced vegetables than to wash whole ones.

Sea Vegetables—Sea vegetables such as kombu can simply be dusted with a clean, damp sponge before soaking and slicing. Nori sheets also do not require washing. With arame and hijiki, sort any hard clumps, as they may contain stones or small snail shells, and discard these. Then place the sea vegetable in a bowl and cover with water. Rinse as is done with grains or beans, repeating once or twice. Wash the sea vegetables quickly, then place them in a colander or strainer and rinse quickly under cold water. Arame does not need to be soaked, simply allow it to sit and drain for three to five minutes before slicing. Once hijiki has been washed, it is then soaked for three to five minutes before slicing. Wakame, dulse, and sea palm can simply be placed in a bowl covered with cold water and washed as is done with hijiki or arame. Pour the water off and repeat once or twice. The sea vegetables are now ready to soak.

Seeds—Seeds are washed in much the same manner as grains and beans. Sort and remove any stones, sticks, or hard shells. Then place the seeds in a bowl and cover with cold water. Stir and pour the water off. When washing sesame seeds, some seeds may float to the top. These are a little too yin or expanded for regular use, and may be slightly spoiled. Skim these off and discard. Repeat the rinsing process once again. Then place the seeds in a strainer and rinse quickly under cold water. The seeds are now ready to roast. Sesame seeds are very small and require a very fine mesh strainer for the final rinsing or they will fall through the strainer.

Others—Dried daikon can be washed by placing it in a bowl of cold water. Stir it around and pour the water off. Place the daikon in a strainer and rinse it very quickly under cold water. It is now ready to soak.

Items such as dried chestnuts and lotus seeds can be washed in the same manner as grains and beans.

CUTTING VEGETABLES

Vegetables can be cut in a variety of shapes, sizes, and thicknesses. By using a wide variety of cutting techniques, we can create many beautiful and varied dishes. The way in which we cut a vegetable can alter the taste and appearance of a dish. Cutting vegetables in a variety of shapes also helps us to balance the other ingredients in our dishes.

The following illustrations show a few of the most commonly used methods for cutting vegetables, together with their Japanese names:

Cutting on a Diagonal (*Hasugiri*)

Matchsticks or Slivers (*Sengiri*)

Cutting into Irregular Wedges
(*Rangiri*)

Cutting into Thin Rounds
(*Koguchigiri*)

Dicing (*Sainome*)

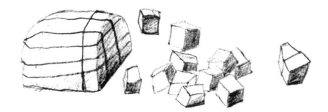

Cutting into Half-Moons (*Hangetsu*)

Cutting into Quarters (*Ichogiri*)

Cutting into Rectangles (*Tanzaku*)

Cutting into Chrysanthemum (*Kikukagiri*)

Cutting into Crescents (*Mawashigiri*)

58

Dicing Onions (*Mijingiri*)

Shaving (*Sasagaki*)

Cutting Leaves

Flower Shapes (*Hanagata*)

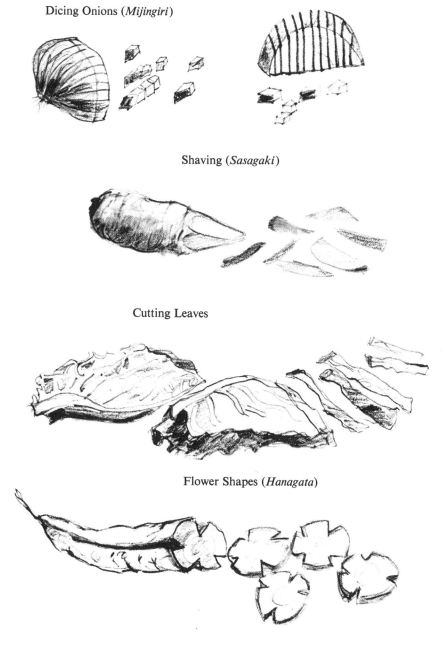

As may have been noticed, macrobiotic cooks often cut vegetables on an angle. This style allows one to create many beautiful cuts and to evenly balance the yin and yang energies in each cut. However, there are also times when cutting straight across may be more appropriate for the dish being prepared. When a dish calls for several cutting styles, be sure to choose those that are generally similar in size and thickness. This will ensure that vegetables will finish cooking at the same time. If, for example, we combine small diced carrot pieces with large chunks or rounds of daikon or squash, the carrots, being small, would still be hard and undercooked when the larger pieces were finished. Also, when using large chunks, make sure that they are cut into bite-sized pieces, or at least cut into a size that is not awkward to eat.

Cutting vegetables properly may seem difficult at first, but with continual practice, one's knife technique can become quite good.

HANDLING A KNIFE

When cutting vegetables, hold them with the fingers curled slightly. Tilt the blade slightly away from the fingers, with the top of the blade resting against the middle or end joint. Then, place the front part of the blade on the vegetable and slide it firmly but gently forward through the vegetable, with a slight downward pressure. Cut the vegetable with the entire length of the blade. It is best not to saw or push down too hard to the extent that the knife tears through the vegetable. This produces jagged cuts that are not so attractive.

SHARPENING A KNIFE

A sharp knife is very important, as this makes it possible to make clean, attractive cuts and allows one to cut much more quickly, thus reducing actual preparation time.

A whetstone or oil stone will be needed to sharpen knives.

The Japanese vegetable knives sold in Europe and America are usually right-handed, and are sharpened only on the right side. If the blade is sharpened on both sides, it will pull to one side when cutting. Left-handed knives can be specially ordered and are slightly more expensive. Left-handers can use the inexpensive right-handed knife until ready to purchase one that is more suited to them.

Sharpening a knife once a week should be enough for normal use.

To sharpen the knife, first wet or oil the sharpening stone. Next, hold the handle in the right hand and place the left thumb, middle and index fingers firmly against the left side of the blade. Tilt the blade so that it comes to about a 25 to 30 degree angle to the stone. Slide the entire length of the blade gently but firmly across the entire length of the stone. Remove the blade and slide it through again. Repeat several times until the blade is sharp. Then, to remove any burrs, flip the blade over and run it very gently through the entire length of the stone.

Once a knife is sharpened, wash it to remove any metal filings and oil. It is now ready to use or to put away. Before putting it away, though, make sure to dry it.

To store a knife so that it can last many years, place it either in a special wooden knife rack or wrap it in a clean kitchen towel. This will help protect the blade.

Sharpening stones tend to become clogged with metal filings or oil. To wash the stone, simply place it under warm water and scrub it clean with a non-abrasive cloth or plastic scrubber. Dry it and place it in a box for storage.

Now that the pantry is stocked with good food, the kitchen is sparkling clean, and the utensils are in their proper places, we are ready to begin cooking. At the conclusion of this book, we discuss other preparatory steps such as how to plan menus and combine dishes properly. Refer to this section for ideas as necessary. When entering the kitchen, do so with confidence and with a calm, peaceful, and loving mind.

Chapter 3
Grains, Including Seitan and Noodles

For many people in the modern world, the idea of using whole grains as principal foods may seem new. Like many of us who grew up in the 1950s and 1960s, family meals were often based around some type of animal-food dish. Vegetables were used mostly as garnishes to these main dishes, and grains were pretty much limited to chemically treated white bread, rolls, or buns, occasional three-minute white rice, and breakfast cereals. Grains were not really thought of as main foods. Bread, for example, was not viewed as the Staff of Life, but as a vehicle for a hamburger, hot dog, or the contents of a sandwich.

The disappearance of grains from American dinner tables, which I and many others experienced, is largely a twentieth-century phenomenon. It is the result of a number of factors, including affluence, modern agricultural practices, and modern nutritional theories.

In the field of nutrition, for example, the prevalence of the "four food groups" concept contributed to this change. This view, which everyone remembers from high school and which is still taught today, has led to the mistaken notion that meat and animal products, dairy, and fruits and vegetables, are on equal footing with grains in the human diet. This is further reinforced by labeling grains and their products as "breads and cereals." It is no wonder that the average person would look elsewhere for principal foods, since "breads and cereals" are thought to be fattening.

Eating whole grains helps us to get back in touch with human tradition. Early Americans and other preindustrial peoples around the world looked to whole grains as their main foods, with fresh vegetables, beans, and other agricultural products serving as supplementary foods. They ate grains directly in forms as diverse as corn fritters, kasha, barley porridge, rice *kayu*, and countless others. Their intake of animal food was generally much less than it is at present.

As we mentioned in Chapter 1, the modern way of eating is increasingly associated with chronic illness. In January, 1987, for example, the American Cancer Society reported that one out of ten American women will develop breast cancer at some point, an all time high. A decade ago, the chances of getting breast cancer were one in thirteen. In an interview with the *Boston Globe*, Dr. Virgil Loeb, president of the American Cancer Society stated that fat in the diet and obesity were both factors in the development of the disease.

People often equate the modern diet with status and prosperity. The popular notion that we in the modern world are "the best fed people in history" contributes to this association. However, the rise of degenerative diseases in the twentieth century is forcing a reassessment of our definition of prosperity. Should not our definition include a long, productive, and active life, together with the foods that make that quality of life possible? Are not good health and sound mind at the root of prosperity and an adequate standard of living?

One of the major contributions of macrobiotics has been the reintroduction of whole grains—the Staff of Life—into the diets of modern people. In the sections that follow, we present practical and convenient ways for everyone to begin cooking and eating whole grains everyday.

BROWN RICE

Be selective when buying brown rice. A large percentage of green grains in the rice indicates that it is not yet mature, while rice that is broken or chipped has not been properly milled. Rice in this condition begins to oxidize from exposure to the air, resulting in the disruption of its natural balance of carbohydrates, minerals, and vitamins. It is already starting to lose its *Ki* or life energy. Rice that has been grown and milled properly is vibrant with a life-force that will remain intact for thousands of years, and even if then planted, will sprout and grow.

In terms of yin and yang, rice is the most balanced of all grains. This is reflected in its natural balance of minerals, protein, and carbohydrates. This is one reason why brown rice is the most suitable grain for daily consumption. Also, it is the most biologically developed grain. Since humans are the most biologically developed species in the animal kingdom we should eat our counterpart in the vegetable world.

Cereal grains can comprise 50 to 60 percent of our daily food, and brown rice can be our main or primary grain. It can be eaten everyday and the other grains used as supplemental side dishes. If we eat brown rice daily, our condition can improve rapidly, and we can more easily become happy, healthy, and satisfied in whatever we are doing.

Pressure-cooking is the best way to prepare brown rice. Rice will cook quickly and thoroughly, and taste sweet when made this way. Pressure-cooked rice accelerates physical, mental, and spiritual development to an extent no other cooking method can.

A cook can continually reflect on the quality of his or her cooking. If family members do not eat much rice, then perhaps something is wrong with our preparation. Our condition changes daily and thus the way in which we cook rice also changes. Cooks are encouraged to always try to improve their rice. If, for example, it is burnt on the bottom, the flame may be too high, so lower it the next time. The flame may not be high enough if the rice is too wet. Dry rice indicates that probably not enough water was used, and if the rice is too mushy, probably too much was used. The best rice is well cooked with each grain separate. It tastes sweet and becomes sweeter the more it is chewed. Needless to say, all of our food needs to be thoroughly chewed, to the point where it becomes liquified, before it is swallowed. Grains are digested primarily in the mouth through their interaction with saliva. If they are not well chewed they cannot be properly digested.

Never fill the pot more than half full with grain when pressure-cooking rice or other grains. This will bring the cooker to about 70 percent of its capacity after water has been added. If too much grain is put in the pressure cooker, it will not cook as well.

How rice is grown is also important. There is a world of difference between organic rice and rice grown with chemicals. I understood this more clearly when I lived in Japan almost ten years ago.

One spring day, I went with friends to a large organic farm nestled in the mountains around Kyoto. There I saw row after row of organic daikon, Chinese cabbage, carrots, and other vegetables, together with acres of organic rice seedlings. The people at the farm were especially proud of the fact that their grains and vegetables were grown entirely free of chemical fertilizers and insecticides, and without animal fertilizer. Their crops were fertilized only with leaves, straw, and grass from the surrounding mountains.

To illustrate the importance of organic growing, the farmers produced two sample jars of brown rice: one that had been grown organically on their land, and another that had been grown somewhere else with chemical methods. The rice was several years old, and the organic sample looked and smelled fresh and alive. The chemicalized rice, however, had turned black and had a terrible, putrefying smell. This simple demonstration convinced me that organically grown rice was far superior to chemically cultivated varieties.

A big improvement in the quality of the brown rice that we use occurred several years ago with the introduction of home rice hulling machines. Freshly hulled rice is even better than regular brown rice, as it retains its natural Ki and nutrients right up until the time that it is cooked. It has a richer, more deliciously sweet flavor, and since it does not sit exposed in a bag, is cleaner and easier to wash. Unhulled paddy rice is now available through organizations like the Kushi Foundation, and can be ordered directly from growers such as Lundberg Farms in California. (Information on rice hulling machines can also be obtained from the Kushi Foundation, 17 Station Street, Brookline, MA 02146.)

Pressure-cooked Brown Rice #1

1 cup brown rice, washed
1¼–1½ cups water
pinch of sea salt

Place rice in the pressure cooker and add water. Place cooker on a low flame for about 10 to 15 minutes. Add salt and cover the cooker. Turn flame to high. Bring up to pressure. Reduce the flame to medium-low and place a flame deflector under the cooker. Cook for 50 minutes. Allow pressure to come down and remove cover. Let rice sit for about 4 to 5 minutes. Remove and place in a rice bowl. Garnish and serve.

Pressure-cooked Brown Rice #2

1 cup brown rice, washed
1¼–1½ cups water
pinch of sea salt

Place rice in pressure-cooker and add water and salt. Place cover on pressure cooker. Turn flame high. When gauge begins to hiss or jiggle remove pot from flame, place flame deflector on top of the burner, and then place pressure cooker on top. Reduce flame to medium-low and cook for 50 minutes. When rice is done, remove from burner and allow pressure to come down. This will take approximately 15 to 20 minutes, depending on the number of cups of rice cooked. Before removing the top from the pressure cooker, lift the gauge to make sure that the pressure is completely out of the cooker. Remove cover. Remove rice from pot with a bamboo rice paddle, one spoonful at a time, and smooth each spoonful into a wooden bowl, so that the bottom (most yang) part of the rice and the top (most yin) part are evenly distributed.

Pressure-cooked Brown Rice #3

1 cup brown rice
2 cups water
pinch of sea salt

Wash the rice and allow to drain. Heat a stainless steel skillet and dry-roast the rice until light, golden brown.

Place in a pressure cooker with water and salt. Turn flame to high. Bring to pressure, reduce flame to medium-low and place a flame deflector under the cooker. Pressure-cook for 40 to 45 minutes. Remove from flame and allow pressure to come down. Remove cover and allow to sit 4 to 5 minutes. Remove rice and place in a serving bowl.

Boiled Brown Rice

1 cup brown rice (unroasted or roasted)
2 cups water
pinch of sea salt

Wash rice. Place in heavy pot. Add water and salt. Cover with a heavy lid. Bring to a boil, lower flame to medium-low and simmer for 1 hour or until all water has been absorbed. Remove and serve.

If roasting rice, add 2½ cups water per cup of rice.

Soft Brown Rice (Rice Kayu)

1 cup brown rice
5 cups water
pinch of sea salt

Wash rice. Cook as for pressure-cooked or boiled rice, only not all of the water will be absorbed. This rice is very smooth and creamy.

This makes a very good breakfast cereal and is also good for people who have digestive problems or any other type of sickness. For variety, cook in vegetables such as Chinese cabbage or daikon, or an umeboshi plum.

Basic Fried Rice

4 cups cooked brown rice
1–2 Tbsp sesame oil (light or dark)
1–2 Tbsp tamari soy sauce
1 cup sliced scallions

Brush skillet lightly with oil. Heat and add rice. (If rice is dry, add a few drops of water to moisten.) Place cover on skillet and cook on low flame for 10 to 15 minutes. Add tamari and scallions. Cover and cook 5 to 7 minutes longer. Do not mix until just before serving. There is no need to stir. Make sure to keep the flame low or the rice may burn. Mix and serve hot.

For variety, use onions, parsley, or a combination of vegetables such as onions and carrots, daikon and daikon leaves, onions and beans, Chinese cabbage and mushrooms, or onions and celery. Ingredients such as toasted nori squares, fresh or dried tofu, corn, tempeh, burdock, lotus root, or other seasonal vegetables may also be added.

Pressure-cooked Rice with Beans

1 cup brown rice
10%–20% beans
1¼–1½ cups water
pinch of sea salt

Azuki, kidney, or pinto beans are boiled ½ hour first, then allowed to cool. Add beans and cooking water to rice. Chick-peas are soaked overnight, cooked for ½ hour, allowed to cool, and added to the rice with cooking water. Black beans (Japanese soybeans) can be dry-roasted after washing, and then added to the rice.

Most beans can be soaked and added to the rice, but discard the soaking water. However, the soaking water from azuki beans may be used.

Wash grain and beans. Cook or soak as mentioned above. Add beans and cooking water to rice after it has cooled. The cooking water from the beans should be counted as part of the 1¼ to 1½ cups of water in the recipe. Pressure-cook 50 minutes, and remove as with plain rice.

Brown Rice with Chestnuts

1 cup brown rice
10% dried chestnuts
1¼–1½ cups water
pinch of sea salt

There are two ways to prepare this dish. The first way is to wash the chestnuts, dry-roast until golden brown, and then soak for 10 to 15 minutes before adding to the rice.

The second way is to soak the chestnuts for several hours before adding to the rice.

Add water, salt, and cook as for plain rice.

Brown Rice and Lotus Seeds

1 cup brown rice, washed
¼ cup white or red lotus seeds, soaked 3–4 hours
1¼–1½ cups water
pinch of sea salt

Place rice, lotus seeds, and water in pressure cooker. Put on a low flame for 10 to 15 minutes. Add sea salt and cover. Turn flame to high and bring to pressure. Cook as for plain rice.

Gomoku

1 cup brown rice, dry-roasted
1 Tbsp dried lotus root, soaked
   ½ hour
1 piece dried tofu, soaked 10
   minutes in warm water, rinsed
   in cold water, and diced
3 shiitake mushrooms, soaked,
   stems removed, and diced
1 Tbsp dried daikon, rinsed,
   soaked 3–5 minutes, and sliced
1 strip kombu, 2 inches long,
   soaked and diced
¼ cup seitan, cubed
¼ cup carrots, diced
¼ tsp scallion root, finely
   chopped
1½ cups water
chopped scallions for garnish

Add all ingredients to pressure cooker and cook as for plain rice. Remove from flame, allow pressure to come down, and remove cover. Allow to sit 4 to 5 minutes. Remove and place in a serving bowl. Garnish and serve.

Variations: Rice may also be cooked with diced vegetables, vegetable water, soaking water from kombu, wakame, or shiitake mushrooms, with bancha tea, or other ingredients. When using bancha tea instead of plain water, add a couple of drops of tamari soy sauce to the bancha and rice as well as the correct proportion of sea salt. There are thousands of variations that can be used when cooking rice. Please use imagination to create delicious rice dishes throughout the year.

Sushi

Sushi is a traditional Japanese dish. It is very attractive as a party dish, or handy to take on picnics, while traveling, for special meals, or as a snack.

nori
cooked brown rice
carrots, cut intostrips
scallion leaves
umeboshi or umeboshi paste

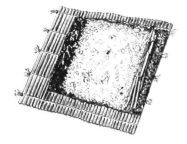

Step 1: Roast one side of a sheet of nori over a flame until it turns green, and place on a bamboo sushi mat. Wet both hands with water, and spread cooked brown rice evenly on the sheet of nori. Leave about ½ to 1 inch of the top of the nori uncovered by rice, and about ⅛ to ¼ inch of the bottom uncovered.

Step 2: Slice a carrot into lengthwise strips 8 to 10 inches long and about ¼ inch thick. Place carrot strips in water with a pinch of sea salt. Boil for 2 to 3 minutes. Carrots should be slightly crisp. Remove and allow to cool. Separate the green leaf portion of several scallions from the roots, so that each strip is about 8 to 10 inches in length. Place carrot and scallion strips approximately ½ to 1 inch from the bottom of the sheet of nori. Then lightly spread 1/16 to ⅛ teaspoon puréed umeboshi along the carrot and scallion strips (entire length).

Step 3: Roll up the rice and nori, using a sushi mat, pressing the mat firmly against

the rice and nori until it is completely rolled up into a round log shape. The vegetables should be centered in the roll. If they are not centered, they were probably placed too far from the bottom edge of the nori and rice.

Step 4: Wet a very sharp knife and slice the roll into rounds approximately ½ to 1 inch thick. The knife may need to be moistened after each slice. If this is not done it may not slice properly. In this case the nori may tear and the rice often sticks to the knife.

Step 5: Arrange rounds on a platter with the cut side up, showing the rice and vegetables.

As a variation put strips of fish, pickles, deep-fried tofu, or other root or green vegetables inside the sushi. If going on a trip or picnic, or if it is a hot day, umeboshi or pickles will help keep the rice from spoiling. For leftover sushi that has become slightly sour or dried out, deep-fry it in hot sesame oil to create a delicious, crunchy snack.

Rice Ball (Musubi)

2 cups cooked brown rice (or 2 handfuls)
1 sheet nori
1 umeboshi plum

Roast the nori (shiny, smooth side up) over a flame by holding it 10 to 12 inches above the flame. Rotate it until the color changes from black to green (about 3 to 5 seconds). Fold the nori in half and tear. Then fold in half again and tear so that there are 4 equal-sized pieces of nori (about 3-inches square).

Wet hands in a dish of water with a pinch of salt diluted in it. Take half of the rice in the hands and form the rice into a ball, as would be done with a snowball, or into a triangle by cupping the hands into a ∨ shape. Pack the rice to form a solid ball or triangle. With the thumb, press a hole into the center, and place half of the umeboshi inside. Then pack the rice ball again to close the hole. Place the toasted nori one piece at a time on the rice ball until the ball is completely covered with nori. The nori will stick to the rice ball. It may be necessary to wet the hands occasionally, to keep the rice and nori from sticking to them. Do not use too much water. The less water used in making a rice ball, the better it will taste and the longer it will keep. The umeboshi inside helps to keep the rice from spoiling, if it is not eaten immediately, and aids in the digestion of the rice and nori. Two pieces of nori, each 3-inches square, are sufficient to cover the rice ball.

Rice balls make a delicious fun snack anytime. They are good for traveling and as lunches for children or adults. When making a rice ball for children, use less or no umeboshi depending on the age of the child. Repeat until all rice and nori are used.

Many interesting conversations develop when one eats a rice ball in a public place, such as on buses, trains, or airplanes.

Rice balls can also be made without using nori. Just simply pack the rice into a ball and eat it as is or roll it in a few roasted sesame seeds.

As a variation, place a small piece of pickle or vegetable inside the rice ball.

OTHER GRAINS

Millet

Millet is one of the more widely used of the cereal grains. It still forms a major part of the diet of about one-third of the world's population, particularly in places like China, Japan, Korea, India, and Africa. We use it quite often in our home as a supplement to rice. It is delicious in soups, stews, combined with vegetables, croquettes, burgers, combined with rice, or just plain.

Boiled Millet with Vegetables

1 cup millet, washed
1 onion, sliced in half-moons
1 cup buttercup squash or
   carrots, cubed or cut in large
   chunks
3 cups boiling water
sesame oil (optional)
pinch of sea salt

Brush pot very lightly with sesame oil. (If not using oil, eliminate sautéing the vegetables.) Sauté vegetables for 3 to 5 minutes on low flame. Add millet to vegetables and dry-roast for 3 to 5 minutes. Add boiling water and salt. Bring to a boil. Turn flame to low, cover, and simmer for 30 to 35 minutes or until water is absorbed.

Pressure-cooked Millet with Seitan and Vegetables

1 cup millet, washed
1 cup cauliflower, flowerettes
½ cup cooked seitan, diced
1½ cups water
1 Tbsp chopped parsley for
  garnish

Place millet, cauliflower, seitan, and water in cooker. Cover, turn flame to high and bring up to pressure. Reduce flame to medium-low and place a flame deflector under it. Cook for 15 minutes. Remove from flame and allow pressure to come down. Remove millet and place in a serving bowl. Garnish with chopped parsley.

Soft Millet

Cook same as boiled millet, only add 5 cups of boiling water instead of 3. This makes a very good breakfast cereal. To pressure-cook soft millet, add 4 to 5 cups water, and sea salt, and cook 15 to 20 minutes. If desired, vegetables such as corn, onions, carrots, squash, cauliflower, or other items may be added.

Millet Croquettes with Vegetable-Kuzu Sauce

3 cups cooked millet
½ cup diced onion
¼ cup diced celery
1 Tbsp chopped parsley
dark sesame oil

Place ingredients in a bowl and mix thoroughly. Take a handful at a time and form the millet into balls or thick patties. Heat oil and deep-fry croquettes until golden brown. Remove and drain on paper towels. Place in a serving dish. Pour Vegetable-Kuzu Sauce (below) over the croquettes, garnish, and serve.

Vegetable-Kuzu Sauce

2 cups water
½ cup onions, sliced in half-
  moons
½ cup carrots, cut into
  matchsticks
2–3 tsp kuzu, diluted in 3 tsp
  water
tamari soy sauce
½ tsp grated ginger
1 Tbsp chopped scallions, chives,
  or parsley

Place water in a saucepan. Bring to a boil. Add onions, cook 1 minute, then add carrots. Cook 2 to 3 minutes. Reduce flame to low. Add diluted kuzu, stirring constantly to avoid lumping. Cook until translucent. Season with a small amount of tamari. Add ginger and mix. Pour sauce over croquettes and garnish with chopped scallion, chives, or parsley, and serve.

Oats

Oats are high in vitamin B, protein, and minerals, and are related to rice and barley. It seems wasteful that 95 percent of the oats grown in the United States are consumed by animals, while only 5 percent of the total crop is consumed by humans. This grain makes a very delicious morning cereal, and can be used in making desserts, and pie crusts. Natural food stores generally carry three types: whole oats, steel-cut oats, which have been steamed and cut into pieces, and rolled oats, which have been steamed and rolled.

Whole Oats

1 cup whole oats, washed
5–6 cups water
pinch of sea salt

Place the whole oats in a pot. Add water and salt. (For a different flavor, roast the oats until light gold.) Cover and bring to a boil. Reduce flame and simmer on a low flame overnight or for several hours. Place a flame deflector under the pot to keep oats from burning. This makes a very good breakfast cereal. Occasionally, add a few raisins or barley malt before when eating.

Pressure-cooked Whole Oats

1 cup whole oats, washed
4 cups water
pinch of sea salt

Instead of boiling, whole oats may be pressure-cooked. First soak the oats for 6 to 8 hours or dry-roast. Add oats, water (soaking water if applicable), and sea salt. Cover and bring to pressure. Reduce flame to medium-low and place a flame deflector under the cooker. Pressure-cook for about 50 to 60 minutes. Remove from flame, allow pressure to come down. Remove cover and serve warm with a favorite garnish or natural sweetener.

Rolled Oats

1 cup rolled oats
2–3 cups water
pinch of sea salt

Roast oats over a low flame for several minutes until they release a nutty fragrance, or to change the flavor somewhat, try not roasting them. Add water and salt. Bring to a boil. Cover and reduce flame to low and simmer for 30 minutes.

For variety, add a sliced onion, or serve with dulse flakes as a garnish.

Buckwheat or Kasha

Traditionally, buckwheat was used as a staple food in Russia and Central Europe. It is the most yang of the cereal grains. It is high in calcium, vitamin B, iron, and minerals. In northern Japan, it is used in making a type of noodle called *soba*. In cold weather, this grain can be used occasionally as a morning cereal or as a supplement to rice. It can also be used in making soup.

There are two types of buckwheat sold in most natural food stores—roasted

72

and unroasted. The roasted variety need only be reroasted for about 3 to 5 minutes. To roast the unroasted type simply place in a dry skillet and roast for approximately 10 minutes or until golden brown, before cooking.

We do not recommend kasha, in most cases, for children under 4 to 5 years old because of its yang qualities.

Kasha

1 cup buckwheat, roasted
2 cups boiling water
1 cup cabbage, sliced in chunks
$\frac{1}{2}$ cup carrots, sliced in matchsticks
pinch of sea salt

Bring water to a boil. Place buckwheat and vegetables in a pot, add boiling water and salt. Bring to a boil, reduce flame to medium-low and cover. Simmer for 20 minutes or until the water has been absorbed.

For variety, sauté cabbage and carrots or onions and chopped parsley in a small amount of dark sesame oil. Cook as above.

For a morning cereal, add 4 to 5 cups of boiling water and cook as above.

Kasha Salad

1 cup buckwheat, roasted
pinch of sea salt
$1\frac{1}{2}$ cups water plus juice from the sauerkraut
1 cup sauerkraut, chopped
1 cup kale, sliced and boiled 1 minute or so
$\frac{1}{2}$ cup red radish, sliced into thin rounds, boiled 1 minute
1 cup boiled tempeh, cut into $\frac{1}{2}$-inch cubes
1 Tbsp chopped parsley, water-sautéed 1 minute
2 Tbsp tamari soy sauce
$\frac{1}{2}$ tsp ginger juice

Place kasha, sea salt, and water in a pressure cooker. Cover and bring to pressure. Reduce flame to medium-low and cook for 10 to 15 minutes. Remove from flame and allow pressure to come down. Remove cover and place kasha in a large mixing bowl. Add sauerkraut, kale, red radish, tempeh, and parsley. Mix well. Add tamari and ginger juice. Mix well again. Place in a serving bowl and serve.

Stuffed Cabbage

1 cup buckwheat, roasted
4–5 cabbage leaves
sesame oil
$\frac{1}{2}$ cup onions, diced
$\frac{1}{2}$ cup carrots, diced
$\frac{1}{4}$ cup mushroom, diced
$\frac{1}{4}$ cup celery, chopped

Remove cabbage leaves from head of cabbage. Try to avoid breaking the leaves, they should be left whole. Boil cabbage leaves in water until tender (about 1 minute) but not soft. Set aside to cool.

Brush pot lightly with sesame oil. Heat pot.

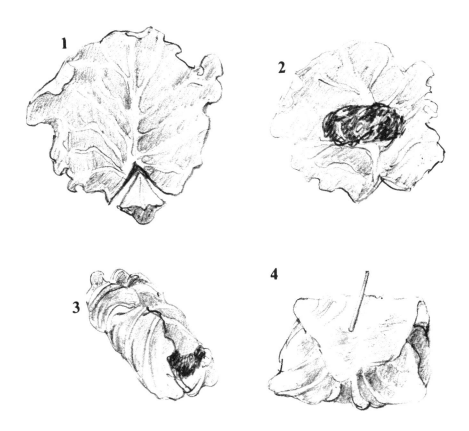

2 cups boiling water
pinch of sea salt
1 strip kombu, 3–4 inches long
2 tsp tamari soy sauce

Add onions, carrots, mushroom, and celery.
Sauté for 5 to 10 minutes. Add buckwheat and
mix with vegetables. Add boiling water and salt.
Bring to a boil. Cover and reduce flame to low.
Simmer 20 to 30 minutes. Remove from flame
and allow to cool. Cut thick portion of cabbage
leaves off the leaves as shown in illustration. Take
a large spoonful of kasha and vegetables and
form by hand into a croquette. Place croquette on
cabbage leaf. Fold sides of cabbage leaf toward
center and roll into a croquette shape. Fasten
leaf with a toothpick.

Place cabbage and kombu in a pot and add
enough water to half cover the stuffed cabbage.
Add a couple of teaspoons of tamari to the water.
Bring to a boil. Cover, reduce flame to low, and
simmer for 20 to 25 minutes. Serve plain or with
a sauce.

Sweet Rice ────────────────────────────

Sweet rice is more glutinous than regular brown rice. Traditionally in Japan it is used in making saké, an alcoholic beverage, and for making mochi, which is pounded into a sticky mass and formed into cakes. Sweet rice is very high in protein and vitamin B. It is a delicious grain and may be eaten by itself or occasionally mixed with brown rice.

1 cup sweet brown rice 1–1¼ cups water pinch of sea salt	Wash rice. Add water and salt. Cook as for regular pressure-cooked brown rice.

Mochi ────────────────────────────

Cook same as above. Remove from pressure cooker and place rice in a wooden bowl. Wet mochi pounder before pounding or rice will stick. Pound the cooked rice with a heavy wooden pestle or mochi pounder (which can be purchased at a natural food store) until the grains are completely crushed and become very sticky. Then wet both hands and form a tablespoonful of rice into a small ball or round cake. Or, spread the mochi on a baking sheet which has been oiled and dusted with rice flour, and allow it to dry for several days. To serve, cut into pieces, and then deep-fry, bake, or pan-fry in a dry skillet over a low flame. As a variation, place pieces of pan-fried or baked mochi in hot tamari soy sauce broth or miso soup several minutes before serving the soup.

Sweet Rice and Chestnuts ────────────────────────────

1 cup sweet brown rice ¼ cup dried chestnuts 1¼–1½ cups water pinch of sea salt	Wash chestnuts and dry-roast several minutes, stirring constantly to avoid burning, over a medium-low flame. Remove chestnuts and soak for 10 to 15 minutes in 1¼ to 1½ cups water. Wash sweet rice and place in pressure cooker. Add chestnuts, soaking water, and sea salt. Cook same as for regular rice. Remove and place in a serving bowl.

Ohagi ────────────────────────────

Ohagi are balls of sweet rice which have been lightly pounded. Prepare same as for mochi, but pound the sweet rice only until the grains are about half crushed. Take about 1 tablespoon of the dough and roll in one of the following nut or seed coatings. These are a great snack item or a delicious party or picnic treat.

Walnut Ohagi

1 cup walnuts **tamari soy sauce**	Dry-roast the walnuts in a skillet and lightly season with tamari. Remove the walnuts from the skillet and chop very fine. Place in a suribachi and grind until fine but not pasty. Add 2 to 3 more drops of tamari and grind again lightly to mix in tamari. Moisten hands lightly with water. Take 1 table-spoon of pounded sweet rice and roll it in the walnuts until it is completely coated. Form into balls or patties. Continue until all walnuts are used. Arrange attractively on a platter.

Sesame Ohagi

1 cup sesame seeds, roasted **tamari soy sauce (optional)**	Place the seeds in a suribachi and grind until about half crushed. Add a couple drops of tamari and grind in lightly. Prepare same as above. For variety, simply roll in plain, roasted, sesame seeds, omitting the tamari. *Variation:* Ohagi can also be made by coating the pounded sweet rice with chestnut purée, or sweet azuki bean purée.

Barley

Barley is believed to be one of the oldest cultivated grains in history. It is also a staple grain in many countries around the world today.

There are several types of barley available in natural food stores. The most common type is *pearled* barley, which is white in color and a little fatter than grains of rice. There are less refined varieties of this grain which are darker in color—often referred to as *hulled* barley—which take a little longer to cook than the whiter variety. There is *pearl* barley, also called *hato mugi*. This variety of barley is not actually a grain but is a wild grass known for its medicinal qualities and is often classified as a grain in macrobiotic cooking. It is white in color and round in shape, with a light tan streak in the middle of the grain. It also has a very strong flavor.

Any of these varieties can be soaked and cooked together with rice or made into soups and stews. Barley can also be milled into flour and combined with wheat flour to make a very delicious bread. It can also be dry-roasted to make teas.

Soft Pearled Barley Cereal

1 cup pearled barley, soaked
  6–8 hours
5 cups water (soaking water)
½ cup onions, diced
2 shiitake mushrooms, soaked,
  stems removed, and diced
pinch of sea salt
chopped scallions for garnish

Place the soaked barley and soaking water in a pressure cooker. Add onions, shiitake and sea salt. Cover and place on a high flame. Bring up to pressure. Place a flame deflector under the cooker and reduce the flame to medium-low. Cook for 50 minutes. Remove from the flame and allow pressure to come down. Place in individual serving bowls and garnish with chopped scallions.

Soft Pearl Barley and Vegetables (*Hato Mugi*)

1 cup pearl barley (hato mugi),
  soaked
5 cups water
½ cup onions, diced
2 shiitake mushrooms, soaked
  and diced
½ cup celery, diced
½ cup carrots, diced
¼ cup daikon, diced
pinch of sea salt

Cook same as above recipe, but only for 30 to 40 minutes.

Corn

Corn was widely used by the American Indians and still is today by Latin and South American people. There are several varieties of corn available today and depending on the variety of corn, the various nutrients are iron, protein, calcium, and vitamin A. Sweet corn is probably the most widely known and used in this country today along with popcorn, which closely resembles the ancient early domestic corn of the American Indians.

Corn is very delicious cooked plain, with other grains such as rice or millet, and in soups and sea vegetable dishes.

Fresh sweet corn is a wonderful summer and late summer treat either boiled or baked. Dry, hard corn must be cooked a long time with wood ash to soften the outer shell. Hard corn is not recommended for children under the age of four to five unless milled and formed into arepas (corn cakes) or other corn products such as tacos or empanadas. Cornmeal is also a delicious breakfast cereal, occasionally, or can be used in making desserts such as corn pudding.

Corn silk, dried, can be used in making a very refreshing summer tea when boiled in water.

Baked Corn

4–5 ears sweet corn

Remove 1 to 2 outer layers of the corn husk, but leave several layers of the husk intact. Also, remove only the dark brown, dried corn silk, and save for making tea. Rinse the corn under cold water for a minute or so. Place in a 350°F oven and bake for 25 to 30 minutes, until done. Remove and place in a serving bowl. Remove husks before eating. For variety, rub a little umeboshi plum on the corn for a delicious flavor.

Sweet corn may also be steamed instead of baked when first prepared in the above manner.

Arepa

Arepa is a traditional South American dish made from cooked, whole, dried corn. It is very delicious and a wonderful treat for both children and adults. The corn is cooked together with wood ash, which helps to soften the hard outer shell of the corn, making it easier to digest. Prepackaged corn dough, called *masa*, can be found in some natural food stores, but make sure that it has been cooked with wood ash and not with lime. The lime may cause serious health problems, especially for pregnant women.

2 cups whole dry corn, washed
1 cup sifted wood ash, tied in
   a cheesecloth or muslin sack
4–5 cups water
⅛ tsp sea salt
dark sesame oil

Place corn, wood ash, and 4 to 5 cups of water in a pressure cooker and cook for 20 minutes or so. Remove from flame, allow pressure to come down, and remove the corn. Place the corn in a bowl and wash thoroughly to remove any wood ash. This may take several washings. Loose corn skins should float to the top while rinsing. Discard these. If they do not, add more wood ash to the sack and pressure-cook another 15 minutes or so.

After rinsing, place the corn back into a clean pressure cooker, add fresh water to cover, and pressure-cook again for about 60 minutes.

Remove from flame and allow pressure to come down. Remove the corn and place in a bowl. Allow to cool completely.

Place the corn in a hand grinder or flour mill (do not use a blender or food processor). After grinding, knead the dough for about 15 to 20 minutes by hand.

Add sea salt and a small amount of water to

make the corn about the consistency of bread dough. Form the dough into several balls a little smaller than fist size. Form these balls into patties or oval cakes so that they are about ½ inch thick. Brush dark sesame oil on a cast-iron skillet and heat up. Place the arepas in the skillet and fry 2 to 3 minutes on each side, or until a crust forms. Be careful not to burn the cakes. Remove the cakes and bake at 350°F for 20 minutes or so, or until the arepas puff up slightly. Test for doneness by using the fingers to tap the arepas. They should make a hollow popping or thumping sound.

The arepas can be eaten plain or with a tamari dip sauce.

For variety, mix in finely chopped vegetables to the dough before cooking.

Seitan

Seitan is very high in protein, calcium, and niacin. It is made from more glutinous varieties of flour. It is traditionally eaten in many countries throughout the world. It can be used in soups, stews, salads, and cooked with vegetables, in *sukiyaki*, sandwiches, or combined with bread crumbs, onions, celery, and mushrooms to stuff a squash. There are many different ways of preparing this food.

I have found that the hard spring wheat flour produces a much softer texture of seitain than the hard winter wheat flour. Hard winter wheat produces a more firm texture. They both produce about the same amount of gluten and both result in delicious seitan.

I have a very quick method of making seitan and it produces almost the same amount of seitan as does the long method described in most macrobiotic cook books.

Seitan

3½ lbs whole wheat flour
8–9 cups water, warm
1 strip kombu, 3 inches long
¼–⅓ cup tamari soy sauce

Place flour in a large pot. Add the warm water to make a consistency of oatmeal or oatmeal cookie batter. Knead 3 to 5 minutes or until all the flour is mixed with the water and becomes firm. Cover with warm water and let sit 5 to 10 minutes. It can sit longer than this without hurting the seitan.

Knead again in the soaking water for about 1 minute. The water will become cloudy and milky. Pour off the cloudy water into a jar. (Save the soaking and the majority of the rinsing water.) Place the sticky gluten in a large strainer. Place strainer in a large pot or bowl. Pour cold water over the gluten and knead the gluten in the strainer. Repeat until the bran and starch are almost all washed out. Alternate between warm and cold water when rinsing and kneading the gluten.

This alternating water temperature helps the bran to wash out more easily. The first and last rinse should always be with cold water to contract the gluten into a large ball. Save the white liquid from the first 3 to 4 rinsings of the gluten. This is called *starch water* and is used as a thickening agent for stews or gravies, or if allowed to sour for 3 to 4 days, bread can be made with the water. This sour starch water acts as a sourdough starter.

After the bran and starch has been rinsed out of the gluten in the strainer, wash again in a bowl for 2 to 3 minutes with cold water to remove any remaining bran. The gluten should now form a sticky ball. Separate the gluten into 5 to 6 pieces and form balls. Drop balls into 6 cups of boiling water, and boil for 5 minutes or until the balls float to the top. Remove and cut into cubes for soup, strips if they are to be sautéd with vegetables, or leave whole to make sandwiches.

Place the kombu in the boiling water and add tamari. Place cubed, sliced or whole pieces of gluten into the tamari water. Bring to a boil. Reduce flame to low, cover pot, and simmer for 35 to 45 minutes. The seitan is now ready to use.

Seitan Stew

seitan and seitan-tamari cooking water
1 medium onion, cut in thick wedges
2 carrots, cut in irregular or rolling method shape
1 stalk burdock, sliced on thin diagonal
1 cup Brussels sprouts, cut in half

Place the seitan and seitan-tamari cooking water in the pot. Add onions, carrots, burdock, Brussel sprouts and celery. Add enough cold water, if needed, to cover the vegetables. Bring to a boil. Reduce flame to low and simmer until vegetables are done. Add starch water, stirring constantly until thick. Bring to a boil. Reduce flame to low. Add tamari to taste, cover, and simmer for 15 to 20 minutes. If the stew is too thin, add a little

80

¼ cup celery, cut on thin
  diagonal
1–2 cups seitan starch water
  (from rinsing gluten)
tamari soy sauce

more starch water. If too thick, add more cold
water for desired consistency.

Seitan-Barley Soup

seitan and seitan-tamari cooking
  water
½ cup barley, soaked 6–8 hours
  in 5 cups water
1 medium onion, sliced
2 carrots, cut in irregular or
  rolling method shape
¼ cup mushrooms, sliced
½ cup celery, sliced
tamari soy sauce
chopped scallions, chives, or
  parsley for garnish

Place barley and soaking water in a pressure
cooker. Pressure-cook 30 to 40 minutes. Add
onions, carrots, mushrooms, and celery. Add
the seitan and seitan-tamari cooking water.
Bring to a boil. Reduce flame to low and simmer
uncovered about 30 minutes. Add tamari to taste
if necessary and simmer for another 5 to 10
minutes. Place in individual serving bowls.
Garnish with chopped scallions, chives, or parsley,
and serve.

Sautéed Vegetables and Seitan

Slice the seitan. Sauté sliced kale and carrots in dark sesame oil for 2 to 3 minutes.
Add seitan slices and ¼ cup seitan-tamari cooking water. Simmer seitan and
vegetables in it until kale and carrots are tender and all liquid has evaporated.

Stuffed Cabbage with Seitan

Boil several whole cabbage leaves about 5 minutes until tender. Remove from
water, drain, and wrap the cooked seitan (2 inches in size) inside the cabbage
leaves. Fasten with a toothpick. Place one 3-inch piece of kombu in the bottom of
a skillet. Place cabbage rolls on top. Add 1 cup of water and 1 tablespoon of
tamari soy sauce to the skillet. Cover and bring to a boil. Reduce flame to low and
simmer 20 to 30 minutes. Remove cabbage rolls and drain. Place on a serving
platter. Add a small amount of diluted kuzu to the remaining liquid in the skillet.
Stir constantly until thick. Pour the sauce over the rolls and garnish with chopped
scallions or parsley. Serve.

Seitan Croquettes

When the bran and starch have been rinsed out of the gluten as explained in the
seitan making recipe, do not boil in water. Instead, separate the gluten into 5
equal pieces and form into balls. Pull the gluten into flat pieces and wrap one
2-inch-long by ⅛-inch-wide piece of carrot and burdock inside each piece of
gluten. Deep-fry in hot sesame oil until gluten is golden brown. Remove and
place on a paper towel to allow oil to drain off. Place a 3- to 4-inch strip of kombu

on the bottom of a pot. Place pieces of deep-fried gluten on top of the kombu and add water to cover. Add 2 tablespoons of tamari soy sauce. Bring to a boil. Reduce flame to low, cover, and simmer for 30 to 45 minutes. Add 4 cups starch water and $\frac{1}{2}$ cup diced onions to create a sauce. Stir starch water in gently. Add 1 tablespoon tamari and simmer for another 15 to 20 minutes.

As a variation, wrap cauliflower, daikon, or onions inside the gluten. Or, add diced celery and mushrooms to the sauce.

Wheat

Wheat is seldom used in its whole form as it may be difficult to digest if not properly cooked and well chewed, but there are many delicious dishes that can be prepared using whole wheat berries. Wheat is more often used in its flour form to make seitan, fu, noodles and pasta, bread, and pastries.

Brown Rice with Wheat Berries

1 cup brown rice, washed
$\frac{1}{4}$ cup wheat berries, washed and dry-roasted until golden brown
$1\frac{1}{2}$–$1\frac{3}{4}$ cups water
pinch of sea salt

Place rice, wheat, and water in a pressure cooker. Place on a low flame for 10 to 15 minutes. Add sea salt and cover. Turn flame to high and bring up to pressure. Reduce flame to medium-low and place a flame deflector under the cooker. Cook for 50 minutes. Remove from flame and allow pressure to come down. Remove cover and let sit 4 to 5 minutes. Place rice in a wooden serving bowl. Garnish and serve.

Azuki Beans with Wheat Berries

1 cup azuki beans, soaked 6–8 hours
$\frac{1}{4}$ cup wheat berries, soaked 6–8 hours
1 strip kombu, 3–4 inches long
water (soaking water may be used)
$\frac{1}{8}$–$\frac{1}{4}$ tsp sea salt
chopped scallions for garnishs

Place kombu on the bottom of a pot. Place azuki beans and wheat berries on top of the kombu. Add water to just cover. Bring to a boil, cover, and reduce the flame to medium-low. Simmer $1\frac{1}{2}$ to 2 hours or until 70 percent done, adding water, occasionally as needed, just to cover. Add sea salt and simmer another $\frac{1}{2}$ hour or so until soft. Remove, place in a serving bowl, garnish and serve.

Noodles

I use a variety of noodles and pasta in our home. For example, there are several types of Japanese noodles available in this country, such as *upon, somen,* and soba. There are several types of udon available. Some are made with 100 percent whole wheat flour, while others are made with varying proportions of whole wheat and unbleached or sifted wheat flours. All of these are fine for regular consumption. The same is true for somen, a thin, very light tasting Japanese noodle. Soba, a buckwheat noodle, originated in the colder, northern climates of Japan. There are several types of soba, such as 100 percent buckwheat flour; those made with varying proportions of buckwheat and wheat flours; *ito* soba, a thin soba noodle similar to somen; *jinenjo* soba, made with buckwheat flour and jinenjo (a wild mountain potato from Japan) flour. All of the various Japanese noodles contain salt, and it is not necessary to add salt to the cooking water as with European and American pastas, which do not contain salt.

There are also European and American whole wheat pastas and spaghetti, which come in various shapes and sizes. There are elbows, spirals, ribbons, lasagne, shells, rigatoni, ziti, and spaghetti to choose from. When cooking these pastas, use a pinch of sea salt.

Any whole grain noodle may be used in soups, salads, fried with vegetables, boiled and served with a little miso or tamari broth, or simply cooked and eaten plain with a little tamari soy sauce and scallion garnish.

To cook any noodle or pasta, first bring a pot of water to a boil. If cooking Japanese noodles, do not add any salt to the cooking water. If using European or American pasta, add a pinch of sea salt to the boiling water. Reduce the flame to medium-low and simmer several minutes until done. To test for doneness, take one noodle or piece of pasta and slice or bite in half. When done, the noodle or pasta should be the same color inside and out. If the center is white and the periphery is dark, it is not quite done, so continue to cook. When done, remove and place in a strainer or colander. Rinse with cold water until the noodles or pasta are completely cool before using. The noodles may also be eaten hot, without rinsing, but the Japanese noodles may be a little salty tasting. Serve with a few drops of tamari soy sauce and garnish with chopped scallions if unwashed.

Fried Udon or Soba

1 package (8 oz) udon or soba
1 Tbsp sesame oil
½ cup carrots, matchsticks
1 cup sliced or shredded cabbage
1–2 Tbsp tamari soy sauce
½ cup sliced scallions

Cook noodles as above, then wash under cold water and allow them to drain for several minutes. Add oil to a skillet and heat up. Add carrots and cabbage. Sauté vegetables for about 5 minutes. Place udon or soba on top of the vegetables. Cover the skillet and cook on a low flame for several minutes, until the vegetables are done. (Some combinations of vegetables will take longer to cook than the combination I have given.) Add tamari to taste and the scallions. Cook for another 3 to 5 minutes. Mix noodles and vegetables near the end of cooking. This will keep the noodles from burning and allow the vegetables to cook faster. Make sure to keep the flame fairly low to avoid burning the vegetables. Serve hot or cold.

As a variation, use onions and cabbage; scallions, Chinese cabbage, and tofu or tempeh; scallions, dried tofu and mushrooms; or other vegetable combinations. Please experiment.

Udon or Soba and Broth

1 package (8 oz)udon or soba
1 strip kombu, 3 inches long
2 dried shiitake mushrooms, soaked and sliced
4 cups water
2–3 Tbsp tamari soy sauce
sliced scallions for garnish
1 sheet toasted nori, cut in 1-inch squares

Cook noodles, wash, and drain. Place kombu, and shiitake in a pot and add water. Bring to a boil. Reduce flame to medium-low and simmer for about 10 minutes. Remove kombu. (Either slice the kombu into small pieces and add again to the soup or leave it out and use it in some other dish.) Reduce the flame to low. Add tamari to taste and simmer for 3 to 5 minutes. Place noodles in the pot of broth to warm them up. Do not boil them. Serve immediately. Garnish with slices of shiitake, scallions, and 1-inch squares of nori.

For a variety of clear broths, which can be used for noodles, refer to the soup section.

Noodle water may be saved and used as a beverage, or as a soup stock. Slightly soured noodle water may be used as a starter for sourdough bread, as it helps unyeasted bread to rise.

For variety, vegetables such as cabbage, onions, squash, carrots, broccoli, kale, and others, may be added to the unseasoned broth water in various combinations and cooked until tender. Then season with tamari or miso.

Soba Sushi

1 package (8 oz) jinenjo soba, cooked, rinsed, and drained
3–4 sheets nori, toasted
3–4 thin strips of scallion or several sprigs of cooked watercress

Place a sheet of toasted nori on top of a bamboo sushi mat (sudare). Place cooked soba on top of the nori so that it covers three-fourths of the sheet and is about $\frac{1}{2}$ inch thick. Place strips of scallion or several sprigs of watercress across the width of the nori about 2 inches from the bottom. Roll up as for rice sushi. Slice same as for rice sushi. Arrange attractively on a serving platter.

Udon or somen may be used in place of soba for variety, as may other vegetable combinations.

Noodle Salad

(See Chapter 8 on Salads for recipe.)

Chapter 4
Soups and Soup Stocks

Preparing soups and stews has always been one of my favorite areas of cooking. Soups can be thick and creamy, chunky and rich, or simple and elegant. They can be warming or cooling depending on the season of the year and method of preparation. For a fussy child who does not always eat his or her vegetables, a very mildly seasoned soup can be one way to make sure the child eats vegetables. There are many different textures and flavors which can be created when preparing soups by using various cooking methods, seasonings, and garnishes, as well as ingredients.

Although soups comprise only about 5 percent (or 1 to 2 bowls) of our daily food intake, they are a very important part of our diet. Soups provide extra liquid and various nutrients, they stimulate our appetites, and prepare our digestive system for the remaining part of our meal. They contribute to creating a healthy blood condition, as well as intestinal conditions.

There are many methods of preparing soups to create balance with seasonal change, our age, our physical and mental condition, and our activity or work. Soups are usually served at the beginning of a meal and, ideally, should complement the dishes to follow, in terms of color, taste, texture, and aroma. For instance, if the other dishes in the meal are rich and hearty, to make balance, prepare a simple or clear broth soup. If the meal as a whole is simple and light, prepare a thick, hearty, rich soup or stew. This same principle applies to seasonal changes. For a cold winter day, we may prepare a thick, heavier and richer soup or stew to generate body warmth. During the hot summer months, lighter, more cooling soups, made with less seasoning can be made.

The following are several methods which can be used to prepare soups and stews:

1. **Method #1**—*Boiling Water:* When using this boiling method, bring water to a boil first and then add various vegetables and other ingredients. Cook several minutes until tender, reduce the flame and season. This method is very nice for miso soup. It has a refreshingly light, upward energy quality.

2. **Method #2**—*Layering Method:* Various ingredients are layered, in a pot, with the most yin (softer) vegetables or ingredients on the bottom of the pot and the more yang (harder) ingredients on the top. For example, to make a millet soup, place diced kombu on the bottom of the pot. Next, diced onions are layered on top of the kombu, and diced celery on top of the onions. Layer diced carrots on top of the celery. Diced or quartered burdock is layered on top of the carrots. Finally, layer millet on top of the burdock, as millet is a grain and more yang than vegetables.

    Add enough cold water to very lightly cover the millet. Add a pinch of sea salt. Bring to a boil, reduce the flame to medium-low. Cover and do not mix or stir until the end of cooking. As the millet begins to absorb water and expand, add only enough water to lightly cover the millet. This may need to be done several times until the millet is soft. Once the vegetables and millet are soft, add more water to obtain the desired consistency (it may be thick like a stew or a thin soup, whichever is desired). Then add a little more sea salt to create a mild salty taste and continue to simmer until all ingredients are soft and creamy. This results in a beautiful creamy, pale, or soft yellow soup, if seasoned with sea salt. If seasoning this soup with tamari soy sauce instead of sea salt, add the tamari soy sauce in the last 10 to 15 minutes of cooking time. This results in a darker color soup and a different flavor. This soup may also be seasoned with puréed miso instead of sea salt or tamari soy sauce. If using miso, make sure to add it in the last 2 to 3 minutes of cooking, after reducing the flame to low. When seasoned with miso, this soup has a darker color and richer flavor.

    The layering method can be used not only for soups but with grain, bean, sea vegetable, and vegetable side dishes as well. Using the layering method results in a very calm, relaxing, peaceful energy because the food is basically undisturbed while cooking. The energy and flavors of the food mix naturally with the rising yin energy and flavors and the more yang descending ones. This method can be used several times per week.

3. **Method #3**—*Cold Water:* Place vegetables or other ingredients in cold water and bring to a boil or pressure-cook until done. Then season and serve several minutes later. This is a slightly stronger preparation, but is also very delicious.

4. **Method #4**—*Sautéing:* Another way of preparing soups, on occasion, is to sauté the vegetables in oil first and then add water and cook until soft and tender. Season the soup, simmer several minutes, and then garnish and serve. Sautéing the vegetables first results in a richer flavor and a strong energy. This method can be used more during cooler weather or seasons.

One of my favorite soups is a French onion miso soup using this method. It is very sweet and rich.

Other Comments

Usually, soups are simmered using one of the above methods but occasionally they may be pressure-cooked, especially in the case of beans or thick stews, if a very soft texture is desired, or if in a hurry.

Soups may also be prepared with a soup stock as a base before adding other ingredients. There are many types of seasonings which can be used when making soups such as: miso, tamari soy sauce, sea salt, umeboshi or umeboshi paste.

Miso Soups

There are many types of misos available which vary in color, taste, and energy.

The most important and most often used is *mugi miso*, which has been fermented for twenty-four to thirty-six months. Mugi miso, sometimes called barley miso, is made from barley, soybeans, sea salt, water, and a miso bacteria starter called *koji*. This is the best miso to use for everyday cooking and is especially important for those with a serious illness. This two-year-old miso is dark in color, rich in flavor, and has a moderate salty taste. It should not be confused with *mellow* or *light* barley misos, which are usually lighter in color, saltier in taste, and fermented for a shorter period of time.

Of course other misos can be used, if one's condition is generally strong, but these are generally used occasionally for variety. Some of the other types of miso are: *genmai* (brown rice); *Hatcho* (soybean); and *kome* (white rice). Genmai is generally lighter in flavor and recommended during warmer months, occasionally. Kome is very similar to genmai. Hatcho miso is aged for over three years and has a deep, dark color, and a strong, rich flavor. Hatcho is generally used in colder weather or for making strong condiments such as tekka.

There are also light, quickly fermented misos such as white, yellow, red, buckwheat, and natto miso which are used less frequently. These can be occasionally used in soups, dips, and sauces, by those in relatively good health.

Miso soup can be served for any meal. When preparing it for breakfast, it is best if simply made and light in taste, while miso soup for dinner can be a little stronger and more hearty, if desired.

Miso has started to become more widely known for its antitoxic properties, including the power to offset nuclear radiation. Following the Chernobyl accident, as a radioactive cloud diffused across Western Europe, natural food shops there experienced a run on macrobiotic staple foods. Within a week, their shelves were cleaned of items such as miso and sea vegetables. This trend continued, so that by the end of the year, the leading exporters of traditional, natural miso in Japan reported a sevenfold increase in sales over previous years: mostly to Western Europe.

Below are a variety of recipes for preparing hearty and nourishing miso soup.

Basic Miso Soup (*Wakame and Onion*)

1 oz (approximately ½ cup) dry wakame, soaked
1 cup onions, sliced in half-moons
4–5 cups water
1½–2½ Tbsp puréed miso

Wash wakame twice under cold water very quickly to remove any dust, and soak for 3 to 5 minutes. Slice into ½-inch pieces. Bring the water to a boil and add the onions. Reduce the flame and simmer for approximately 3 to 5 minutes, or until the onions are tender. Add the wakame and simmer another 5 minutes or so. Reduce the flame to very low, so that the water is not boiling or bubbling. Purée the miso with ¼ cup of water. (Add approximately ½ teaspoon of puréed miso to each cup of water.) Stir the miso gently to mix in with the soup. Simmer for 2 to 3 minutes, garnish and serve.

As a variation, use wakame, onions, and tofu; daikon and daikon greens; wakame, onions, and carrots; onions and squash; Chinese cabbage and carrots; cabbage, carrot and onion; as well as other combinations.

Daikon-Shiitake Miso Soup

1 cup daikon, sliced in thin rounds, halved, or quartered
3 shiitake mushrooms, soaked, stems removed, and sliced
4–5 cups water
¼ cup wakame, soaked and sliced
1½–2½ Tbsp puréed barley (mugi) miso
sliced scallions for garnish

Bring the water to a boil and add the shiitake. Cover, reduce the flame to medium-low, and simmer 5 to 10 minutes. Place the daikon in the pot, cover, and simmer 2 to 3 minutes. Add the wakame, cover, and simmer about 5 minutes. Reduce the flame to very low, add puréed miso, cover, and simmer 2 to 3 minutes. Garnish and serve.

Chinese Cabbage Miso Soup

1–1½ cups Chinese cabbage,
 sliced
¼ cup tofu, diced
4–5 cups water
½ cup onions, sliced in half-
 moons
¼ cup carrots, cut in matchsticks
⅛ cup wakame, soaked and
 sliced
1½–2½ Tbsp puréed miso
sliced scallions for garnish

Bring the water to a boil and add the onions. Reduce the flame to medium-low and cover. Simmer 2 to 3 minutes. Add the carrots, simmer 1 to 2 minutes. Next, add the wakame and simmer 3 to 5 minutes. Add the Chinese cabbage and tofu. Simmer 1 to 2 minutes. Reduce the flame to very low and add the puréed miso, cover, and simmer 2 to 3 minutes. Garnish and serve.

Carrot and Burdock Miso Soup

1 cup carrot, cut in matchsticks
1 cup burdock, shaved
¼ cup wakame, soaked and
 sliced
½ cup onions, sliced in half-
 moons
4–5 cups water
1½–2½ Tbsp puréed miso
chopped parsley for garnish

Bring the water to a boil. Add onions, cover, and reduce the flame to medium-low. Simmer 2 to 3 minutes, add the burdock and simmer 3 to 4 minutes. Add the carrots and wakame, cover, and simmer 3 to 4 minutes longer. Reduce the flame to very low. Add the puréed miso and simmer 2 to 3 minutes longer. Garnish and serve.

Daikon and Celery Miso Soup with Sweet Rice Dumplings

1 cup daikon, sliced in thin
 rectangles
½ cup celery, sliced on a diagonal
4–5 cups water
⅛ cup wakame, soaked and
 sliced
½ cup daikon greens
1½–2½ Tbsp puréed miso
sliced scallions for garnish
Dumplings:
 ½ cup sweet rice or brown
 rice flour
 ¼ cup boiling water
 small pinch of sea salt

Bring water to a boil and add the daikon. Cover, simmer 1 to 2 minutes. Add the celery and cover. Simmer 2 to 3 minutes. Add the wakame and simmer 3 to 5 minutes.

While the wakame is cooking, mix the rice flour, boiling water, and salt together in a bowl for the dumplings. With both hands, form a heaping teaspoon of the mixture into a small ball. With the thumb, make a light thumbprint into the dumpling. Repeat until several dumplings are made.

Place the dumplings into the soup, together with the daikon greens. Simmer, covered, until the dumplings float to the top of the soup. Reduce the flame to very low and add the puréed miso. Simmer 2 to 3 minutes. Garnish and serve.

This soup is a real favorite in our house, on

a cold winter morning. It becomes very thick and creamy because of the dumplings.

Koi-koku (Carp Soup)

1 small or medium carp, whole, cut in chunks (Only have the bitter bone and insides removed. Leave on head, scales, bones, tail, and fins. If the carp is female, leave the eggs in.)
dark sesame oil
burdock (twice the volume of carp), shaved
1 cup used bancha twigs
water
puréed barley miso
grated ginger
sliced scallions for garnish

Place a small amount of sesame oil in a pressure cooker and heat it up. Add the burdock and sauté 3 to 5 minutes. Wrap the used bancha twigs in a cotton cheesecloth or linen sack and tie tightly. Place the sack of twigs on top of the burdock. Place the chunks of carp on top of the sack and burdock. Add water to cover the carp. Pressure-cook for 2 hours. Bring pressure down and remove the cover. Reduce the flame to low and add a small amount of puréed miso, for a moderate salt taste. Simmer for several minutes. Add a small amount of grated ginger and simmer 1 to 2 minutes longer. Garnish and serve hot.

For a less strong soup, add carrots cut in matchsticks, or celery and onions for a regular, mild fish soup.

The carp soup with just the burdock is often recommended for persons with a weakened condition. It helps restore energy and vitality. Trout may be substituted if carp is not available, but only cook for 1 hour.

Quick Miso Soup

1 cup water
$\frac{1}{8}$–$\frac{1}{4}$ cup sliced scallions
$\frac{1}{2}$–1 tsp puréed miso
half sheet toasted nori, cut into 1-inch squares

Bring the water to a boil. Reduce the flame to low, add the scallions and miso. Simmer 1 to 2 minutes. Garnish with nori and serve.

This soup is quick to prepare for those who are traveling or in a hurry.

Grain Soups

Millet Soups

$\frac{1}{2}$ cup millet, washed
1 strip kombu, 4–5 inches long, soaked and diced
1 onion, diced
$\frac{1}{2}$ stalk of celery, halved and

Set the kombu on the bottom of the pot. Place the onions on top of the kombu. Next, add a layer of celery on top of the onions and then a layer of carrots. Then place a layer of burdock and finally a layer of millet. Do not mix.

sliced diagonally
1 carrot, diced or quartered
1 small burdock stalk, halved or
    quartered
4–5 cups water
¼–½ tsp sea salt
sliced scallions, celery leaves,
    or sprig of parsley for garnish

Gently add enough water just to cover the top of the millet, without disturbing the layered ingredients. Add a pinch of sea salt and turn the flame to high. Bring to a boil, reduce the flame to medium-low, and simmer. When the water starts to be absorbed by the millet and the grains expand, add enough water to lightly cover again. Repeat this process until the millet is soft and starts to become creamy.

When the millet is completely cooked, add 4 to 5 cups more water and the remaining sea salt. (For a thick soup or stew, add less water; for a thin soup add more.) Simmer for another 20 to 25 minutes until the soup becomes very soft and creamy. Garnish with sliced scallions, celery leaves, or a sprig of parsley

This layering method can be used in preparing just about any grain, bean, or vegetable soup.

Rice and Pumpkin Soup

2 cups cooked rice
1 cup Hokkaido pumpkin (or
    buttercup squash cut into
    ¼–½-inch chunks)
½ cup diced onion
5–6 cups water
¼–½ tsp sea salt

Place the onions on the bottom of the pot. Add the pumpkin. Place the rice on top of the pumpkin. Add the water and a small pinch of sea salt. Bring to a boil, reduce the flame to medium-low and simmer for about 45 minutes to 1 hour. Add the remaining sea salt to taste and cook for another 15 to 20 minutes.

Barley-Lentil Soup

½ cup barley, washed and
    soaked
¼ cup lentils, washed
1 strip kombu, 4–5 inches long,
    soaked and diced
½ cup onions, diced
5–6 cups water
¼ cup celery, diced
5–7 fresh mushrooms, sliced
¼–½ tsp sea salt
sliced scallions for garnish

Set the kombu on the bottom of the pot. Place the onions in the pot. Set the barley on top of the onions. Place the lentils on top of the barley. Add water. Bring to a boil, reduce the flame to medium-low and simmer until the barley is almost done. Add the celery, mushrooms, and sea salt. Cook for another 15 to 20 minutes. Garnish and serve.

For a variation, a combination of barley, kidney beans, onions, celery, and mushrooms is delicious.

Cream of Corn Soup

2 ears fresh sweet corn removed
   from the cob
4 cups water
sesame oil
1 cup onions, diced
¼–½ tsp sea salt
¼–½ cup corn flour
¼ cup celery, diced
chopped scallions, parsley, or a
   sprig of watercress for
   garnish

Boil the corncobs in 4 cups of water. Save the water for the soup. Brush a pot with a very small amount of sesame oil. Sauté the onions and sweet corn. Add a pinch of sea salt. Add the corn flour to the onions and sweet corn. Mix so that the vegetables become coated with the flour.

Add the water, gradually, to the flour and vegetables, stirring gently but constantly to avoid lumping of the flour. Bring to a boil, reduce the flame to medium-low and simmer about 30 minutes. Add the celery and remaining sea salt. Cook another 15 to 20 minutes. Garnish with chopped scallions, parsley, or a sprig of water-cress.

As a variation, omit the corn flour and season with tamari soy sauce instead of sea salt.

Rice Soup (*Ojiya*)

2 cups cooked rice
1 strip kombu, 3 inches long,
   soaked and diced
3 shiitake mushrooms, soaked,
   and sliced
½ cup daikon, sliced in rectangles or quartered
4 cups water
1½–2½ Tbsp puréed miso
½ cup scallions for garnish

Place the kombu, shiitake, daikon and rice in a pressure cooker. Add water, cover, and bring up to pressure. Reduce the flame to medium-low and place a flame deflector under the cooker. Pressure-cook for 30 minutes. Remove and allow the pressure to come down. Remove the cover and mix in the puréed miso. Reduce the flame to very low. Simmer 2 to 3 minutes. Garnish and serve hot.

Cream of Vegetable Soup

1 cup cooked brown rice
½ cup oatmeal
½ cup onions, diced
¼ cup celery, diced
½ cup carrots, sliced in rounds
1 cup broccoli, sliced
4–5 cups water
¼–½ tsp sea salt
chopped scallions for garnish
½ sheet toasted nori, cut into
   squares or strips

Place the rice, oats, and water in a pot, and cover. Bring to a boil. Reduce the flame to medium-low and simmer about 10 to 15 minutes. Add the onions, celery, carrots, and broccoli. Cover and simmer until the vegetables are tender. Season with sea salt and cook another 5 to 10 minutes. Garnish with scallions and nori squares and serve.

Other variations which can be made using this rice and oat base are: cream of celery; cream of mushroom; cream of cauliflower; cream of carrot; cream of broccoli; or cream of corn soup. For a smoother texture soup, purée the rice and oats in a hand food mill before adding the vegetables.

Bean Soups

Azuki Bean Soup

1 cup azuki beans, washed and soaked 6–8 hours
1 strip kombu, 3–4 inches long, soaked and sliced
1 cup onions, diced
$\frac{1}{2}$ cup buttercup squash, cubed
$\frac{1}{2}$ cup carrots, sliced
4–5 cups water
$\frac{1}{4}$–$\frac{1}{2}$ tsp sea salt
tamari soy sauce to taste (optional)

Place the kombu, onions, squash, and carrots in a pot. Add the beans. Add water (including soaking water from the beans and kombu). Cover and bring to a boil. Reduce the flame to medium-low and simmer about $1\frac{1}{2}$ hours or until the beans are about 80 percent done. Season with sea salt and a little tamari, if desired, and continue to cook another 30 minutes or so until the beans are soft. Garnish and serve.

Lentil Soup

1 cup lentils, washed
1 strip kombu, 3–4 inches long, soaked and diced
1 cup onions, diced
$\frac{1}{2}$ cup carrots, diced
$\frac{1}{4}$ cup burdock, quartered
4–5 cups water
1 Tbsp chopped parsley
$\frac{1}{4}$–$\frac{1}{2}$ tsp sea salt

Place the kombu and onions on the bottom of a pot. Then layer carrots and burdock on top. Place the lentils on top of the burdock. Add the water and bring to a boil. Reduce flame to medium-low and cover. Simmer for 45 to 50 minutes. Add the chopped parsley and sea salt. Simmer another 20 minutes or so and serve. If some of the water evaporates, add a little more to make it the desired consistency.

Split-Pea Soup

1 cup split-peas
1 cup onions, diced
$\frac{1}{2}$ cup carrots, quartered
$\frac{1}{4}$ cup soaked wakame, sliced
$\frac{1}{2}$ cup cooked seitan, cubed
4–5 cups water
$\frac{1}{4}$–$\frac{1}{2}$ tsp sea salt

Cook same as for the lentil soup. This soup should be creamy and may require a little more cooking than the lentils. Garnish and serve.

As a variation, add $\frac{1}{4}$ cup diced jinenjo, or even cooked elbow noodles at the end of cooking.

Kidney Bean Soup

2 cups kidney beans, soaked 6–8 hours
1 strip kombu, 3–4 inches long,

Place kombu, onions, celery, carrots, corn, and beans in a pressure cooker. Add water, cover, and bring to pressure. Reduce the flame to

soaked and diced
1 cup onions, diced
¼ cup celery, sliced on a
    diagonal
½ cup carrots, sliced in rounds
½ cup fresh sweet corn
5–6 cups water
¼–½ tsp sea salt
chopped scallions for garnish

medium-low and cook about 1 hour. Remove and allow pressure to come down. Remove cover and season with sea salt. Simmer uncovered for another 10 to 15 minutes. Garnish and serve.

For a different, more rich flavor, season with a little puréed miso instead of sea salt.

Lima Bean Soup

1 cup large lima beans, soaked
    6–8 hours
1 strip kombu, 3–4 inches long,
    soaked and diced
½ cup kurumabu (large rounds
    of fu), soaked and cubed
2 cups cabbage, sliced in chunks
4–5 cups water
¼ cup bonito flakes
¼–½ tsp sea salt
sliced scallions for garnish

Place kombu, fu, cabbage, beans, and water in a pressure cooker. Cover and bring to pressure. Reduce the flame to medium-low and cook for 50 minutes. Remove and allow pressure to come down. Remove cover, add bonito flakes, and season with sea salt. Simmer 15 to 20 minutes longer. Garnish and serve.

Soybean Stew

1 cup yellow soybeans, soaked
    6–8 hours
1 strip kombu, 3–4 inches long
    soaked and diced
¼ cup celery, diced
⅛ cup dried daikon, washed,
    soaked, and sliced
¼ cup dried tofu, soaked and
    cubed
½ cup carrots, diced
¼ cup lotus root, diced or
    quartered
⅛ cup burdock, quartered
¼ cup cooked seitan, diced
4–5 cups water
tamari soy sauce
sliced scallions for garnish

Layer kombu, celery, dried daikon, dried tofu, carrots, lotus root, burdock, seitan, and soybeans in a pressure cooker. Add water to cover the beans. Bring up to pressure. Reduce the flame to medium-low and cook about 45 to 50 minutes. Allow the pressure to come down, remove cover, and season lightly with tamari. Continue to simmer, uncovered, for another 10 to 15 minutes. Garnish and serve.

Black Bean Soup (Turtle Beans)

1 cup black beans
4–5 cups water
1 cup onions, diced

Place the beans in a pressure cooker with water. Bring up to pressure. Reduce the flame to medium-low and cook for 45 to 50 minutes.

¼–½ tsp sea salt
chopped parsley or scallions for
  garnish

Allow pressure to come down. Remove the cover
and add the onions and sea salt. Simmer for
another 20 minutes until the onions are soft. If
desired, add a little tamari soy sauce to taste.
Garnish with chopped parsley or scallions and
serve.

Chick-pea Soup

1 cup chick-peas, soaked 6–8
  hours
1 strip kombu, 3–4 inches long
⅛ cup burdock quartered
½ cup onions, diced
½ cup carrots, diced
¼ cup celery, diced
4–5 cups water
1½–2½ tsp puréed miso
chopped scallions or parsley for
  garnish

Place kombu, chick-peas, vegetables, and water
in a pressure cooker. Cover and bring up to
pressure. Reduce the flame to medium-low and
pressure-cook for 1 to 1½ hours. Allow the
pressure to come down. Remove the cover, season
with miso, and cook for several minutes longer
on a very low flame. Garnish with scallions or
parsley and serve.

Vegetable Soups

French Onion Soup

2 cups onions, sliced in very thin
  half-moons
1 strip kombu, 3–4 inches long,
  soaked and sliced in matchsticks
3–4 shiitake mushrooms, soaked
  and sliced
4–5 cups water
dark sesame oil
pinch of sea salt
2–3 Tbsp tamari soy sauce
¼ cup deep-fried whole wheat
  bread cubes
sliced scallions for garnish

Place kombu and shiitake in 4 to 5 cups of water
including the soaking water from the kombu
and shiitake mushrooms. Cover and bring to
a boil. Reduce the flame to medium-low and
simmer 3 to 4 minutes. Sauté the onions in a
small amount of dark sesame oil for about 5
minutes. Add the onions to the water and add
a pinch of sea salt. Simmer 25 to 30 minutes.
Add the tamari and simmer for another 10
minutes. Garnish with deep-fried bread cubes
and sliced scallions.

Puréed Squash Soup

4–5 cups buttercup squash, or
  medium Hokkaido pumpkin,
4–5 cups water
½ tsp sea salt
1 cup onions, diced

Remove skin from squash. (Save skin, if un-
waxed. It can be cut into matchsticks and cooked
tempura-style, or used to make miso soup.)
Place squash in a pot with water. Add a pinch
of sea salt. Bring to a boil. Cover and reduce

sliced scallions for garnish
toasted nori strips for garnish

the flame to medium-low. Simmer until the squash is soft (about 10 to 15 minutes). Remove the squash and purée it in a hand food mill. Place the puréed squash in a pot, add the diced onions and remaining sea salt. Bring to a boil. Reduce flame to medium-low and cook for another 20 minutes. Garnish with scallions and nori strips. This soup should be rather thick and creamy.

Vegetable Soup

½ cup leeks, sliced in 1-inch pieces
1 cup onions, cut in thick wedges
½ cup celery, sliced on a thick diagonal
½ cup dried tofu, soaked and cubed
1 cup carrots, cut in irregular shapes
¼ cup burdock, sliced diagonally
dark sesame oil
1 strip kombu, 3–4 inches long, soaked and cut into 1-inch cubes
4–5 cups water
pinch of sea salt
1–2 Tbsp tamari soy sauce
sliced scallions for garnish

Sauté the leeks and onions in a small amount of dark sesame oil. Place the kombu, leeks, onions, celery, dried tofu, carrots, and burdock in a pressure cooker. Add water and a pinch of sea salt. Cover and bring to pressure. Cook for 10 to 15 minutes. Allow the pressure to come down and remove the cover. Season with tamari and simmer for another 10 minutes. Garnish and serve.

This soup may be boiled for 45 to 60 minutes instead of pressure-cooking.

Puréed Carrot Soup

4 cups carrots, grated finely
1 cup onions, finely minced
4–5 cups water
¼ tsp sea salt
chopped parsley for garnish
½ sheet toasted nori, cut in strips for garnish

Place the carrots, onion, and water in a pot. Add a pinch of sea salt. Bring to a boil. Cover and reduce the flame to medium-low. Simmer for about 25 to 30 minutes. Add the remaining sea salt and cook another 10 minutes. Garnish with parsley and nori strips and serve.

Cream of cauliflower or summer squash soup can be prepared using this method. In this case, before seasoning, purée in a hand food mill. Then season and cook 10 minutes longer.

96

Cream of Mushroom Soup ─────────────────────────────

3 cups fresh mushrooms, sliced
1 cup onions, minced
dark sesame oil
tamari soy sauce
4–5 cups water
1 cup oatmeal
¼–½ tsp sea salt
sliced scallions for garnish

Sauté the mushrooms and onions several minutes in a small amount of dark sesame oil and several drops of tamari. Add water and oatmeal to the sautéed vegetables. Cover and bring to a boil. Reduce the flame to medium-low and simmer 30 minutes or so. Season with sea salt or tamari and simmer another 10 minutes. Garnish and serve.

Soup Stocks ───────────────────────────────

There are many soup stocks that we can create and use as a base for clear broth soups or grain and vegetable soups or stews. A simple clear broth soup can be an elegant, and beautiful complement to the more hardy or complex dishes to follow in a meal, occasionally. A variety of soup stock bases for soups can each add a unique flavor.

The following are just a few of the soup stocks we use in macrobiotic cooking.

Kombu Stock (Dashi) ─────────────────────────

This delicious sea vegetable complements just about any vegetable, grain, or bean it is cooked with. It is the most widely used soup stock in macrobiotic cooking. Wash the kombu off quickly, with a clean, damp sponge. Add a 3- to 5-inch piece of kombu to 1 quart of cold water. Boil for 3 to 5 minutes. Remove kombu. Save the kombu and use in other dishes or dry it out and use it again for soup stock. The stock is now ready to use.

Shiitake Mushroom Stock ─────────────────────

Soak 5 or 6 shiitake mushrooms in water for several minutes. Remove stems and place the shiitake and soaking water in 2 quarts of water. Bring to a boil and simmer 5 to 10 minutes. Remove the shiitake and use again in another recipe or slice them and add to the soup. Cut off the woody stems if adding the mushrooms to a soup. Shiitake combine very well with kombu to make another delicious soup stock. They are especially good to balance animal food or salty dishes. Because of shiitake's yin qualities, we do not recommend their use often for those with weak conditions.

Dried Vegetable Stock ───────────────────────

Slice root vegetables, such as daikon, carrot, or turnip into rounds or dice them. Thread or tie them on a string and hang them in a shaded but warm place to dry out. When they are about half dried, they are very sweet. Add to 1 quart of water and boil for 3 to 5 minutes. Remove from water and use the water for soup stock. These vegetables can also be stored in an air-tight container, once they are completely dried and saved for future use.

Fresh Vegetable Stock

Vegetable roots, stems, tops, or leaves can be used for making soup stock. Boil them in 1 quart of water for 5 to 10 minutes and then remove and throw away the vegetables. Use the stock for any vegetable, grain, or bean soup. Be careful not to add too many strong tasting vegetables, such as burdock, celery, and others, to a soup stock as these will overpower the taste of sweeter vegetables such as carrots, onions, cabbage, and others. Also, make sure that the vegetables are thoroughly cleaned before using.

Grain Soup Stock

Roast $\frac{1}{2}$ to 1 cup of grain until it is golden brown and gives off a nutty fragrance. Boil in 1 quart of water for 5 minutes and remove grain and use the liquid.

Fish Stock

Tie fish heads and bones in a cheesecloth sack, and boil for several minutes. Remove fish sack from water and use the stock as a base for a delicious soup or stew. Dried bonito flakes or dried fish such as *chuba* or *chirimen* can be boiled in water 3 to 5 minutes to make a stock as well.

These fish stocks combine very well with kombu stock as a base for vegetable soups.

Clear Broth Soups

Clear Broth Soup with Chinese Cabbage

$\frac{1}{2}$ **cup taro potato, peeled, washed, and cut in chunks**
1–1$\frac{1}{2}$ quarts kombu and bonito flake stock
2 cups Chinese cabbage, sliced
$\frac{1}{2}$ **cup carrots, cut in flower shapes, parboiled**
tamari soy sauce
$\frac{1}{2}$ **tsp ginger juice**
sliced scallions for garnish

Place the stock in a pot and bring to a boil. Add the taro chunks, cover, and simmer until tender. Add the Chinese cabbage and carrot flowers. Cover and simmer 1 to 2 minutes. Reduce the flame to low and season lightly with tamari. Simmer 1 to 2 minutes. Add the ginger juice just before serving. Garnish with scallions and serve.

Clear Broth Soup with Tofu

1 strip kombu, 3–4 inches long, soaked
2 shiitake mushrooms, soaked
4–5 cups water
2–3 Tbsp tamari soy sauce
2 cups tofu, cubed
¼ cup scallions, sliced
¼ cup carrots, cut in flower shapes, parboiled

Place the kombu and shiitake in a pot and add water. Bring to a boil. Cover and boil for 10 to 15 minutes. Remove the kombu and shiitake. (Either use the kombu and shiitake in another soup or dry them out again and use later.) Add the tamari and simmer for 3 to 4 minutes. Add the tofu and simmer on a low flame for 5 to 10 minutes. Place soup in soup bowls and garnish with scallions and carrot flowers.

Clear Broth Watercress Soup

½ bunch watercress, washed
1 strip kombu, 3 inches long
4–5 cups water
½ cup cauliflower, flowerettes
2–3 Tbsp tamari soy sauce
4–5 slices lemon, cut in half

Make a soup broth by boiling the kombu in covered pot for 10 to 15 minutes. Remove the kombu, add the tamari, and simmer for 3 to 4 munites. Cook the cauliflower, separately until tender. Remove and set aside. Boil the watercress for 1 minute, rinse under cold water, and set aside. Place 2 to 3 sprigs of cooked watercress, 1 cauliflower flowerette, and ½ slice of lemon in each serving bowl. Pour a cup of hot tamari-kombu broth over the vegetables and lemon. Serve hot.

Fish Soup

Fish and Vegetable Stew

1 lb white-meat fish, cut in large chunks
½ cup onions, cut in thick wedges
½ cup celery, cut on a thick diagonal
1 cup carrots, cut in chunks
¼ cup leeks, sliced
¼ cup burdock, shaved
1 strip kombu, 3–4 inches long, soaked and diced
5 cups water
pinch of sea salt

Place the kombu, onion, celery, carrot, leeks, and burdock in a pot. Add water and a pinch of sea salt. Cover and bring to a boil. Reduce the flame to medium-low and simmer until the vegetables are tender. Add the fish, cover, and continue to cook until the fish and the vegetables are soft. Season with a small amount of tamari and add the ginger juice. Cook another 2 to 3 minutes. Garnish with sliced scallions and serve.

For a little thicker and creamier stew, thicken with either diluted kuzu, arrowroot, or whole wheat pasty flour.

tamari soy sauce
$\frac{1}{2}$ tsp ginger juice
sliced scallions for garnish

Sometimes I make dumplings out of whole wheat pastry flour, sea salt, and water. This mixture should be like a thick batter. Let it sit overnight in a warm place to ferment slightly. This helps the dumplings to rise a little. When adding to the soup, place 1 tablespoon at a time on top of the soup until there is 1 dumpling for each person. Cover and simmer 3 to 5 minutes until done.

Koi-koku

(See miso soup section of this chapter for recipe.)

Chapter 5

Vegetables

Nature very generously supplies us with a vast selection of various shapes, sizes, colors, tastes, and textures of vegetables. Each type of vegetable is unique, supplying us with different nutrients as well as energy. We can create a variety of tastes, textures, and energies by using a wide variety of cooking methods. Also, the seasoning and cutting styles that we choose greatly affect the taste, texture, and energies of vegetables.

Several cooking methods which we can use to prepare vegetables, as well as other foods, are steaming; boiling; sautéing; baking; pressure-cooking; broiling; deep-frying; pickling or pressing; as well as using raw vegetables occasionally.

For persons with serious illnesses we do not recommend baking or pressure-cooking vegetables because of the more yang energy associated with these two cooking methods. It is best to use more moist or lighter methods such as boiling, steaming, and others for preparing vegetables in the case of serious illness.

For those in generally healthy conditions, baking and pressure-cooking vegetables can be used very occasionally. When baking vegetables it is best to have a more moist preparation and avoid very dry baked preparations. This can be done by adding water to the vegetables and by keeping them covered during baking.

Steaming

Steaming foods is a very refreshing and light method of cooking, which requires very little time. The foods do not retain as much liquid as with boiling, and they keep their bright colors more easily. Steaming can be used for most vegetables, either sliced or sometimes whole, or steaming can be used to heat up leftover foods. There are two primary ways in which to steam food:

Place about ½ inch of water in a pot. Set a collapsable stainless steel vegetable steamer down inside the pot, or place a Japanese wooden steamer, on top of the pot. Place the vegetables in the steamer. Cover and bring the water to a boil. Steam until tender (approximately 5 to 7 minutes depending on the size and thickness of the vegetables).

The second method can be used, if there is not a vegetable steamer handy. Place about ¼ inch of water in the bottom of a pot. Add the vegetables and bring to a boil. Lower the flame to medium and steam until done. (Steamed vegetables are best if slightly crisp but not raw. Be careful not to overcook them.)

Save the vegetable water from the steamed vegetables for use as a soup stock, or a base for a bechamel or kuzu sauce.

If steaming several kinds of vegetables, it is best to steam each type separately to insure proper cooking. Then mix them together when they are done. Also, if the stems of the vegetables are hard, it is best to steam them separately from the leaves or at least chop the stems very fine before steaming.

This cooking method can be used daily.

Boiling

Boiling is one of the most often used cooking methods and can be used at least once a day or more.

There are several ways in which to prepare boiled vegetables:

- **Boiling Method #1**—With this method the vegetables can be either sliced or cooked whole. If using several types of vegetables, boil them separately, cooking milder vegetables such as onions, Chinese cabbage, or carrots first, and stronger tasting ones such as celery, burdock, watercress, and others, toward the end of cooking.

  This method is used very often for green leafy vegetables, in which the vegetables are dipped into rapidly boiling water and cooked for a very short time, until the vegetables have a crisp taste and the colors are deep and vibrant. The vegetables are then removed, drained, and allowed to cool. This method of cooking is referred to as *ohitashi style*, and is used often in preparing boiled salads.

Ohitashi-Style Watercress

1 bunch watercress, washed,   Place about ½ inch of water in a pot and bring

uncut
water

to a rapid boil. Dip the watercress in the water and move it around. When the water comes to a boil again, cook the watercress another 30 seconds or so. Remove, drain, and allow to cool. Arrange, whole or sliced, on a plate or bowl, garnish with a lemon slice or twist, and serve.

Boiled Kale and Carrots

2 cups kale, sliced
½ cup carrots, sliced on a thin
   diagonal
water

Place about ½ inch of water in a pot and bring to a boil. Add the carrots to the water and boil about 1 minute. Remove and drain. Next, place the kale in the water and cook about 1 minute, until bright green and slightly crisp. Remove, drain, and mix together with the carrots. Place the vegetables in a bowl and serve.

Boiled Salad

(See Chapter 8 for recipe.)

• **Boiling Method #2**—With this method of boiling, vegetables are sliced into large chunks, rounds, or occasionally left whole, such as with onions. The vegetables are cooked in a small amount of water, over a low flame for a long period of time (35 to 45 minutes), until very soft, juicy, and sweet. A pinch of sea salt may or may not be added at the beginning of cooking, and the vegetables are seasoned with a little tamari soy sauce at the end of cooking. This method of cooking is referred to as *nishime style* and may be enjoyed several times per week, especially in cooler weather.

Nishime Vegetables

1 strip kombu, 6–8 inches long,
   soaked and cubed
¼ cup celery, sliced in thick
   diagonals
1 cup daikon, cut in thick
   rounds
½ cup butternut squash, sliced
   in large chunks
½ cup carrots, sliced in chunks
water
pinch of sea salt
tamari soy sauce

Place the kombu in the bottom of a heavy stainless steel pot. Layer the celery, daikon, squash, and carrots on top of the kombu in that order. Add enough water to cover only about ½ inch up the vegetables. Add a small pinch of sea salt. Cover and bring to a boil. Reduce the flame to medium-low and simmer about 35 to 40 minutes until the vegetables are soft. Add a small amount of tamari, cover, and continue to cook another 10 minutes. Remove the cover, shake the pot gently to coat the vegetables with the sweet cooking juice, and continue to cook until almost all liquid is gone.

For a variation add dried tofu, tempeh, pan-fried or deep-fried tofu, fu, seitan, and, of course, a variety of other vegetables as well, as long as the items are cut into large bite-size chunks or rounds.

Whole Onions with Miso

4–5 medium-sized onions, peeled and washed
1 strip kombu, 6–8 inches long, soaked and cubed
2 cups water
2 tsp barley miso
2 tsp kuzu, diluted
1 Tbsp chopped parsley for garnish

Make ¼-inch shallow slits in the top of each onion to create a pinwheel effect. (Make sure not to cut the bottom of the onion where the root was attached or the onion will fall apart while cooking.) Place the kombu in the bottom of a pot and set the onions, standing with the slit side up, on top of the kombu. Add water. Purée the miso and put a dab on top of each onion. Cover and bring to a boil. Reduce the flame to medium-low and simmer about 25 to 30 minutes or until the onions are tender but not falling apart. If it is not salty enough, add a very small amount of puréed miso to the cooking water. Remove the onions and place them in a bowl so that they are standing up. Add the diluted kuzu to the cooking water, stirring to avoid lumping, and cook until thick. Pour the kuzu sauce over the onions and garnish with chopped parsley.

Daikon, Daikon Greens, and Kombu

2 cups daikon, sliced into ½-inch thick rounds
1 cup daikon greens, chopped
1 strip kombu, 6–8 inches long, soaked and cubed
water
pinch of sea salt
tamari soy sauce

Place the kombu in the bottom of a pot and set the daikon rounds on top. Add about ½ inch of water and a small pinch of sea salt. Cover and bring to a boil. Reduce the flame to low and simmer 35 to 40 minutes until the daikon is soft. Season with a small amount of tamari, cover, and simmer another 5 minutes. Place the daikon greens on top of the daikon, cover, and cook until tender, but still bright green. Mix and place in a serving bowl.

Place any leftover liquid in the serving bowl, thicken with kuzu to make a sauce, or save for soup stock.

As a variation, use shiitake, lotus root, burdock, daikon, kombu, and pan-fried or deep-fried tofu or tempeh.

● **Boiling Method #3**—This method of boiling vegetables is similar to nishime. It is referred to as *nabé-style* cooking using an earthenware cooking pot, or as *sukiyaki* or *udon-yaki* using a cast iron skillet. Sukiyaki usually includes meat but delicious substitutes include seitan, tempeh, tofu, or even fish or shellfish. This is a very colorful, one dish meal that is served in the nabé or skillet. It is usually served with a dip sauce made with either miso or tamari soy sauce, for dipping vegetables, udon, or other foods into as they are eaten.

Udon-Yaki

1 package (8 oz) udon, cooked eldante, rinsed
1 strip kombu, 6–8 inches long, soaked
3 shiitake mushrooms, soaked and stems removed
4–5 daikon rounds
4–5 pieces deep-fried tofu, drained
4–5 cups water (including soaking water from kombu and shiitake and also cooking water from daikon)
tamari soy sauce
4–5 slices cooked seitan
4–5 broccoli spears
4–5 carrot slices, $\frac{1}{4}$-inch thick diagonal
4–5 butternut squash slices, $\frac{1}{4}$ inch thick
4–5 buttercup squash slices, $\frac{1}{4}$ inch thick
2–3 onion rounds, $\frac{1}{4}$ inch thick
Dip Sauce:
1 cup water
tamari soy sauce
$\frac{1}{2}$ tsp grated ginger
1 tsp sliced scallions

After soaking the kombu, slice it into $2\frac{1}{2}$- to 3-inch-long strips about $\frac{1}{4}$ inch wide, and tie the strips into bows, with a knot in the center of each strip. Place the kombu bows in a stainless steel pot. Take the shiitake and make a $\frac{1}{8}$-inch X in the top of each, and place them in the pot with the kombu. Place the daikon and tofu in the pot. Add about $\frac{1}{2}$ inch of water to the pot. Bring to a boil, cover, and simmer 35 to 40 minutes until the daikon and kombu are tender. Season with a small amount of tamari, cover, and cook another 10 minutes. Remove and place on a plate. Save the cooking water.

Prepare a broth for the nabé with the cooking water from the daikon, and the soaking water from the shiitake and kombu. Place it in a pot and bring to a boil. Cover and simmer 2 to 3 minutes. Season lightly with tamari and simmer 1 to 2 minutes longer. Remove from flame and pour the broth into the nabé or cast iron skillet. Place the cooked noodles in the broth.

Quickly, attractively, arrange the daikon, shiitake, kombu, tofu, seitan, broccoli, carrots, squash, and onion slices on top of the noodles. Cover the nabé and place it on a high flame. Bring to a boil, reduce the flame to medium-low, and simmer until the vegetables are tender but still bright and colorful. Remove from the flame and remove the cover.

To prepare the dip sauce, place water in a pot. Add enough tamari to create a slightly salty taste. Bring to a boil, reduce the flame to low and simmer 2 to 3 minutes. Turn off and add the ginger and sliced scallions. Pour into 4 to 5 individual serving cups for dipping.

Place nabé on the table and have each person serve themselves at the table.

This is a real favorite in our home.

- **Boiling Method #4**—This method is referred to as *kinpira-style* or *nitsuke-style* boiling.

Kinpira style is a combination of sautéing and boiling which is used primarily with root vegetables that are shaved, cut in matchsticks, or thinly sliced. (Oil may be omitted for those on oil-restricted programs and vegetables can be simply water-sautéed.) Kinpira vegetables are seasoned with tamari soy sauce when about 75 to 80 percent done, and cooked until no liquid remains. Sea vegetables such as arame and hijiki are often prepared with the kinpira style of cooking as well.

Nitsuke style involves cooking vegetables a moderate amount of time. The juice from cooking may be cooked down or served with the vegetables, such as with dried daikon-kombu dishes.

Kinpira Burdock and Carrot

2 cups carrots, matchsticks
2 cups burdock, shaved
dark sesame oil
water
tamari soy sauce

Place a small amount of dark sesame oil in a skillet and heat up. Add the burdock and sauté 3 to 4 minutes, mixing occasionally to evenly sauté. Place the carrots on top of the burdock. Do not mix. Add enough water to half cover the vegetables. Bring to a boil. Cover and reduce the flame to medium-low. Simmer about 10 minutes or until the vegetables are about 75 to 80 percent done. Season lightly with tamari, cover, and continue to cook several more minutes until done. Remove the cover and cook off any excess liquid. Mix and place on a serving dish.

As a variation, add lotus root slices, a little ginger juice at the end, or even prepare a kuzu sauce for this dish. Seitan strips are also very delicious.

Dried Daikon, Shiitake, and Kombu

2 cups dried daikon, soaked and sliced
3 shiitake mushrooms, soaked, stems removed, and sliced
1 strip kombu, 6–8 inches long, soaked and sliced in thin matchsticks

Place the kombu in a skillet. Set the shiitake on top. Place the dried daikon on top of the shiitake. Combine the soaking water from the daikon (if very dark and bitter, do not use), shiitake, and kombu. Add enough soaking water to the skillet to half cover the daikon. Periodically while cooking, a little more liquid may need to be

water
tamari soy sauce

added, so do not discard leftover soaking water. Cover and bring to a boil. Reduce the flame to medium-low and simmer about 35 to 40 minutes. Add a small amount of tamari and continue to cook until almost all or all of the liquid is gone.

Sautéing

Sautéing is a commonly used method of cooking in macrobiotic kitchens. There are several methods of sautéing using oil, oil and water, or just water. Just about any type of vegetable can be used in sautéing, as long as it is cut thinly for most sautéing. For long sautéing, the vegetables can be sliced a little thicker. Any method chosen results in a delicious, rich flavor.

• **Sautéing Method #1**—Cut the vegetables into matchsticks, thin slices, or shave them. Brush a skillet with a small amount of light or dark sesame oil. Heat the oil. Add the vegetables and a pinch of sea salt to bring out the sweetness of the vegetables. Sauté the vegetables by moving them from side to side with chopsticks to help them cook evenly. Sauté for 5 minutes on a medium flame. Reduce flame to low and sauté for another 10 minutes or so, gently mixing occasionally to avoid burning the vegetables. Season to taste with sea salt or tamari soy sauce and sauté 2 to 3 minutes longer.

• **Sautéing Method #2**—This method uses oil and water. The vegetables can be cut into matchsticks or shaved. First, sauté the vegetables in a small amount of sesame oil over a medium flame for approximately 5 minutes. Then add enough water to almost half cover the vegetables. Add a pinch of sea salt, cover, and cook until the vegetables are tender. Season with tamari soy sauce or sea salt to taste near the end of cooking. Remove the cover and simmer until any remaining water has evaporated. This method is often referred to as kinpira.

• **Sautéing Method #3**—Stir-frying vegetables in a wok or skillet is a very quick method that the Chinese use. Use a small amount of oil, a high flame, and stir the vegetables constantly. This results in a crispy, brightly colored dish.

• **Sautéing Method #4**—Water-sautéed vegetables are great for those with restricted oil intake. Simply add 2 to 3 tablespoons of water to a skillet, bring to a boil, add the vegetables and sauté in the same way as for oil sautéing. Season with tamari soy sauce at the end of cooking and continue to cook 2 to 3 minutes longer. Remove cover and cook off any remaining liquid.

• **Sautéing Method #5**—Long-time sautéed vegetables are cut into larger slices or chunks and sautéed on a low flame, with or without oil (use water instead), and without stirring or mixing until about half done. Then continue to cook on a low flame until tender. Season with sea salt or tamari soy sauce when the vegetables are about 80 percent done.

Sautéed Chinese Cabbage

4 cups Chinese cabbage, sliced
   on a wide diagonal
dark sesame oil
tamari soy sauce

Place a small amount of oil in a skillet and heat up. Add the cabbage and sauté, gently pushing the cabbage around the skillet until half done. Add a small amount of tamari and continue to sauté until done.

Kinpira Lotus Root and Onions

2 cups lotus root, sliced thin
1 cup onions, sliced in half-
   moons
dark sesame oil
water
tamari soy sauce

Place a small amount of oil in a skillet and heat up. Add the onions and sauté for 2 to 3 minutes. Add the lotus root. Add enough water to half cover the vegetables and bring to a boil. Reduce the flame to medium-low and cook another 10 to 15 minutes until about 80 percent done. Add a small amount of tamari, cover, and cook another 5 minutes, or until done. Remove the cover and cook off all remaining liquid.

Kinpira Burdock and Carrot

(See Boiling—Kinpira style in this chapter for recipe.)

Stir-fry Chinese-style Vegetables

$\frac{1}{2}$ cup onions, sliced in thick
   half-moons or wedges
2 cups broccoli, spears
$\frac{1}{2}$ cup carrots, sliced in matchsticks
$\frac{1}{2}$ cup tofu, cubed
1 cup mung bean sprouts,
   washed
dark sesame oil
tamari soy sauce
1 cup water
1 tsp kuzu, diluted
$\frac{1}{2}$ tsp ginger juice

Place a small amount of oil in a wok and turn flame to high. Add onions and sauté by constantly stirring for 1 to 2 minutes. Add the broccoli, carrots, and tofu. Sauté until half done. Add the sprouts and a small amount of tamari. Continue to sauté until the vegetables are tender but still brightly colored and crispy. Remove and place in a serving bowl.

For the sauce, pour the water in the wok. Add the diluted kuzu, stirring constantly, and cook until thick and translucent. Add a small amount of tamari for a mild taste and simmer 2 to 3 minutes. Add the ginger juice and stir. Pour the sauce over the stir-fried vegetables and serve.

Water-sautéed Carrot Tops and Sesame Seeds

2 cups carrot tops, very finely
   chopped
water

Place enough water in a skillet to just barely cover the bottom and bring to a boil. Add the carrot tops and sauté 2 to 3 minutes until all

108

¼ cup roasted sesame seeds
tamari soy sauce

water is gone and the carrot tops are done.

Place the sesame seeds in a suribachi and grind as for gomashio. Add a few drops of tamari and grind into the seeds.

Mix the carrot tops together with the sesame seeds. Place in a serving bowl.

Baking

Baking vegetables is a method that can be used in preparing squashes and root vegetable dishes.

Squashes can be halved, seeds removed, and baked on an oiled baking sheet until done, or winter squashes such as blue hubbard, buttercup, or Hokkaido pumpkin can be stuffed and baked whole. Vegetables such as carrots or burdock can be wrapped in pastry, baked whole, and sliced when done.

Vegetables can also be sliced and baked in a covered casserole dish with a little water for a more moist vegetable dish.

Baked Summer Squash

2–3 lb summer squash,
dark sesame oil
tamari soy sauce

Remove stem and cut the squash in half. With a knife, make diagonal slashes in the skin of the squash about ⅛ inch deep. Then make diagonal slashes in the opposite direction, thus creating XX's on the surface skin. Place the squash on a

lightly oiled baking pan or cookie sheet.
Lightly brush the top of the squash with sesame
oil or omit if oil intake is to be restricted. Bake
the squash at 375°F for about 20 minutes. Then
place a couple of drops of tamari on top of
each piece of squash and bake for 15 to 20
minutes longer or until the squash is done. By
cutting and baking the squash in this manner
the squash looks like baked fish.

Baked Winter Squash

Butternut, buttercup, Hokkaido pumpkin, acorn, and hubbard squash require
more time to bake. Brush a baking pan or cookie sheet lightly with sesame oil.
Cut the squash in half and clean out the seeds. Place on the baking pan with the
skin side up. Lightly oil the skin of the squash and bake for 1 to 2 hours or until
done, at 375° to 400°F. Season the squash by rubbing a pinch of sea salt on the
inside of the squash before cooking, or by adding a little tamari soy sauce at the
end. Seasoning may be omitted entirely if desired. Turn the halved squash upside
down during the final 10 minutes of cooking to let some of the liquid evaporate
from the squash.

Baked Stuffed Squash

The halved squash may also be stuffed with rice and vegetables or bread crumbs,
onions, celery, and seitan. Cover the baking dish to allow the rice and vegetables
to cook. Bake at 375° to 400°F until tender. Remove the cover the last 10 to 15
minutes to allow any excess liquid to evaporate. Garnish and serve.

Whole squashes may also be stuffed and baked. First cut a circular hole in the
top of the squash. Then clean out the seeds. Stuff the squash with a mixture of
grain (rice, millet, couscous, or wild rice) and vegetables, or even bread cubes,
seitan, and vegetables, and bake until done. The baking time will differ depending on the size and type of squash.

Test the squash for doneness by poking a chopstick or fork into the squash. If
it goes through easily, it is done. If it is still hard, bake it longer.

Baked Carrots or Burdock in Pastry

Make a dough and roll it out as for a pie. Wrap partially boiled vegetables such
as whole carrots or burdock in the pastry dough and bake them whole at 375°F
until the crust is golden brown and the vegetables are tender. When done, slice
the roll into rounds and serve.

Arame or hijiki rolls can also be made in the same manner by wrapping the
cooked sea vegetable in pastry dough as for strudel, and baking as above. Cut into
rounds and serve.

110

A vegetable or sea vegetable pie can also be made in the same manner as for a fruit pie.

Pressure-cooking

Because vegetables require little cooking time compared to other foods and because we generally use pressure-cooking with many grain dishes and some bean dishes, we generally do not recommend pressure-cooking vegetables. It is best to use other cooking methods for vegetables.

Occasionally, when in a hurry, large chunks of root or ground vegetables can be pressure-cooked 3 to 5 minutes.

Of course, when vegetables are combined with grains, beans, or in soups, they can be pressure-cooked to create many delicious dishes.

Broiling

Usually, we use broiling for fish, shellfish, and tofu, as broiling vegetables may make them a little bitter, but occasionally we use broiling to prepare shish kebabs or skewered vegetables.

Shish Kebabs

Attractively arrange vegetables such as onion wedges, broccoli spears, cauliflower flowerettes, mushroom caps, carrot chunks, cooked seitan, tofu or tempeh chunks on a shish kebab skewer or bamboo skewer and broil under the broiler until done, basting occasionally with a sauce made from water, tamari soy sauce, ginger juice, and mirin to prevent burning. This only takes several minutes. Fish or shellfish can also be used instead of seitan, tofu, or tempeh.

Broiled Stuffed Mushroom Caps

8–10 large stuffing mushrooms, stems removed
$\frac{1}{4}$ cup cooked seitan, finely chopped or ground
1 Tbsp onions, minced
1 Tbsp carrots, finely diced
1 tsp chopped parsley

Mix the seitan, onion, carrot, and parsley together. Stuff each mushroom with the mixture. Set the mushrooms on a baking sheet and place under the broiler. Broil until the mushrooms are tender and juicy.

Deep-frying Including Tempura

Vegetables that are dipped in batter and deep-fried are known as *tempura*. The best quality vegetable oil to use in making tempura is sesame oil. Corn oil is more yin and expands quickly, bubbling up over the sides of the pot. Fill a 10- or 12-

inch cast iron skillet, Dutch oven, or stainless steel pot with about 2 to 3 inches of sesame oil. Heat the oil to about 350°F. Be careful not to let the oil smoke. To test for the right temperature, drop a small morsel of batter into the hot oil, if the oil is ready, it should sink to the bottom of the skillet and almost immediately rise to the surface. Dip the vegetables one at a time in the batter and gently drop into the oil. Do not add too many pieces to the skillet at one time. When one side becomes golden brown, turn over with chopsticks or a wire strainer and brown the other side. Remove the vegetables from the oil and place on a wire tempura rack or on paper towels allowing the excess oil to drain off the vegetables. To keep the vegetables crisp, place them on a cookie sheet in a warm oven (200°F). Serve hot with dip sauce.

Tempura Batter #1
$\frac{1}{2}$ cup whole wheat pastry flour
$\frac{1}{2}$ cup corn flour (or sweet rice flour)
$\frac{1}{4}$ tsp sea salt
1–1$\frac{1}{4}$ cups water

Tempura Batter #2
1 cup whole wheat pastry flour
$\frac{1}{4}$ tsp sea salt
2 level tsp arrowroot flour or kuzu, diluted
1–1$\frac{1}{4}$ cups water

Mix dry ingredients. Then add water and stir until the batter is smooth. Some of the batter will separate from the dipped vegetables when they are added to the hot oil. If too much of the batter separates the batter is too thin. Simply add a little more flour. If none of the batter separates, the batter is probably too thick. Just add a little more water to thin out. It is best to prepare a batter a few minutes before dipping the vegetables in it and keep it in a cool place until ready to use. When the batter is exposed to the warm air in the kitchen, it may become a little too thick. If so, just add a little water to obtain desired consistency again.

Hundreds of different vegetables and even apple slices can be cooked tempura style. Examples include carrots, cauliflower, broccoli, Brussels sprouts, mushrooms, lotus root, kale, dandelion leaves and roots, parsley, carrot tops, squash, celery, celery leaves, green and yellow string beans, onions, burdock, seitan, tofu, and many others. If the vegetables are wet, first dry them off with a paper towel then dip them into the batter. Tofu should be drained of excess water first before deep-frying.

Also, seafood such as shrimp, haddock, sole, squid, clams, oysters, smelt, and others can be deep-fried in basically the same manner. Please see the section in this cookbook on the preparation of fish for instructions on fish tempura.

Vegetables such as carrots and burdock, can be cut into matchsticks, or vegetables can be diced and added directly to the batter. Place a tablespoon of the vegetable batter mixture into the hot oil and deep-fry until golden brown.

To clean the oil, skim it with an oil skimmer to remove chunks of batter debris. Also, drop an umeboshi plum into the hot oil and deep-fry it until it becomes charred. This will remove any odors from the oil. For instance, if fish has previously been deep-fried, it is desirable to remove the odor of the fish from the oil before vegetables are cooked in it to prevent the vegetables from tasting like fish.

The oil can be stored in a glass jar. It should be tightly covered and kept in a dark or cool, shaded place.

We recommend that tempura be served with a dip sauce made of grated daikon or ginger and tamari soy sauce to help digest the oil and flour.

Tamari-Daikon Dip Sauce	*Tamari-Ginger Dip Sauce*
$\frac{1}{4}$ tsp grated daikon	$\frac{1}{8}$ tsp grated ginger
1 Tbsp tamari soy sauce	1 Tbsp tamari soy sauce
2 Tbsp water	2 Tbsp water

Mix ingredients and heat up. Serve in a small cup or bowl. Each person should have one dish of the sauce to dip the tempura in.

Plain grated daikon (about a tablespoonful with a drop of tamari poured on it to each person) can be served instead of the dip sauce or in addition to the dip sauce.

Aveline Kushi's Miso Stuffed Lotus Root

1 section lotus root, fresh, washed
2 Tbsp organic roasted tahini
1 Tbsp barley miso
$\frac{1}{4}$–$\frac{1}{2}$ tsp grated ginger
1–2 tsp minced parsley
$\frac{1}{4}$ cup whole wheat flour
$\frac{1}{2}$ cup tempura batter
(see previous recipe)

Cut the ends off the lotus root and boil in water for 5 to 10 minutes. Combine the tahini, miso, ginger, and parsley, and mix. Gently pound one of the open ends of the lotus root into the bowl of miso mixture. As it is pounded the miso will fill the hollow lotus chambers. When the chambers are full of the miso mixture, place the lotus in a dish and let it sit for 1 hour. The miso will draw liquid out of the lotus root. Next, roll the lotus root in this liquid and then roll the lotus in whole wheat flour until completely coated. Place the lotus in tempura batter and deep-fry (whole) until golden brown (2 to 3 minutes). Remove, drain, and allow to cool. When cool, cut the lotus root into $\frac{1}{4}$-inch rounds and arrange attractively on a platter. Garnish and serve 1 or 2 slices to each person, as this is quite a yang dish.

Deep-fried Lotus Chips

1 section lotus root, 6–8 inches long, washed and sliced into thin rounds
dark sesame oil (for deep-frying)
tamari-ginger dip sauce (see previous recipe)

Place the oil (2 to 3 inches) in a pot and heat up. When the oil is hot, deep-fry several lotus slices until crispy and golden brown. Remove and drain. Repeat until all the lotus slices have been deep-fried. Serve with a tamari-ginger or tamari-daikon dip sauce.

Chapter 6

Beans, Including Tofu and Tempeh

BEANS

Beans and bean products are a good source of protein, fat, iron, various vitamins and minerals, as well as carbohydrates as can be seen from the following chart. Some studies of vegetable-protein eaters indicate that not only do they have low cholesterol levels, but vegetable protein helps to break down built-up cholesterol.

Smaller beans such as azuki, lentil, and chick-peas, which are lower in fat, are recommended for regular use; medium-sized beans such as navy, northern, kidney, pinto, soybeans, and so on, are used occasionally; while larger, fattier beans such

Nutritional Content of Various Beans and Bean Products
(Measurements are per 100 grams.)

	Protein	Carbohydrate	Iron	Vitamin A	Vitamin B	Calcium
Azuki	21.5 g	58.4 g	4.8 mg	6 I.U.	2.5 mg	75
Lentils	24.7 g	60.1 g	6.8 mg	60 I.U.	2.0 mg	79
Chick-peas	20.5 g	61.1 g	6.9 mg	50 I.U.	2.0 mg	150.0
Pinto beans	22.9 g	63.7 g	6.4 mg	—	2.2 mg	135
Natto	16.9 g	11.5 g	3.7 mg	—	1.1 mg	103
Kidney beans	22.5 g					
Soybeans	34.1 g	33.5 g	8.4 mg	80 I.U.	2.2 mg	226.0
Tofu	7.8 g		1.7 mg		0.5 mg	146.0
Dried tofu	53.4 g		9.4 mg		0.6 mg	590.0
Black beans	22.9 g	—	7.9 mg	—	2.2 mg	
Dried peas	24.1 g	60.3 g	5.1 mg	170 I.U.	3.0 mg	64
Tempeh	(Vitamin B_{12} 1.5–6.3 mg per 100 g [3.5 oz.])					

(Information from U.S. Department of Agriculture and the Japan Nutritionists Association. From *The Book of Macrobiotics* by Michio Kushi.)

as lima beans are used less often. For those with serious illness, the smaller beans are used almost exclusively because of their low fat content, while other beans such as black beans, black soybeans, soybeans, and so on, are used on occasion.

Digestibility of beans is greatly affected by whether the beans are soaked or not, cooked long enough, chewed properly, or by eating too much.

One cup of vegetable protein per day is sufficient for most vegetarian or macrobiotic people.

There are several ways in which to prepare beans. The most common ways are boiling and baking, but beans may also be pressure-cooked occasionally, for those in generally good health.

Washing

Before cooking beans, sort out any stones or clumps of soil. Then wash very well with cold water. This usually takes about three rinsings to thoroughly clean the beans.

Soaking and Precooking

There are several ways in which to soak or precook beans to make them more digestible.

Method #1—Wash beans and place in a cooking pot. Add water to cover. Bring to a boil and cook about 5 to 10 minutes. Remove from flame and let soak 5 to 6 hours. Some people have found this method very helpful in eliminating intestinal gas, and providing a softer texture to the bean dish.

Method #2—Wash beans and cover with warm water. Allow to soak 5 to 6 hours.

This produces a softer texture bean, makes them more digestible, and reduces the soaking time considerably.

Method #3—Wash beans and cover with cold water. Soak 6 to 8 hours. This results in a firmer texture bean, which may be more appropriate for bean salads, but requires a longer soaking period. For a softer texture, cook longer.

Parboiling

Parboiling may be used in some cases when beans such as azuki, kidney, and so on, are to be pressure-cooked with rice. First wash the beans. Then place in a pot and cover with water. Bring to a boil, reduce the flame to medium-low, and simmer about 20 minutes. Remove and allow to cool slightly before combining with rice. The cooking water from the beans may be used as part of the water measurement when cooking the rice. This method gives a much darker red color to the beans, which is very attractive. Soaking creates a less colorful effect.

Roasting

Roasting may be used occasionally for soybeans in soybean stew; soybean and sea vegetable dishes; soybean relish; or when regular soybeans or black soybeans are combined with rice and pressure-cooked. Wash the beans and dry-roast until the skin begins to split. Do not roast too long or over a very high flame as they may become bitter tasting. When roasting the beans, be sure to stir and move them around constantly to evenly roast and prevent burning. After the beans have been roasted, combine them with rice and pressure-cook as per normal rice. These are usually the only beans we roast as they are more yin and have a high fat content. More yang beans would become very bitter if roasted. Soaking is best for more yang beans.

Cooking Times of Beans (per 1 cup)

	Boiling		Pressure-cooking	
	Water (cup)	Time (hour)	Water (cup)	Time (hour)
Azuki	3–3½	2½	2–2½	½
Lentils	3–3½	1½	—	—
Chick-peas	3–4	4	2–2½	1½
Kidney beans	3–3½	2½	2–2½	1
Pinto beans	3–3½	3	2–2½	1–1¼
Soybeans	3–3½	3	2–2½	1
Black beans	3–3½	2½	2–2½	½
Black soybeans	3–3½	2–3	2–2½	1
Split peas	3–3½	1½	—	—
Red lentils	3–3½	1½	—	—
Navy beans	3–3½	2½	2–2½	½
Northern beans	3–3½	2½	2–2½	½
Lima beans	3–3½	2½–3	2–2½	1

Soaking Water

The soaking water, for most beans, is discarded. The exceptions to this are azuki beans, which have a very low fat content, and black soybeans, which are soaked in salt water to keep thin skins on. For other beans, we discard the soaking water and cook in fresh cold water.

Baking

When baking beans, usually we use kidney, pinto, navy or northern beans. First wash, then soak using one of the above mentioned methods. Then cover with water and bake covered at about 300° to 350°F for 5 to 6 hours, adding water periodically as needed. For a sweeter flavor, mix in sliced vegetables or add a little sweetener such as barley malt or rice syrup.

Shocking Method

A third way of cooking beans is by a method called the shocking method. Place 1 cup of beans in a pot and add only enough water to lightly cover the surface of the beans. As the beans cook, they will begin to expand and the water will be absorbed. As this happens, add only enough cold water to lightly cover the surface of the beans again. Repeat this process until the beans are approximately 80 percent cooked (about 2 hours), add ¼ teaspoon of salt and cook until water evaporates (about 15 to 20 minutes).

Kombu

We recommend using a 3- to 4-inch strip of kombu when cooking beans. Kombu, because of its high mineral content, helps to soften the hard outer shell of the beans and aids in their digestion.

Place the kombu under the beans on the bottom of the pot, add water and either boil, pressure-cook, or bake as per instructions.

Seasonings

Sea salt is used in seasoning most beans, but tamari soy sauce or miso in some cases may be more appropriate, depending on the bean being cooked.

Seasonings such as sea salt, miso, and tamari soy sauce are added to the beans when they are about 70 to 80 percent done. If the seasoning is added before they are 70 to 80 percent done they do not cook properly and may be very hard in texture. The high sodium content will contract the outer skin of the beans making it difficult for them to cook properly.

Also, when we season beans with sea salt, we use between ⅛ to ¼ teaspoon per cup of beans. Whatever seasoning chosen, the taste should be moderate, not overly salty.

Seasonings for Various Beans

	Sea Salt	Miso	Tamari Soy Sauce
Azuki	×	—	—
Lentils	×	×	×
Chick-peas	×	×	×
Kidney beans	×	×	×
Pinto beans	×	×	×
Soybeans	×	×	×
Black beans	×	—	×
Black soybeans	×	—	×
Split peas	×	×	×
Navy beans	×	×	×
Northern beans	×	×	×
Lima beans	×	×	×

× yes   — no

The following are suggestions on how to cook some of the different beans.

Azuki Beans

The best quality azuki beans for medicinal purposes or for general health maintenance are the Japanese variety, which are dark red in color and very shiny. These beans grow in the rich volcanic soil of northern Japan and are known for their medicinal qualities and benefits to the excretory system. They are high in protein as well as iron. They make great soups, bean side dishes, and are used in making some desserts and candies.

Azuki Kombu Squash

1 cup azuki beans, washed and soaked
1 strip kombu, 3–4 inches long
1 cup hard winter squash (buttercup or butternut squash, or Hokkaido pumpkin)
water
⅛–¼ tsp sea salt

Place the kombu on the bottom of the pot. Add squash on top of the kombu. Place the soaked azuki beans on top of the squash. Add enough water (soaking water may be included) to just cover the squash, not the beans. Bring to a boil. Reduce the flame to medium-low, cover, and cook until about 80 percent done (about 1½ to 2 hours). Add water, occasionally, as needed, but only to just cover the beans. Season with sea salt and cook until done, which will probably take another ½ hour. Remove, garnish, and serve.

Azuki Beans and Wheat Berries

(See Chapter 3 on Grains for recipe.)

Lentils

These beans require no soaking and cook very quickly compared to other beans. They may be used in making soups, bean side dishes, pâté, dips, or lentil burgers. Lentils are always boiled. Do not pressure-cook as they will clog the valve.

Lentils and Vegetables

1 cup lentils, washed
½ cup onions, diced
⅛ cup celery, diced
¼ cup carrots, diced
1 strip kombu, soaked and diced
water
sea salt

Place the kombu on the bottom of a pot. Layer the onions, celery, and carrots in that order on top of the kombu. Place the beans on top of the vegetables. Add water to just cover the vegetables. Bring to a boil. Reduce the flame to medium-low, cover, and simmer about 45 minutes to 1 hour, adding water occasionally as needed just to cover the beans. When the beans are 70 to 80 percent done, season with sea salt and continue to cook several more minutes until done. Do not add any more water after adding the sea salt. Remove, garnish, and serve.

Chick-peas (Garbanzo)

Chick-peas grow in more warm climates such as Portugal, Africa, and the Middle East, where they are often cooked with or used as a complement to wheat couscous, and bulgur. These beans can be used to make soups, stews, salads, dips such as hummus, cold soup called *gazpacho*, cooked with rice, or simply as a bean side dish.

Chick-peas require quite a bit longer to cook than most beans. They are very sweet tasting beans and are real favorite for both young and old. They may be boiled or pressure-cooked.

Chick-peas and Kombu

1 cup chick-peas, soaked
1 strip kombu, 6–8 inches long,
  soaked and diced
water
sea salt
1 Tbsp chopped parsley

Place kombu in a pressure cooker. Add beans and about 2 to 2½ cups of water. Cover and bring up to pressure. Reduce flame to medium-low and cook for about 1 to 1½ hours. Remove from flame and allow pressure to come down. Remove cover and season with sea salt. Leave uncovered and continue to cook until soft and most of the liquid has evaporated. Mix in the parsley and place in a serving dish.

Hummus

Cook same as above. When the beans are done, purée them in a hand food mill. Place a small amount of organic toasted tahini, chopped or grated raw onion, a little umeboshi paste, and a little chopped parsley in a suribachi. Grind until smooth. Mix in the puréed chick-peas. If too thick, add a little water to produce the desired consistency. Serve with warm pita bread or any other favorite whole grain bread. Great for sandwiches, parties, or just a snack!

Pinto Beans

Often referred to as brown beans or speckled beans, pinto beans are cooked in the same manner as kidney beans.

Pinto Beans with Vegetables

1 cup pinto beans, soaked
½ cup onions, diced or cut in wedges
¼ cup celery, sliced on thick diagonal
⅛ cup fresh sweet corn
¼ cup carrots, cut in chunks
1 strip kombu, 3–4 inches long, soaked and diced
water
⅛–¼ tsp sea salt
chopped scallions for garnish

Place kombu on the bottom of the pot. Layer onions, celery, corn, and carrots on top of the kombu. Place the soaked beans on top of the vegetables. Add water to just cover the beans. Bring to a boil. Cover and reduce the flame to medium-low. Simmer about 2 hours or until 70 to 80 percent done. Add water, occasionally, as needed just to cover the beans. When 70 to 80 percent done, season with sea salt and continue to cook until tender, which may take approximately ½ hour or so. Remove, garnish, and serve.

Kidney Beans

Kidney beans are often referred to as red beans and are probably most well known in a dish called *chili con carni*. These beans are a real favorite in our house because of their rich delicious flavor. People with serious illnesses may have to avoid or temporarily restrict their intake of these beans because of their higher fat content, as compared to smaller beans. For those in generally good health, kidney beans may be enjoyed occasionally in soups, stews, salads, bean side dishes, spreads and dips, or combined with rice. Kidney beans go great with corn bread, corn on the cob, arepas, tacos, or enchilada and tortillas. They may be boiled, pressure-cooked or baked.

Kidney Beans with Miso

1 cup kidney beans, soaked
1 strip kombu, 3–4 inches long,

Use the shocking method of cooking as described in the introduction. Season with miso the last 10

120

soaked and diced
water
1½–2 tsp puréed barley miso

to 15 minutes of cooking. Instead of miso, sea salt may be used as a seasoning.

Japanese (Hokkaido) Black Soybeans

Japanese black soybeans are very sweet and delicious beans that come from northern Japan. They are known for their medicinal qualities, especially for the female reproductive system when prepared as a tea. They are often used in holiday cooking in Japan as a bean side dish, black bean rice or in mochi. They are usually cooked plain without vegetables as the color of the beans turns the vegetables a dark purplish-black color, which is not so attractive. These beans can occasionally be sweetened with a little barley malt or rice syrup for a special treat.

They may be roasted occasionally, and cooked with rice, but the primary method of cooking them is boiling without kombu.

Black soybeans are also the only beans that are soaked and cooked with salt water to keep the skins on. They are then cooked and seasoned with a little tamari soy sauce to make the skins shiny.

They are also washed differently than all other beans. To wash, take a clean, damp kitchen towel and place the beans on it. Cover the beans up in the towel and gently but firmly roll or knead the towel over the beans. Repeat this 2 to 3 times, rinsing and wringing out the towel occasionally. The beans are now ready to soak or dry-roast, before cooking them.

1 cup black soybeans, washed
2½–3 cups water
¼ tsp sea salt
tamari soy sauce
barley malt, rice syrup, or mirin

Place the beans in a bowl, add water and sea salt. Soak overnight or 6 to 8 hours. Place the beans and soaking water in a heavy stainless steel pot, bring to a boil, reduce flame to medium-low and leave uncovered. A gray foam will float to the top of the beans. Skim off and discard this foam along with any loose skins. It may be necessary to add water occasionally just to cover the beans. When the beans are about 80 percent done (about 2 to 2 ½ hours), add a few drops of tamari. Cook until almost all the liquid is gone. Then mix the beans to coat them with the remaining sweet juice. Sweeten these beans, occasionally, by adding a little barley malt, rice syrup, or mirin.

Soybeans

Soybeans are often referred to as the king of the bean family because of their high protein content. Remember, however, that they are also very high in fat and are thus a more yin bean. They need to be cooked with more yang vegetables such as root, round, or ground vegetables.

They are probably best known for their use in making tofu, tempeh, miso, natto, okara, and tamari soy sauce. They are also delicious as a bean side dish, stews, or cooked with rice. Soybeans have a very rich, delicious flavor that is unique. Unless cooked properly they can be difficult to digest.

A couple of favorite dishes which I learned from Mrs. Kushi are:

Soybean Stew

1 cup soybeans, soaked 6–8 hours with kombu
1 strip kombu, 3–4 inches long, soaked and diced
$\frac{1}{8}$ cup celery, diced
$\frac{1}{8}$ cup dried daikon, soaked and chopped
1 shiitake mushroom, soaked and diced
2 pieces dried tofu, soaked and diced
$\frac{1}{8}$ cup burdock, diced
$\frac{1}{4}$ cup lotus root, diced
$\frac{1}{4}$ cup seitan, diced
water
tamari soy sauce
ginger, grated (optional)
chopped scallions for garnish

Layer in a pressure cooker from bottom to top in this order: kombu, celery, dried daikon, shiitake, dried tofu, burdock, lotus root, seitan, and soybeans. Add water to about 2 to 3 inches above the beans. Cover and bring up to pressure. Reduce the flame to medium-low and cook for 50 minutes. Remove and allow pressure to come down. Remove cover and mildly season with tamari. Continue to cook another 15 to 20 minutes. Just before serving, an optional small amount of grated ginger may be added. Place in individual serving bowls, and garnish with chopped scallions.

For small children, omit the ginger.

Soybean Relish

1 cup soybeans, washed and dry-roasted
1 strip kombu, 3–4 inches long, soaked and diced
water
dark sesame oil
$\frac{1}{8}$ cup burdock, diced
$\frac{1}{4}$ cup lotus root, diced
$\frac{1}{2}$ cup carrots, diced
puréed barley miso
ginger juice
1 Tbsp chopped chives or scallions

Place kombu on the bottom of a pressure cooker. Add soybeans and water to almost cover. Bring up to pressure. Reduce flame to medium-low and pressure-cook for about 30 to 40 minutes. Remove from flame and allow pressure to come down. Remove and drain soybeans.

Place a small amount of dark sesame oil in a skillet and heat up. Sauté burdock, lotus root, and carrots several minutes until tender but still firm. Add the drained soybeans and a small amount of puréed barley miso. Cover and simmer 2 to 3 minutes. Add a very small amount of fresh ginger juice and chopped chives or scallions. Remove cover and sauté until all liquid is gone. Mix, then place in a serving dish.

This dish, if mildly seasoned, can be a bean side dish. If salty, serve in very small amounts as a condiment with rice.

TOFU

When I first wrote this cookbook in 1978, tofu was an item found only in natural food stores and familiar mostly to macrobiotic or vegetarian people. Today it can be found in almost every major supermarket chain across the country. Many people use it as a protein source or are at least aware of what tofu is. Chinese, Japanese, macrobiotic, and vegetarian tofu dishes are becoming more popular as people are seeking to prevent illness, reduce cholesterol levels, and generally improve their health.

Tofu is a wonderful vegetable-quality, high-protein source, which is made from soaked, ground, and cooked yellow soybeans.

Tofu can be boiled, baked, pan-fried, broiled, deep-fried, sautéed, pickled, or for those in generally good health, it can be occasionally eaten raw, garnished with chopped scallions, ginger, and tamari soy sauce in the hot summer months. It can be used to create many delicious healthy meals for all family members. Tofu can be bought prepackaged or made at home.

Homemade Tofu

3 cups soybeans
water
4½ tsp *nigari* (special salt made from sea water)

Soak beans in water overnight and drain. Grind the beans in an electric blender. If one has time and patience, they can be ground in a hand food mill. Add the beans to about 6 quarts of fresh cold water and bring to a boil. Reduce the flame to medium-low and simmer for about 5 minutes. (Do not cover the beans as they will foam over the top of the pot.)

Place a cotton cloth or several layers of cheesecloth in a strainer and pour the liquid through the strainer. Fold the corners of the cloth together to form a sack. Squeeze the liquid soy milk out of the sack. Save the pulp in the sack. This pulp is called *okara* and can be used to prepare a delicious dish for which there is a recipe later in this section.

Place the liquid soy milk in a bowl and sprinkle the ground nigari over it. (Grind the nigari in a suribachi or blender until it is a fine powder.) Stir the liquid and nigari very gently. Let this liquid sit for 15 to 20 minutes. The tofu liquid should start to curdle. Most natural food stores sell special wooden or stainless steel tofu boxes. One of these, or a strainer or colander will be needed.

Line the box or strainer with cheesecloth and gently spoon the tofu liquid into the box. Cover the top with a layer of cheesecloth. Place a wooden lid on top of the box or a light disc or plate on top of the strainer so that it rests on the cheesecloth and tofu. Place a small weight on the lid. Let this sit for approximately 1 hour or until a cake is formed. Then very carefully place the tofu in a dish of cold water for about ½ hour. Refrigerate until ready to use.

When storing tofu in the refrigerator, make sure to keep it covered with fresh water in a bowl, as it will spoil very easily if exposed to warmth. Tofu will keep for several days like this.

Summer Scrambled Tofu and Corn

1 cake (1 lb) tofu
3 ears fresh sweet corn, removed
   from cob
dark sesame oil
tamari soy sauce
½ cup chopped scallions

Lightly brush a skillet with oil, and sauté the corn for 2 to 3 minutes. With both hands, mash tofu into small pieces. Place the tofu on top of the corn and cover. Simmer several minutes until corn is done and the tofu is light and fluffy. Season with a small amount of tamari (should not be brown or salty) and garnish with chopped scallions.

As a variation sauté onions, corn, carrots, and tofu, or onions, corn, cabbage, and tofu. As an option, season with a pinch of sea salt or a small amount of umeboshi vinegar instead of tamari, to keep the color of the tofu more white, or to create a different flavored tofu.

Okara

Okara is the soybean pulp remaining after making tofu. It is best used immediately as it has a tendency to spoil more quickly than tofu. It is lower than tofu in protein content and slightly sweeter. It is an occasional item for those in generally good health.

Sautéed Okara with Vegetables

2 cups fresh okara
¼ cup burdock, cut in matchsticks
2 shiitake mushrooms, soaked

Add a small amount of dark sesame oil to a skillet and heat up. Place the burdock in the skillet and sauté 2 to 3 minutes. Add the shiitake and sauté 1 to 2 minutes. Next, add the celery,

and sliced
¼ cup celery, sliced on a thin
   diagonal
½ cup carrots, cut in matchsticks
¼ cup green string beans, sliced
   on a thin diagonal
dark sesame oil
water or kombu stock (optional)
tamari soy sauce
¼ cup almonds, finely chopped
   and tamari-roasted
⅛ cup chopped scallions

carrots, and green beans and sauté 2 to 3 minutes. Add the okara, a small amount at a time, and sauté several minutes until all the okara has been added and sautéed. If too dry, add a few drops of water or kombu stock while sautéing. Add a small amount of tamari for a mild taste and then mix in the almonds and chopped scallion. Mix well, and place in a serving dish.

Ganmodoki (Tofu and Jinenjo Patties)

Squeeze water out of the tofu using the same process explained later for dried tofu, pressing between two boards. Then place the tofu in a piece of cheesecloth and squeeze out any remaining liquid.

1 cake (1 lb) tofu, drained
½ cup diced onions
½ cup grated jinenjo mountain
   potato
¼ cup carrots, cut in thin
   matchsticks
⅛ cup burdock, cut in thin
   matchsticks
pinch of sea salt
arrowroot flour
grated daikon
tamari soy sauce

Place tofu in a suribachi and grind. Mix in onions, jinenjo, carrots, and burdock. Add a pinch of sea salt and mix. Form the mixture into ½-inch patties or cakes. Coat with arrowroot flour. The patties may also be wrapped in roasted strips of nori. Deep-fry the patties until golden brown on both sides. Serve with grated daikon and tamari soy sauce, or a ginger-tamari dip sauce.

For variation, add very finely chopped shiitake mushrooms; or finely chopped kombu, hijiki, or lotus root to the patty mixture.

These patties can be served with either a tamari-kuzu sauce or a sweet-and-sour kuzu sauce poured over them, and garnished with chopped scallions.

Pan-fried Tofu

4–5 slices of fresh tofu, ½ inch
   thick
dark sesame oil
tamari soy sauce
¼–½ tsp fresh grated ginger
   (optional)
chopped scallions for garnish

Lightly oil a skillet and heat the oil. Place the tofu in the skillet. Add a couple drops of tamari on top of each slice and squeeze a drop of ginger juice on each slice. Fry until golden (2 to 3 minutes). Turn over and fry on the other side until browned. Again add 1 to 2 drops of tamari and ginger juice on top of each slice of tofu. Flip the slices over again and fry several seconds.

Remove, place on a serving platter, and garnish with chopped scallions.

These tofu slices may be eaten as is, used in preparing sandwiches, or sliced and added to nishime or even stews.

Small children do not usually like the taste of ginger as it is very strong. When preparing for children, this may be omitted.

Broiled Tofu

To avoid using oil, broil tofu slices instead of pan-frying them. Simply season as for pan-frying with tamari soy sauce and ginger juice, and broil each side until slightly brown.

Use in the same manner as pan-fried tofu.

Dried Tofu

Dried tofu is tofu that has been frozen and dried to remove water. It is high in protein, fat, calcium, and iron. It can be purchased in most natural food stores or can be made at home, although the texture will be very different. Dried tofu can be used much the same way as fresh tofu in soups, stews, nishime, sea vegetable and vegetable dishes. Store-bought dried tofu must be soaked in warm water to reconstitute, before using.

Dried Tofu and Carrots

6 slices dried tofu
½ cup carrots, cut in thick matchsticks
2 strips kombu, 6 inches long, soaked
2 thin slices fresh ginger
water
tamari soy sauce

Place the dried tofu in a bowl and cover with hot water. Let sit for about 5 to 7 minutes. Remove, squeeze out water, and rinse under cold water. Squeeze out liquid again. Slice the dried tofu into rectangular shapes about ¼ inch thick.

Slice the kombu into very thin matchsticks. Place the kombu in a pressure cooker. Add the dried tofu, carrots, and ginger slices. Add enough water to just cover the kombu. Add a few drops of tamari. Cover and bring up to pressure. Reduce the flame to low and cook about 5 to 7 minutes. Allow pressure to come down, remove cover, and take out the ginger slices. If there is any remaining liquid in the cooker, simmer uncovered until gone. Remove and place in a serving dish.

Homemade Dried Tofu ———————————————————————————

Gently squeeze the water out of a cake of fresh tofu by placing the tofu on a cutting board with a clean dish towel over it. Then place another thin cutting board or plate on top of the tofu. Place a light weight on top of the board or plate to apply pressure. Prop the boards up so that they are slightly tilted, to allow the excess water to drain off. Let stand for about 1 hour.

Slice the drained tofu into ½-inch-thick slices and place outside in the clean snow overnight or in the freezer. Bring indoors and allow the tofu to thaw out. For best results, freeze for 48 hours to 1 week. To thaw, soak in warm water several minutes and then squeeze out any liquid. Use same as for store-bought dried tofu.

NATTO

Natto is a fermented soybean product that is very high in protein, calcium, iron, and vitamin B (niacin). Some Japanese believe that natto when eaten regularly, keeps the skin young and youthful looking as well as flexible. Those with serious illnesses may have to restrict their intake of natto because of its yin qualities.

Natto has an interesting odor and may take some time to get used to. My observation has been that if a person eats or has eaten much dairy food in the past he is more likely to dislike natto than a person who does not eat dairy or has been macrobiotic for several years and has discharged much of his past dairy food intake.

Natto is usually eaten as a side dish in Japan, with a little tamari soy sauce and chopped scallion; or mixed in a bowl with rice, tamari, and scallions. It can be served on top of buckwheat noodles, udon, or somen, It can also be added to simply made miso soup, occasionally, for those in generally good health.

Homemade Natto ———————————————————————————

To make natto, wash 2 cups of organic soybeans, then soak them in water for 4 to 6 hours. Place the beans in a pressure cooker. Add fresh water to cover the beans. Leave the lid off the pressure cooker, and bring the beans to a boil. Reduce the flame to low and simmer until a white foam floats to the surface. Skim off the foam and discard. Also, loose soybean skins will float to the top. Skim these off and discard.

Repeat this process until the foam stops. Then place the top on the pressure cooker. Do not add salt. Bring up to pressure. Reduce flame to very low. Place a flame deflector under the pressure cooker, and cook for 30 to 45 minutes. Remove from flame and allow the pressure to come down by running cold water over the outside of the pressure cooker. Remove the cover and pour the beans into a strainer. Let beans drain and cool. When the beans are cool, place them in a stainless steel pot.

For the beans to ferment, they need to be mixed with a special type of bacteria starter that is processed in Japan and exported to the United States. This starter can be purchased in most natural food stores.

Lightly sprinkle the starter on top of the beans and mix in well, or mix in 3 ½ ounces of prepackaged natto, purchased at a natural food store, to begin the fermentation process. After mixing, cover the pot or place the beans in small cardboard containers. Place the pot or containers in the oven with a temperature of 102° to 104°F, which is the temperature of the oven when only the pilot light is lit or the inside light is on. If the natto is exposed to a temperature lower or higher than this, it will not ferment properly. Do not open the oven door or uncover the pot or containers.

Let the natto remain in the oven for 20 to 24 hours. Remove from oven and place containers in the freezer. Freezing stops the fermentation process. If left out of the freezer, the beans will continue to ferment until they are inedible. The above quantity of soybeans will yield 12 to 13 containers of natto, about 7½ ounce in weight. To serve, remove individual packages, thaw, and serve as described above.

TEMPEH

Originating in Indonesia and very popular with macrobiotic and vegetarian people in the United States and Europe today, tempeh is a fermented soybean product, that is high in protein and vitamin B_{12}. It can be purchased in most natural food stores across the country, or can be made at home. Kits for making homemade tempeh can be purchased at local natural food stores.

Tempeh is a versatile food which can be used to make soups, stews, nishime, dips, sandwiches, vegetable dishes, salads, and sea vegetable dishes, gomoku, in grain dishes such as fried rice or noodles. It can also be served as a topping for noodles and broth. The main methods of cooking are boiling, pressure-cooking, steaming, sautéing, and deep-frying.

Tempeh, Cabbage, and Sauerkraut

1 cup (10 oz) tempeh, cubed or sliced
2 cups green cabbage, chunks or sliced
¼ cup sauerkraut
¼ cup sauerkraut juice or water
dark sesame oil (optional)

Place a small amount of oil in a skillet and heat up. (To avoid using oil, omit it and simply dry-sauté or toast the tempeh with a little tamari on both sides until browned.) Add the tempeh to the skillet and sauté with a little tamari until golden. Add the sauerkraut on top of the tempeh. Place the cabbage on top of the sauerkraut. Add

tamari soy sauce

sauerkraut juice or water and bring to a boil. Cover and reduce the flame to low. Simmer about 25 minutes. Remove and place in a serving bowl.

Tempeh and Scallions

10 oz tempeh, cubed
1 bunch scallions, sliced
water
tamari soy sauce

Place tempeh in a saucepan and add enough water to half cover the tempeh. Bring to a boil. Cover and reduce the flame to low. Simmer 20 to 25 minutes until almost all the liquid is gone. Add the scallions and tamari, cover, and simmer 1 to 2 minutes. Remove the cover and cook off remaining liquid. Place in a serving bowl.

Sweet and Sour Tempeh

10 oz tempeh, cubed or sliced
1 cup apple juice
2 cups water, vegetable or kombu stock
$\frac{1}{2}$ cup onions, cut in wedges
$\frac{1}{2}$ cup carrots, cut on a diagonal
$\frac{1}{4}$ cup celery, cut on a diagonal
$\frac{1}{4}$ cup broccoli, spears
2–3 Tbsp kuzu, diluted in 2–3 Tbsp water
brown rice vinegar
tamari soy sauce
$\frac{1}{4}$ cup scallions, sliced

Place the tempeh in a pot and add the apple juice and water, or vegetable or kombu stock. Bring to a boil. Cover and reduce the flame to medium-low. Simmer about 20 minutes, add the onions, carrots, and celery. Simmer 1 minute. Place the broccoli in the pot, cover, and simmer until the broccoli is almost tender and still bright green. Reduce the flame to low and add the diluted kuzu, stirring constantly but gently until thick. Add a small amount of brown rice vinegar for a mild sour taste. Add enough tamari for a mild salt taste. Cook 1 minute longer. Remove and place in a serving bowl. Garnish with sliced scallions.

This may be served over brown rice, other grains, deep-fried croquettes, or favorite noodles.

Arame and Tempeh

(See Chapter 7 on Sea Vegetables for recipe.)

Tempeh Shish Kebabs

10 oz (10 pieces) tempeh, sliced in large chunks or cubes
dark sesame oil (optional)
water
2 slices fresh ginger
tamari soy sauce

Place the tempeh in a lightly oiled skillet and pan-fry until golden brown. (To avoid using oil, omit frying and simply boil for 20 minutes.) Add water to half cover the tempeh. Place the ginger slices in the skillet, cover, and bring to a boil. Reduce the flame to medium-low and simmer

5 onion wedges
5 carrot chunks
5 chunks thickly sliced summer
  squash
5–10 broccoli spears
5 fresh mushrooms, washed

about 15 minutes. Add a small amount of tamari and cook until all liquid is completely gone and the tempeh is browned. Discard the ginger or save for future use. Remove tempeh and place on a plate.

Place about 1 to 2 inches of water in a pot and bring to a boil. Add the onions and cook 1 minute. Remove and drain. Add carrots and boil 1 minute or until tender but still a little crisp. Remove and drain. Add the summer squash and cook 1 minute. Remove and drain. Add the broccoli spears and cook until tender but still bright green and slightly crisp. Remove and drain. Place the mushrooms on a cooking sheet and baste with a little tamari. Broil several minutes until tender. Remove and place on a plate.

Take 5 bamboo skewers and attractively arrange the tempeh and vegetables on them, with one piece of onion, carrot, squash, and mushroom on each skewer and 2 pieces of tempeh and broccoli on each skewer. Serve on an attractive serving platter.

Chapter 7

Sea Vegetables

Known for their healing powers, sea vegetables have been proven to help reverse hardening of the arteries, reduce high blood pressure, regress and prevent tumors, and even help eliminate radiation and fallout from our bodies. There are even very ancient records from Egypt as well as modern documents to prove this.

Sea vegetables are very important in macrobiotic cooking and way of eating. They may be used in an infinite number of ways in soups, salads, with vegetables, as a soup base, cooked with beans or grains to aid in digestion, or simply by themselves. They can also be roasted over a flame or in the oven and ground to a powder in a suribachi for use as condiments.

When beginning to eat macrobiotic food items, the taste, texture, and smell of various sea vegetables may be somewhat unusual and foreign. Introduce sea vegetables gradually into one's diet. Properly cooked, one will soon develop a taste for them. If there are difficulties eating sea vegetables at first, here are several suggestions that I found very helpful when preparing them for beginners in my home and cooking classes:

1) Use a larger proportion of sweet tasting vegetables, such as carrots and onions when preparing arame and hijiki side dishes or in soups, to reduce the sea vegetable's strong flavor.
2) When cooking arame and hijiki side dishes, cook until all remaining liquid is gone so that the sea vegetable tastes very sweet.

3) In soups and stews, cut the sea vegetables in tiny pieces and also reduce the amount called for in the recipe until one has adjusted to the flavor of sea vegetables.
4) Do not use the sea vegetable soaking water in cooking if it has a very strong and salty taste. Use fresh water instead.

The most mild tasting sea vegetables are arame, sea palm, nori, and dulse, while kombu, hijiki, and wakame have a slightly stronger flavor. Long-time cooking changes the flavor of sea vegetables so that they become very sweet and the fishy or ocean smell disappears.

I strongly recommend buying all sea vegetables in natural and macrobiotic food stores, as they are of the highest quality and harvested from unpolluted waters.

Since our sea salt contains no added iodine, we rely on the use of sea vegetables in our cooking to obtain iodine.

Sea vegetables are also a good source of calcium, iron, vitamin A, niacin, vitamin C, and protein, as we can see in the following chart.

Nutritional Content of Various Sea Vegetables
(Measurements are per 100 grams edible portion.)

	Calcium	Iron	Vitamin A	Niacin	Vitamin C	Protein	Iodine
Arame	1,170 mg	12 mg	50 I.U.	2.6 mg	0	7.5 g	300
Hijiki	1,400 mg	29 mg	150 I.U.	4.0 mg	0	5.6 g	40
Wakame	1,300 mg	13 mg	140 I.U.	10.0 mg	15 mg	12.7 g	25
Kombu	800 mg	15 mg	430 I.U.	1.8 mg	11 mg	7.3 g	300
Nori	260 mg	23 mg	11,000 I.U.	10.0 mg	20 mg	35.6 g	0.5
Dulse	567 mg	6.3 mg	N/A	N/A	30 mg	25.0 g	150
Agar-agar Kanten	400 mg	5 mg	0	0	0	2.3 g	0.2

(Information from U.S. Department of Agriculture and the Japan Nutritionists Association. From *The Book of Macrobiotics* by Michio Kushi, and U.S.D.A. food tables.)

ARAME

Arame has a very mild, sweet taste and a delicious texture. It is also one of the easiest of the sea vegetables to begin eating. It is black when dried and turns a dark brown color when cooked. I do not recommend soaking arame, as it is originally a large leaf that has been shredded before drying. If we soak it, many nutrients as well as its sweet flavor goes into the soaking water, resulting in a less tasty and less nutritious dish when cooked.

2 cups arame (approximately 1¼ oz dry weight)
1 tsp dark sesame oil

Wash arame quickly under cold water. Place in a strainer and allow to drain 3 to 5 minutes. Slice the arame diagonally into 1-inch pieces.

1 medium onion, sliced in half-
moons
1 carrot, sliced in matchsticks
water
2–3 tsp tamari soy sauce

Place a small amount of oil in a skillet and heat up. Place the onions in the skillet and sauté 1 to 2 minutes. Place the carrots on top of the onions. Next, place the arame on top of the carrots. Add enough fresh water to only cover the vegetables. (Do not mix vegetables and arame until the very end of cooking.)

Bring to a boil, reduce the flame to medium-low and cover. Simmer on a low flame for 35 to 45 minutes. Remove the cover and add a small amount of tamari. Cover again and cook for 7 to 10 minutes longer. Remove the cover, turn the flame to medium-high and cook off any excess liquid. Mix the vegetables and arame together and serve.

As a variation, use sliced lotus root instead of carrots, or lotus slices together with carrots and onions. Strips of deep-fried or pan-fried tofu or tempeh are also very good cooked with arame or hijiki.

Arame with Snow Peas and Tofu

2 cups arame (1¼ oz dry
weight), rinsed, drained, and
sliced
1 cup snow peas, stems removed
and washed
1 cup pan-fried or deep-fried
tofu strips, 2 inches long by
¼ inch wide
dark sesame oil
water
tamari soy sauce

Place a small amount of dark sesame oil in a skillet and heat up. Add the arame and sauté 1 to 2 minutes. Place the tofu on top of the arame. Do not stir. Add enough water to just cover the arame. Cover and bring to a boil. Reduce the flame to medium-low and simmer about 30 to 35 minutes. Season with a small amount of tamari, cover, and simmer another 5 to 10 minutes. Add the snow peas and cook 1 to 2 minutes until bright green but still crispy. Remove the cover and cook off any remaining liquid. Mix and serve.

Water-sautéed Arame with Tempeh

2 cups arame (1¼ oz dry
weight), rinsed, drained, and
sliced
1 cup tempeh, diced
water
½ cup onions, sliced in half-
moons
½ cup carrots, sliced in
matchsticks

Place enough water in a skillet to just cover the bottom and bring to a boil. Add the onions and sauté 1 to 2 minutes. Place the carrots on top of the onions and then the tempeh on top of the carrots. Next, layer the arame on top of the tempeh. Add enough water to just cover the tempeh and bring to a boil. Cover, reduce the flame to medium-low, and simmer about 30 to 35

tamari soy sauce
½ tsp ginger juice
1 Tbsp sliced scallions for
  garnish

minutes. Add a small amount of tamari and cook another 5 to 10 minutes. Remove the cover, add the ginger juice, and cook until all remaining liquid is gone. Mix and place in a serving bowl. Garnish with sliced scallions and serve.

As a variation, sauté, deep-fry, or pan-fry the tempeh and water sauté as above.

HIJIKI

Hijiki has a stronger taste than arame and a considerably different texture. Hijiki often needs to be cooked longer than arame because of its stronger texture and taste.

Hijiki is cooked basically in the same manner as arame and the same combinations of vegetables that are used for arame can be used. Unlike arame, hijiki needs to be soaked 3 to 5 minutes before cooking, to make it soft enough to slice. If the soaking water is too salty or strong, do not use in cooking or dilute it with half fresh water.

Hijiki with Fresh Lotus Root

1 cup hijiki (1–1¼ oz dry
  weight), washed, soaked, and
  sliced
½ cup fresh lotus root, sliced
  in thin half-moons
1 cup onions, sliced in thin half-
  moons
dark sesame oil (optional)
water
tamari soy sauce

Sauté the onions in a small amount of sesame oil for 1 to 2 minutes. Add the lotus slices. Place the hijiki on top of the vegetables. Do not mix. Add enough water to cover only the vegetables. Cover and bring to a boil. Reduce the flame to medium-low and simmer for about 45 to 50 minutes. Season with a small amount of tamari, cover, and cook another 5 to 10 minutes or until hijiki and vegetables are soft and tender. Remove the cover and cook off any remaining liquid. Mix and serve as is or garnish with a few sliced scallions.

As a variation, water sauté instead of oil sautéing. Dried lotus root may be used in place of fresh after soaking for about 1 hour. Dried lotus seeds, that have been soaked for 1 hour, may also be used on occasion.

Hijiki with Green Peas and Sweet Corn

1 cup hijiki, (1¼ oz dry weight)
  washed, soaked, and sliced
1 cup fresh green peas, removed

Sauté the hijiki for 1 to 2 minutes and then add enough water to about half cover it. Bring to a boil, cover, and reduce the flame to medium-

from pod and washed
1 cup fresh sweet corn, removed
from cob
dark sesame oil (optional)
water
tamari soy sauce

low. Simmer about 45 to 50 minutes. Add a small amount of tamari and layer the green peas and corn on top of the hijiki. Do not mix. Cover and simmer about 7 to 10 minutes until the peas and corn are done. Remove the cover and cook off any remaining liquid. Mix and serve.

WAKAME

Wakame is a green colored, rather delicately textured sea vegetable used mainly in soups. There are many delicious wakame side dishes which can be prepared, such as wakame salads, condiments, and nishime-style dishes. Some people find wakame one of the easier sea vegetables to adjust to while others may have a little adjustment period to go through. Sometimes the soaking water from wakame is a little salty. If so, do not use it in preparing wakame dishes, use plain water instead. Wash and soak wakame the same as for hijiki.

Wakame, Onions, and Carrots

2 cups wakame, washed, soaked, and sliced
1 cup onions, sliced in thick wedges
1 cup carrots, sliced in chunks
water
tamari soy sauce

Place the onions and carrots on the bottom of the pot and set the wakame on top. Add water to cover only the vegetables. Cover and bring to a boil. Reduce the flame to medium-low and simmer about 20 minutes or until the vegetables and wakame are tender. (Some varieties of wakame may require longer cooking time.) Add a small amount of tamari and cook for another 10 minutes. Remove the cover and cook off any remaining liquid.

As a variation, add parsnip chunks to this recipe.

Wakame-Cucumber Salad

(See Chapter 8 on Salads for recipe.)

Goma-Wakame Condiment

(See Chapter 10 on Condiments for recipe.)

Baked Wakame and Onions

2 cups wakame, washed, soaked, and sliced

Place the tahini in a suribachi and purée, gradually adding the water. Add the ginger juice and

1 cup onions, sliced in thin half-
   moons
3 Tbsp organic tahini, roasted
1 cup water
½ tsp ginger juice
tamari soy sauce
¼ cup sesame seeds, roasted

several drops of tamari and mix. Place the wakame and onions in a casserole dish. Mix in the sesame seeds and the tahini mixture. Cover the casserole dish and bake at 350°F for about 30 minutes. Remove the cover and bake another 10 to 15 minutes to brown the top and remove most of the excess liquid.

KOMBU

Kombu is a mild tasting, dark green sea vegetable. Unless properly cooked it can be a little tough or slippery. When cooked a long time kombu becomes very soft and sweet. It is used frequently in preparing soups, stews, grains, in vegetable dishes, soup stocks and broths, and beans, as well as pickles and condiments. Kombu cooked with beans or grains makes them sweeter and more digestible. Kombu can be boiled, baked, pressure-cooked or even deep-fried for a delicious, salty snack at parties.

Boiled Kombu and Vegetables

1 strip kombu, 10–12 inches
   long, soaked and cubed
1 cup carrots, cut in chunks
1 cup burdock, sliced on a thick
   diagonal
water
tamari soy sauce

Place the kombu in a pot. Add the carrots and burdock. Add soaking water from the kombu to about half cover the vegetables. Bring to a boil, cover, and reduce the flame to medium-low. Simmer for approximately 30 minutes. Add a small amount of tamari and cook for another 10 minutes. Remove the cover and boil off any remaining liquid.

Baked Kombu and Vegetables

1 strip kombu, 3–4 inches long,
   soaked and cubed
1 cup onions, quartered
1 cup carrots, sliced in chunks
2 cups cabbage, sliced in thick
   chunks
½ cup water
pinch of sea salt

Place the kombu in a baking or casserole dish. Arrange the onions in one corner of the dish, carrots in the center, and cabbage at the other end of the dish, keeping the vegetables separate from each other. Place the water in the dish and sprinkle a pinch of sea salt over the vegetables. Cover and bake at 375°F for 30 to 40 minutes or until the vegetables are soft and tender.

Pressure-cooked Kombu and Dried Tofu

1 strip kombu, 10–12 inches
   long, soaked and sliced across

Place the kombu, dried tofu, and ginger in a pressure cooker. Add only enough water to cover the

136

the width into very thin
matchsticks
6–8 pieces dried tofu, soaked
in warm water 3–5 minutes,
rinsed in cold water and sliced
into ¼-inch-thick rectangles
2 Tbsp fresh ginger, cut into
paper thin slices and sliced
into very thin matchsticks
water
tamari soy sauce

kombu. Place several drops of tamari on the tofu. Cover and bring up to pressure. Reduce the flame to low and cook for about 5 to 7 minutes. Remove and allow the pressure to come down. Remove the cover. If there is any remaining liquid, place the uncovered cooker on a high flame and boil off most of the excess liquid. Mix and serve.

If cooking this for children, leave out the ginger and use a little less tamari.

As a variation, a small amount of dried fish such as chuba or chirimen may be cooked together with this dish, omitting the dried tofu.

Pressure-cooked Kombu-Carrot Rolls

2 wide strips kombu, 10–12
inches long, soaked
4 medium-size carrots, 6 inches
long, washed
10–12 strips of *kampyo* (dried
gourd strips), 3 inches long,
soaked 3–5 minutes (or 10–12
strips of kombu, 3 inches long
and ¼ inch wide, soaked)
water
tamari soy sauce

Slice the long strips of kombu in half. Place one 5- to 6-inch strip of kombu on a cutting surface and place one carrot on top of it. Roll the carrot up in the kombu as tightly as possible, so that it is completely wrapped.

Take three of the short kampyo or kombu strips and tie the kombu-stuffed carrot up by tying the strips into knots around the roll. Tie one knot at each end and one in the middle of the kombu-carrot roll. Repeat until all the carrots have been wrapped in kombu and tied tightly.

Place the 4 kombu-carrot rolls in a pressure cooker and add about ¼ inch of water. Add a small amount of tamari, cover, and bring up to pressure. Reduce the flame to low and cook 3 to 5 minutes. Allow the pressure to come down. Remove the rolls and slice each roll into 3 pieces, so that each piece is still tied together. Arrange on a platter and serve. The kampyo or kombu knots that hold the rolls together can be eaten along with the kombu-carrot pieces.

Instead of pressure-cooking, these rolls can be boiled in a small amount of water for about 45 minutes or so.

As a variation, burdock or small, thin parsnips can be used in these rolls.

Shio Kombu

(See Chapter 10 on Condiments for recipe.)

NORI

Known as laver or sloke in many European countries, nori was traditionally used to prepare a thin laver bread combined with oatmeal. In Japan and other Asian countries it is used in making sushi, rice balls, condiments, as a garnish for soups and noodles, or simply toasted and eaten as a snack.

There are many varieties of dried nori ranging in color from red, to green black, to light green flakes. Sheets of dried nori do not need to be soaked or washed. Simply toast over a flame for several seconds and they are ready to eat or use in cooking. Green nori flakes (*aonori*) is used as a condiment.

Nori has the highest protein and vitamin A content of any sea vegetable. It is also high in vitamin B_{12} and other nutrients as can be seen from the chart at the beginning of this chapter.

Rice Ball (Musubi)

(See Chapter 3 on Grains for recipe.)

Sushi

(See Chapter 3 on Grains for recipe.)

Shio Nori

(See Chapter 10 on Condiments for recipe.)

Watercress Sushi

2 bunches watercress, cooked, rinsed, and allowed to drain
2 sheets nori, toasted
4–6 shiso leaves (from umeboshi container), 4–5 inches long
2 Tbsp sesame seeds, roasted

With both hands, squeeze out excess water from the watercress. Place a sheet of nori on top of a bamboo sushi mat. Take half of the watercress and spread it evenly to cover the lower half of the sheet of nori closest to you.

Take 2 to 3 shiso leaves and lay them lengthwise across the center of the watercress, forming a straight line. Sprinkle 1 tablespoon of the sesame seeds on top of the shiso in a straight line.

Tightly roll up the nori and watercress in the sushi mat just as if making rice sushi. Before unrolling the sushi mat and removing the watercress cylinder, squeeze the mat gently to remove excess water.

Place the nori-covered watercress roll on a cutting board and quickly slice it in half. Slice each half, quickly, into 8 equal-sized pieces about

1 inch long. If the roll is not cut as soon as it is made it falls apart easily. There should now be 8 pieces of watercress sushi.

Repeat the process again until all the watercress and nori are used to make 16 pieces of sushi.

DULSE

Traditionally used in Europe, Canada, and New England, dulse has a red-purple color and, simply eaten dry as a snack or condiment, it is quite salty. Soaked and used in soups and salads it has a very mild flavor and a beautiful light maroon color. Dulse complements oats or oatmeal nicely when used as a condiment.

Dulse Powder ———————————————————————————

(See Chapter 10 on Condiments for recipe.)

Goma-Dulse Powder ———————————————————————

(See Chapter 10 on Condiments for recipe.)

SEA PALM

Sea Palm is a relatively new sea vegetable to appear in natural food stores. It grows on the Pacific coast from Canada to Central California on rocks in rough shore areas. It resembles land palms before it is sliced and dried and is dark green in color. It has long, thin, corrugated lines on it. It can be boiled or steamed and served with either lemon juice or vinegar and tamari soy sauce. It can also be candied or pickled. I really enjoy sea palm and find it deliciously sweet.

Steamed Sea Palm ———————————————————————

2 cups sea palm, washed, soaked, and sliced in 2-inch-long pieces
$\frac{1}{8}$ cup brown rice vinegar
2 Tbsp rice syrup
tamari soy sauce

Steam the sea palm until tender, remove, and allow to cool. Mix together the vinegar, rice syrup, and several drops of tamari. Pour the sauce over the sea palm, mix and serve.

Boiled Sea Palm and Vegetables ————————————————

2 cups sea palm, soaked and
  sliced
1 cup carrots, cut into thick
  matchsticks
½ cup onions, sliced in thick
  half-moons
water
tamari soy sauce

Place the sea palm and vegetables in a pot and add about ½ inch of water. Cover and bring to a boil. Reduce the flame to medium-low and simmer about 30 to 35 minutes or until the sea palm is tender. Season with a small amount of tamari and simmer another 10 to 15 minutes until all remaining liquid is gone.

AGAR-AGAR

Agar-agar, when cooked, forms a substance similar to gelatin. It is used mainly in dessert cooking to make kanten, which is a fruit gelatin, or pudding, custards, and pies. It can also be used to make a vegetable aspic or an aspic with azuki beans and raisins. Agar-agar is almost colorless and odorless. It comes prepackaged in flakes or bars with directions on how to prepare it printed on the package.

Vegetable Aspic ————————————————

5–6 Tbsp agar-abar flakes (or
  read directions on package for
  appropriate amount)
½ cup carrots, cut into
  matchsticks or flower shapes
½ cup onions, sliced in thin
  half-moons
½ cup celery, sliced on a thin
  diagonal
1 quart water, kombu stock, or
  vegetable stock
tamari soy sauce
1 tsp ginger juice

Blanch the carrots, onions, and celery separately for less than 1 minute, remove, and drain. Place the vegetables in a shallow casserole dish.

Place the water or stock in a pot and add the agar-agar flakes. Bring to a boil, stirring occasionally to dissolve the flakes, and then reduce the flame to low and simmer 2 to 3 minutes. Add a few drops of tamari soy sauce and the ginger juice. Mix and pour the hot liquid over the vegetables. Allow to sit in a cool place until gelled. Slice and serve.

As a variation, grated carrots or squash purée can be used to make a delicious vegetable aspic.

Sweet azuki beans or split pea aspics are also very delicious.

Fruit Kanten ————————————————

(See Chapter 13 on Desserts for recipe.)

Chapter 8

Salads

Salads add a very light and refreshing energy to any meal whether it is spring, summer, autumn, or winter.

They can be prepared with grains, beans, noodles, vegetables, sea vegetables, fruit, fish, or shellfish. Salads can be boiled, steamed, served raw, or pressed. There are many delicious salad dressings and garnishes which can be made to enhance the flavor and beauty of salads. Some garnishes which can be used are roasted seeds and nuts, toasted sea vegetables, deep-fried or pan-roasted bread croutons, scallions, chopped shiso leaves, and parsley.

Usually, raw salads are enjoyed more during the warmer months of the year but are occasionally eaten during autumn and winter to balance an overly yang meal or condition. Cooked or pressed salads can be enjoyed year round.

Brown Rice and Vegetable Salad

2 cups brown rice, freshly cooked

When the rice is done, fluff it up with a rice paddle or chopsticks and allow to cool. Mix

1/2 cup broccoli, cut into small flowerettes and parboiled 1–2 minutes

1/2 cup carrots, cut into thick matchsticks and parboiled 1 minute

3 shiitake mushrooms, soaked, diced, and boiled 10 minutes in water, tamari, and barley malt

1 cup tempeh, cubed and either deep-fried, pan-fried, or boiled for 20 minutes

1/2 cup cooked seitan, cubed

1/4 cup celery, diced and par-boiled for 1 minute

1/4 cup almonds, blanched and skin removed

1/8 cup finely minced shiso leaves or 1/4 cup umeboshi vinegar

4–5 lettuce leaves

in all ingredients separately, except for the lettuce leaves. Scoop the rice salad out onto the lettuce leaves and place one on each individual plate.

Brown rice vinegar, lemon juice, or umeboshi vinegar can be used in place of shiso leaves for this recipe to create variations. Other vegetable combinations can be used as well.

Three Bean Salad

1 cup kidney beans, cooked and drained

2 cups green string beans, washed, stems removed, steamed until tender and sliced

1 cup wax beans (yellow), washed, stems removed, steamed until tender and sliced

umeboshi or scallion-parsley dressing

Combine beans and serve with umeboshi or scallion-parsley dressing. Serve cool in summer or room temperature in other seasons.

Chick-pea Salad

1 cup chick-peas, cooked and drained

1/2 head lettuce, shredded

1/2 cup carrots, shredded

1/2 cup cucumber, sliced in quarters

1/4 cup celery, sliced on a thin diagonal

umeboshi, scallion-parsley dressing, or tahini dressing

Combine ingredients and serve with umeboshi, scallion-parsley dressing, or tahini dressing.

Boiled Salad

1 cup Chinese cabbage, sliced in 1-inch-wide diagonals
½ cup onions, sliced in half-moons
½ cup carrots, cut in matchsticks
½ cup celery, sliced on a thin diagonal
1 bunch watercress, washed and sliced in 1–2-inch lengths
tofu dressing

When making a boiled salad, boil the vegetables separately. All of the vegetables may be boiled in the same water, but boil the vegetables that leave the mildest taste first, so that each vegetable retains its own flavor. For example, Chinese cabbage leaves the mildest taste in the water of the above vegetables.

Drop the Chinese cabbage into 1 inch of boiling water. Boil for about 1 to 1½ minutes. Next boil the onions for 1 minute, then the carrots for 1 minute, then the celery for 1 minute, and lastly the watercress, as it has a very strong taste. Watercress only needs to be boiled for a few seconds. All of the vegetables should be slightly crisp but not raw.

Place the vegetables in a strainer or colander and allow to cool. Mix the vegetables together. Serve with tofu dressing or mix the tofu dressing in with the vegetables just before serving.

Noodle Salad

2 cups of whole wheat shells, elbows, or alphabet noodles, cooked, rinsed, and drained
½ cup carrots, shredded
½ cup cucumber, sliced in quarters
¼ cup celery, sliced on a thin diagonal
¼ cup red onions, sliced in very thin half-moons
tahini or umeboshi dressing

Mix noodles and vegetables. Mix together with tahini or umeboshi dressing.

Hijiki Salad

1 cup hijiki, washed, soaked, and sliced
½ cup onions, sliced in half-moons
½ cup sweet corn, removed from cob
1 cup Chinese cabbage, sliced in 1-inch diagonals

Place about ½ inch of water in a saucepan and place the hijiki in it. Bring to a boil. Cover and reduce the flame to low. Simmer 5 to 10 minutes. Remove and drain. Set aside to cool.

Boil the vegetables, separately, in 1 inch of water in the following order: onions, corn, Chinese cabbage, broccoli, and radishes. Remove

½ cup broccoli, cut in small
  flowerettes
½ cup red radish, sliced in thin
  rounds
water
tofu dressing

each vegetable group and allow to drain and cool.
When cool, either mix together with the hijiki
or arrange the ingredients attractively in a bowl,
keeping each ingredient separate from the others.
Serve with tofu dressing.

Wakame Salad

1 cup wakame, soaked and
  sliced
1 cup cucumber, sliced in thin
  rounds
1 cup apple, sliced in small
  pieces
Dressing:
  1 Tbsp barley miso
  1 tsp lemon juice
  ½ cup water

Place about ¼ inch of water in a saucepan and
bring to a boil. Add the wakame, cover, and
reduce the flame to low. Simmer 5 to 10 minutes.
Remove, rinse quickly, and drain.
  Combine the miso, lemon juice, and water and
purée until smooth in a suribachi.
  Place the wakame, cucumber, and apple in a
bowl and pour the miso-lemon dressing over it.
Mix and let sit for 1 hour. Drain off excess liquid
and serve.

Marinated Lotus Root Salad

1 cup fresh lotus root, quartered
  and thinly sliced
1 Tbsp tamari soy sauce
1 Tbsp brown rice vinegar
1 Tbsp mirin
1 tsp roasted sesame seeds
1 tsp scallions, sliced

Mix all ingredients together in a bowl and let sit
for ½ to 1 hour. Drain and serve.
  As a variation, try 1 tablespoon umeboshi
vinegar, ¼ teaspoon ginger juice, and 1 teaspoon
chopped parsley.

Pressed Salad #1

1 cup daikon, sliced in paper
  thin rounds and then thin
  matchsticks
½ cup carrots, sliced in paper
  thin rounds and then thin
  matchsticks
¼ tsp sea salt
1–2 Tbsp brown rice vinegar
1 tsp roasted black sesame seeds

Place daikon and carrots in a pickle press. Add
the sea salt and vinegar. Mix thoroughly. Place
the top on the press and tightly screw down. Let
sit 1 hour. Remove and squeeze out excess liquid
or, if too salty, rinse quickly under cold water.
Place in a bowl and garnish with the roasted
black sesame seeds.

Pressed Salad #2

½ head iceberg lettuce, thinly
  sliced

Place all vegetables in a pickle press. Add the
water and umeboshi vinegar and mix well. Place

1 cucumber, washed and thinly
  sliced
4–5 red radishes, sliced in thin
  rounds
1 stalk celery, sliced on a thin
  diagonal
½ cup red onions, sliced in
  paper thin rounds or half-
  rounds
1 cup water
¼ cup umeboshi vinegar

the top on the press and screw down tightly.
Let sit for 1 hour. Remove, squeeze out excess
liquid, place in a bowl and serve.

As a variation, use Chinese or regular cabbage,
thinly sliced; grated carrot; white onion; or any
other vegetable.

Chapter 9

Salad Dressings, Spreads, Sauces, and Dips

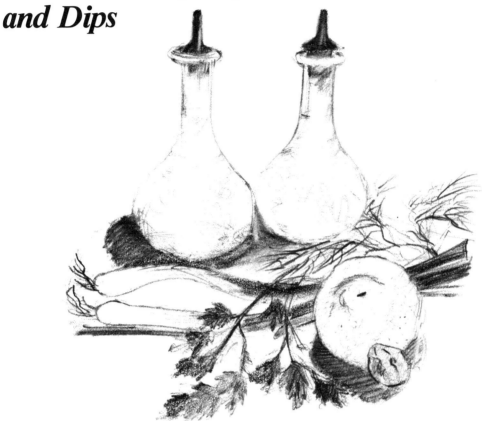

Dressings, spreads, sauces, and dips add a nice touch to many dishes that we prepare. Some are sour tasting, sweet, salty, or slightly bitter, while others are more pungent tasting. They can be used for daily cooking or parties, lunches or holidays. They enhance the taste as well as add to the beauty of many dishes. Make sure that the dressing, spread, sauce, or dip, complements the foods served with it, both in terms of taste and color.

DRESSINGS

Creamy Tofu Dressing

1 cake (16 oz) tofu
1 small onion, grated
1 tsp puréed umeboshi paste, or
   3 umeboshi plums (remove

Purée onion, umeboshi, and water in a suribachi. Purée the tofu in a hand food mill and add to the suribachi. Purée until creamy. Remove and place in an attractive bowl. Garnish with chopped

pits)
¼ cup water
2 Tbsp chopped scallions or sprigs of parsley and slices of parboiled carrots for garnish

scallions, or sprigs of parsley and slices of parboiled carrots. Serve with boiled, raw, sea vegetable, or noodle salads.

Umeboshi Dressing

2 umeboshi plums, pits removed
½ tsp parsley, chopped
½ tsp onions, grated
¼ tsp warm sesame oil (optional)
½ cup water (or more if desired)

Purée umeboshi, parsley, and onion together in a suribachi. Add the warm oil and purée. Add the water and mix. Serve with raw, boiled, noodle, grain, or bean salads.

Scallion-Parsley Dressing

¼ cup scallions, finely sliced
1 Tbsp parsley, chopped
¼ tsp warm sesame oil (optional)
1 cup umeboshi juice or ¼ cup umeboshi vinegar

To make the umeboshi juice, take 3 to 4 umeboshi plums and place in 1 cup of water. Place in a glass jar and shake well. Allow to sit for 1 hour. Drain the water from plums. Save the plums, they can be used again.

Place the scallions, parsley, warm sesame oil, and the umeboshi juice in a suribachi and purée. Serve over raw, boiled, noodle, grain, or bean salads.

Umeboshi-Tahini Dressing

2–3 umeboshi plums, pits removed
1 Tbsp organic tahini roasted
1 small onion, diced or grated
½–¾ cup water

Purée the onion, umeboshi, and tahini in a suribachi. Add the water gradually and purée until creamy. Serve on raw, boiled, noodle, hijiki, or couscous salads.

Miso Dressing

3 Tbsp barley miso
2 Tbsp brown rice vinegar
½ cup water
½ small onion, grated
1 tsp parsley, minced

Place all ingredients in a suribachi and purée until smooth. Serve on vegetable or wakame salads.

Green Goddess Dressing

3 umeboshi plums, pits removed

Blend all ingredients together in a suribachi or

2 Tbsp onions, grated
1 cup water
½ cup parsley, finely chopped
¾ cup cooked brown rice,
   ground in a hand food mill
2 Tbsp organic tahini, roasted
1 Tbsp tamari soy sauce
1 tsp sweet brown rice vinegar

blender until creamy and smooth. Serve with raw, boiled vegetable, or sea vegetable salads.

Tamari-Ginger Dressing

¼ tsp ginger, grated
1 tsp parsley, chopped
½ cup water
¼ cup tamari soy sauce

Place the ginger and parsley together in a suribachi and purée several seconds. Add water and tamari and mix. Serve with raw, boiled vegetable, grain, or noodle salads.

SPREADS

Miso-Tahini Spread

6 Tbsp organic tahini, roasted
1 Tbsp mugi or brown rice miso
2 Tbsp scallions, chopped

Roast tahini and miso in a dry skillet, using a medium-low flame until golden brown. Add the scallions and stir constantly to avoid burning. Remove from the flame and place in a bowl. Serve on fresh, toasted, or steamed whole grain bread or crackers.

Miso-Sesame Spread

Prepare in the same way as Miso-Tahini Spread, except substitute sesame butter instead of tahini.

Onion Butter

10 medium onions, diced
dark sesame oil
pinch of sea salt
water

Place a small amount of dark sesame oil in a pot and heat up. Add the onions and a pinch of sea salt. Sauté 3 to 5 minutes or until translucent. Add enough water to just cover the onions. Bring to a boil, reduce the flame to low, and simmer several hours until the onions are dark brown and very sweet. Occasionally, during cooking it may be necessary to add a small amount of water to prevent burning. Add when necessary but only in small amounts. When the onion butter is done, allow to completely cool before storing in a glass container. Either use immediately on a favorite bread, toast, or crackers, or store in the refrigerator until needed.

Carrot, squash, apple, or pear butter may also be made using this same cooking method.

To avoid oil, omit the oil and water sauté.

These vegetable butters may be seasoned with tamari soy sauce or miso at the end of cooking for a different flavor instead of using sea salt, if desired.

Other Spreads

Spreads can be made from a variety of vegetables and fruits, for example squash, onions and miso; squash and apples; apple butter; tahini, scallion or chives and miso; tofu, umeboshi and scallions; and so on. Please experiment.

SAUCES

Béchamel Sauce

dark sesame oil
1 medium onion, diced
½ cup whole wheat pastry flour or rice flour
3 cups water, vegetable stock, or kombu soup stock
1 Tbsp tamari soy sauce

Brush the skillet lightly with sesame oil. Sauté onions until they become transparent. Add the flour and toast for 2 to 3 minutes. Stir so that each piece of onion is coated with flour. Gradually, add the water and stir constantly to avoid lumping. Add tamari, and bring to a boil. Cover, reduce the flame to low, and cook for 10 to 15 minutes. Place a flame deflector under the skillet to prevent burning. Stir occasionally to prevent sticking.

As a variation add diced celery and/or sliced mushrooms.

This sauce is very good when served occasionally, over kasha, millet, or seitan. However, thick, heavy sauces should be used only on occasion, since they may be a little difficult to digest if eaten regularly. Kuzu sauces may be used more frequently.

Kuzu Sauce

1 Tbsp kuzu

Dilute the kuzu in a small amount of water and

1 cup vegetable stock or water **tamari soy sauce**	add to the vegetable stock and stir constantly. Bring to a boil. Reduce the flame to low and simmer for 3 to 5 minutes. Add tamari to create a mild taste. Serve over vegetables, tofu, or add to a Chinese-style vegetable dish.

Miso-Lemon Sauce

2 Tbsp miso **6 tsp lemon juice (or tangerine juice)** **2–3 Tbsp water**	Mix ingredients together until creamy and heat up in a skillet. Serve on bread, toast, or serve with vegetables as a condiment. Tahini may also be added occasionally.

DIPS

Chick-pea Dip

2 cups chick-peas **1 onion, diced** **2 Tbsp parsley, chopped** **2 umeboshi plums, pits removed** **chopped scallions for garnish**	Cook the chick-peas as described in bean section. Purée onion, parsley, and umeboshi in a suribachi. Add to the chick-peas and chick-pea cooking water. Purée the chick-peas in a hand food mill. Garnish with chopped scallions. Serve with bread, corn chips, crackers, or pita bread.

Tofu Cheese Dip

1 cake (1 lb) fresh firm-style tofu, drained **barley miso** **2 Tbsp sliced scallions** **water**	Wrap the tofu in a thin layer of clean cheesecloth. Pack barley miso on all sides, top and bottom of the tofu. Let sit 2 to 3 days. Remove the miso-packed cheesecloth and rinse the tofu under cold water.

Place the scallions in a suribachi and grind 1 to 2 minutes. Crumple the pickled tofu into the suribachi and purée until smooth. Add a small amount of water and purée until creamy. Serve on a favorite bread, crackers, rice cakes, or corn chips.

Chives or parsley may be substituted for scallions for a variation.

Tofu Dip

Use the same recipe as for Tofu Dressing in the previous chapter. Serve on bread, with corn chips or crackers.

Chapter 10
Condiments and Garnishes

CONDIMENTS

In macrobiotic eating we use a wide variety of condiments but consume them in small quantities because of their yang qualities. Condiments aid in digestion, are a good way to take in extra salt and minerals in a balanced way, and are also a delicious addition to meals. In fact, they are sometimes too delicious and it is easy to take in too much of them. Condiments are usually quite salty or pungent, and are used sparingly. We generally do not serve salty or pungent condiments to children as they cannot tolerate or do not like these tastes as much as adults.

Condiments also provide a good source of extra minerals in our diet. When making them for children we use much, much less salt and try to make more sweet tasting condiments.

Miso-Scallion Condiment ————————————————————

2 cups scallions, chopped (chop
   the roots very fine and sauté
   first)
1 Tbsp barley miso
1 tsp dark sesame oil
2 Tbsp water

Sauté the scallions in dark sesame oil for 2 to 3 minutes. Purée the miso in a suribachi with a small amount of water. Add miso to scallions and gently mix. Place on a low flame and cover and cook for 5 to 10 minutes. Serve with grain, noodle, or vegetable dishes.

Instead of scallions, chives, carrot tops, green peppers, onion or parsley may be used.

Tamari Soy Sauce ————————————————————

Tamari soy sauce is the name given to the soy sauce that is traditionally processed without chemicals, sugar, or preservatives. Real tamari is different. It is a by-product of miso and is darker in color and used less often in everyday cooking. In this book, tamari soy sauce refers to traditionally processed soy sauce and not the tamari which is a miso by-product. I recommend using tamari soy sauce mainly in cooking or in the preparation of medicinal foods. If necessary, a small amount may be added at the table to soups or noodles to enhance their flavor. It can also be used when eating natto. Tamari soy sauce should generally not be used on rice to enhance the flavor. We can, however, make sea vegetable condiments cooked with tamari and eat them with grains.

Shio Kombu ————————————————————

2 strips kombu, 10–12 inches
   long, dusted off, soaked and
   cubed
water
tamari soy sauce

Place the kombu in a pot and just cover with a mixture of half water and half tamari. Bring to a boil, cover, and reduce the flame to medium-low. Simmer until the kombu is soft and then cook off most of the remaining liquid. Only 2 or 3 pieces are eaten with the meal as this condiment is quite salty. To prepare this as a side dish, not a condiment, reduce the tamari content considerably.

Variations of this condiment can be made by adding dried fish such as chirimen or chuba; thin matchstick pieces of ginger; thinly sliced shiitake; or even barley malt or rice syrup for a sweet condiment.

Shio Nori ————————————————————

5 sheets nori, unroasted, cut or
   torn into 1-inch pieces

Place the nori in a saucepan and add enough water to just cover it. Bring to a boil, cover, and

water
tamari soy sauce

reduce the flame to low. Simmer about 20 to 30 minutes until almost all the liquid is gone. Add several drops of tamari and cook several more minutes until it becomes a thick black pasty consistency. This should have a milder salt taste than shio kombu. One to 2 tablespoons may be eaten with a meal.

For a saltier condiment, add more tamari. For a sweeter condiment, add a small amount of barley malt, rice syrup, or mirin.

Umeboshi

Umeboshi is a variety of plum that has been pickled in sea salt with shiso leaves. It aids in digestion. Umeboshi may be used in making rice balls; sushi; soups; dips, sauces, and salad dressings; with cooked vegetables; rubbed on sweet corn; as a condiment served with rice; in medicinal preparations; as well as other dishes. Shiso leaves may be used in preparing condiments as well.

Shiso-Nori Condiment

2 tsp shiso leaves, very finely chopped and dry-roasted 2–3 minutes
¼ cup sesame seeds, roasted
2 Tbsp aonori (green nori flakes)

Place the shiso in a suribachi and grind slightly. Add the sesame seeds and nori flakes and mix. Store in a sealed glass container. Sprinkle occasionally on grains, vegetables, or noodle dishes.

Gomashio

Gomashio is made from roasted black or tan sesame seeds and sea salt. It may be sprinkled over rice, other grains, or vegetables. Sesame seeds are high in protein, calcium, phosphorus, iron, vitamin A, and niacin. Gomashio provides an excellent balanced way of taking in salt and oil, as the salt is coated with oil and aids in digestion. However, it should be used moderately. The recommended proportions for gomashio are 1 part sea salt to 8 to 14 parts sesame seeds. For children, use much less salt or none at all. Gomashio adds a slightly nutty flavor to foods.

The key to making good gomashio is good health and patience. It should not be made quickly. To store gomashio, place it in a jar and cover tightly. Try to make it fresh every week. The black seeds contain less oil than the tan ones and are a little more bitter, but delicious.

1 cup sesame seeds
1½–2 Tbsp sea salt, dry-roasted 2–3 minutes and ground in

Wash the sesame seeds and drain. Roast them in a dry skillet over a medium-low flame. Stir continuously with a wooden spoon, shaking the

a suribachi

skillet from time to time so that the seeds roast evenly. When the seeds give off a nutty fragrance, darken in color, and begin popping, take a seed and crush it between the thumb and index finger. If it crushes easily, it is done. If not, continue to roast.

Pour the seeds, immediately, into a suribachi. The seeds will burn if left in the skillet after the flame has been turned off.

Slowly grind the seeds together with the roasted, ground sea salt in an even circular motion, until each seed is about half crushed. Gomashio should not be ground too fine. Do not hurry. Store in a tightly sealed container after the seeds have cooled.

Sea-vegetable Powders

Sea-vegetable powders can be made by roasting either wakame, kombu, kelp, or dulse in a 350°F oven until they become dark and crisp, but not burnt. Then grind them into a powder in a suribachi. Sea-vegetable powders are rich in protein, calcium, iron, and minerals.

To make different condiments, roast sesame seeds (60 percent) and grind together with the sea vegetable (40 percent). Grind the sea vegetables first before adding the sesame seeds and then grind again until the seeds are half crushed.

In cases of anemia, a condiment made from roasted kombu and roasted chirimen (small dried fish), which are ground together into a powder, is very high in calcium and iron. It can be sprinkled on rice occasionally.

Tekka

$\frac{1}{3}$ cup burdock, finely minced
$\frac{1}{3}$ cup carrots, finely minced
$\frac{1}{3}$ cup lotus root, finely minced
$\frac{1}{2}$ tsp ginger, grated
$\frac{1}{4}$ cup dark sesame oil
$\frac{2}{3}$ cup Hatcho miso

Mince the vegetables as finely as possible. Heat a cast iron skillet, and add half of the oil. Heat the oil and sauté the burdock, carrot, lotus root, and ginger. Add the remaining oil and the miso. Reduce flame to very low and cook for 3 to 4 hours. Stir frequently until all the liquid evaporates and tekka becomes as dry and black as possible.

Tekka helps to make the blood very rich and strong and is high in protein, iron, and niacin. This is a very strong, yang condiment, so use it sparingly. A small pinch is sufficient on occasion.

GARNISHES

Garnishes are added to many macrobiotic dishes for aesthetic reasons, taste, light energy, and to help stimulate our appetite.

There are many items which can be used as garnishes, such as: sliced scallions, chives or parsley; diced onions; grated ginger; daikon or carrot; celery, daikon or watercress leaves; lemon juice, rind, or slices; tangerine juice or slices; toasted nori squares or strips; horseradish; red radish slices; black and tan roasted sesame seeds; roasted sunflower or pumpkin seeds; various nuts, roasted and chopped; shiitake mushrooms; dried fish; fruit slices; wasabi (grated Japanese horseradish); fresh dill or parsley sprigs; carrot flowers; or washed leaves; pine needles; flowers from our yards; and many, many, other items!

Chapter 11
Pickles

Pickles were originally created to help people naturally adapt to the changing of the seasons, strengthen the digestive system, aid in digestion, and stimulate appetite. In temperate climates, pickling was developed as a way of naturally storing vegetables during the winter, while in warmer climates, it was found that pickled vegetables do not spoil easily. Also, certain types of pickles produce a naturally cooling effect during hot weather, while others produce warming or strengthening effects during cooler seasons.

There are a wide variety of methods which can be used in making pickles. By varying factors such as time, pressure, salt, or seasoning agents, and types of vegetables, either more yin or more yang pickles can be produced.

A lighter, refreshing pickle can be made during warmer weather, to balance a heavy or more yang meal, or for those who wish to limit their salt intake. These light pickles or quick pickles can be made in anywhere from a few hours, or days, to several weeks and usually keep for several days or weeks depending on the salt content.

A stronger, long-time pickle is more often used in colder weather or for those with more weak conditions. These pickles may take anywhere from several weeks to several months to pickle and store well for many weeks or months.

In general, to maintain health, ingredients like spices, sugar, and commercial vinegars are not recommended for making pickles. Naturally made macrobiotic pickles are usually made with sea salt, rice bran, wheat bran, umeboshi, rice flour, tamari soy sauce, or miso as pickling agents. Ginger and natural herbs such as fresh dill can be used. For those in fairly good health, a dash of red pepper can occasionally be used. Natural grain sweeteners are also used occasionally.

Listed in the following pages are several basic methods for making pickles. If pickles are too salty, simply soak them in cold water about ½ hour before serving, to draw the salt out, or quickly rinse them.

Long-term Salt Pickles

5 lbs Chinese cabbage
¼–½ lb sea salt

A heavy ceramic crock or wooden keg will be needed for this pickle. Remove leaves from the cabbage and wash under cold water. Quarter the hearts of the cabbage and wash them. Then, set aside and let dry for about 24 hours.

Place a thin layer of sea salt on the bottom of the crock, several pinches will do. Place a layer of several cabbage leaves in the crock. Sprinkle sea salt on top of the leaves. Next, add another layer of leaves, pointing in the opposite direction. Repeat this until all the cabbage is used or until the crock is filled.

Rock or bricks

Plate or lid

Place a wooden lid or plate in the crock that fits down inside on top of the cabbage and salt. Place several clean, heavy rocks or clean bricks on top of the lid or plate. Cover the crock with a thin layer of clean cheesecloth to keep dust out. Leave in a dark, cool place for 1 to 2 weeks or longer. Remove, wash under cold water, slice, and serve.

Daikon, daikon leaves, carrots, or other vegetables may also be pickled in this manner.

Miso Pickles

Miso pickles are very strong and usually quite salty. They require no pressure to prepare. First, wash root vegetables such as daikon or carrots. Then tie a rope around them and hang in a shaded warm place for about 24 hours or until they can be bent in a semicircle. Place the whole vegetables in the miso and leave for 1 to 2 years.

To make a quicker miso pickle, cut the vegetables into rounds after drying and place in the miso. Thinly sliced vegetables take 3 to 7 days, thicker slices 1 to 2 weeks to pickle. Usually, root vegetables are more appropriate to pickle in miso than greens.

Miso Pickled Cucumbers

1 cucumber, washed
barley miso

Slice the cucumber into $\frac{1}{8}$- to $\frac{1}{4}$-inch thick rounds. Place on a clean dish towel or paper towel and squeeze some of the liquid out. Place the slices in a small jar filled with miso. Leave 1 to 2 days. Remove, rinse, and serve.

Pickled Tofu in Miso

(See Chapter 9 on Salad Dressings, Spreads, Sauces, and Dips for recipe.)

Tamari Pickles

Mix half water and half tamari soy sauce in a bowl or glass jar. Slice vegetables such as rutabaga, cauliflower, onions, daikon, broccoli, carrots, celery, turnips, or other vegetables (even greens), and place in the tamari-water. Leave 4 hours to 2 weeks in the water.

Vegetables may be pickled raw or blanched and cooled first. Mirin or a grain sweetener may be added for a sweeter flavor. For a sour taste, use brown rice vinegar. Remove when done, rinse, and eat or store in a container until used. The longer the pickles are allowed to set, the saltier the flavor.

Tamari-Onion Pickles

2 cups onions, sliced in thin
half-moons, parboiled 30
seconds
½ cup shiitake mushroom,
sliced thin and boiled 10–15
minutes
1 cup water
½ cup tamari soy sauce
1 tsp brown rice or sweet rice
vinegar
1 Tbsp barley malt or rice syrup

Allow the vegetables to cool and then place in a quart glass jar. Pour a mixture of half water and half tamari over the vegetables to cover them. Add the vinegar and barley malt or rice syrup. Cover and shake to mix. Allow to sit 2 to 3 days or up to 1 week. Remove, rinse, and serve.

Small onions may be pickled whole, either raw or parboiled for 1 to 2 minutes.

Nuka Pickles (Rice Bran)

Nuka is the bran of milled rice. It can be used to make many kinds of deliciously sweet pickles.

When our family lived in Japan, some of the most wonderful pickles that we tasted were made with nuka.

Since organic white sushi rice has become popular we are now able to purchase organic nuka, which is ideal and preferable.

Many vegetables can be pickled in nuka such as: Chinese cabbage, daikon, daikon greens, turnip and their greens, *mizuna* (an Oriental vegetable), carrots, and even flowers from mustard plants that are going to seed.

There are two ways in which to prepare these nuka pickles. One method is to layer roasted nuka and salt between layers of vegetables. The other is to prepare a thick paste from roasted nuka, salt, and water, and to insert vegetables into it.

If nuka is not available, substitute with wheat bran or brown rice flour.

Kyoto-style Chinese Cabbage Nuka Pickles

This is a deliciously sweet pickle recipe which I learned from a good friend, Satchiko Shimooka, while our family lived in Kyoto, Japan.

4–5 heads Chinese cabbage,
washed and quartered
sea salt
nuka (rice bran), roasted

Dry the cabbage in the sun for 2 days. This will make the cabbage become very sweet. Sprinkle a small amount of sea salt on the bottom of a wooden keg or ceramic crock. Layer the cabbage, little by little, in the crock, alternating the direction of the layers. Between each layer of cabbage sprinkle a few pinches of sea salt. Repeat until cabbage is used up. On top of the last layer of cabbage also sprinkle sea salt.

Place a lid on top of the cabbage, so that it

fits down inside the crock, resting on top of the cabbage. Place a heavy weight on top of the lid. Set in a cool place. The water level should rise up to the lid within about 10 hours. If it does not, either more weight or more salt is needed.

When the water level rises up to the lid, drain off all the salty water and remove the cabbage.

Once again layer the cabbage in the crock, except this time sprinkle a thin layer of roasted nuka between each layer of cabbage. Replace the lid and the weight. Keep in a cool place for about 1 week. The pickles are now ready to rinse, slice, and eat.

The reason for draining off the salty water is that it produces a lighter, less salty, and more sweet pickle. It takes about 1 week for the nuka to produce enzymes. The smell of the pickles will change during this 1 week period.

Rice Bran Pickles #1

10–12 cups nuka (rice bran)
1–1½ cups sea salt
1 strip kombu, 6–8 inches long
3–5 cups water
½ cup Hatcho miso

Roast the nuka in a dry skillet, over a medium-low flame until it releases a somewhat nutty aroma. Do not scorch or burn. Allow to cool. Add the salt, kombu, and water to a pot and boil until the salt dissolves. Allow to cool. Mix the salt water and kombu with the nuka and miso to form a thick paste. Place the nuka paste in a wooden keg or ceramic crock and press down firmly.

When using root vegetables such as daikon, wash off any soil and hang the roots in a shaded, warm place until they can be bent in a semi-circle. Leaves are best washed and allowed to dry for 1 day to remove excess liquid before pickling.

Insert vegetables into the paste so that they are completely covered and the vegetables do not touch each other. Press the paste down until firm again. Place a lid inside the crock and set a stone on top to apply pressure. Keep in a cool room and cover with a thin piece of cheesecloth to keep the dust out. When water comes out, turn the mixture and press down firm again. If water rises to the surface too fast, there is too much pressure. If it rises too slowly, there is not enough pressure. Once water comes out, reduce the pressure.

Whole vegetables such as daikon may take from 3 to 5 months before they are ready. More yin vegetables, such as Chinese cabbage require only 1 to 2 weeks in the nuka paste. For quicker pickles, simply slice vegetables very thin, tie in a cheesecloth sack and insert in the nuka. These take only 2 to 3 days. If the vegetables are cut into rounds or 2- to 3-inch pieces, they will require less time. Firmer root vegetables are best for this type of pickle.

Whenever the paste becomes too soft or new vegetables are added, add a little more salt to the paste and roasted nuka, a little at a time. In this way the same paste can be used for several years.

Rice Bran Pickles #2

10–12 cups nuka or wheat bran, dry-roasted
1–1½ cups sea salt

Combine roasted nuka or wheat bran with sea salt and mix well. Place a thin layer of the salt-bran mixture on the bottom of a wooden keg or ceramic crock. Then add a layer of vegetables. Then sprinkle another thin layer of the nuka and salt mixture on top of the vegetables. Repeat this layering until the nuka mixture is used up or until the crock is full. Always make sure that the bottom and the top layer of the keg is comprised of the nuka mixture.

Place a wooden lid or a plate on top of the vegetables and nuka. The plate should be slightly smaller in circumference than the crock, so that it will fit inside. Place a heavy weight, such as a large, clean rock or bricks on top of the plate. After several days or a week, water will begin to be squeezed out of the vegetables and rise to the surface of the crock. When this happens, remove the heavy weight and replace with a lighter weight on top of the plate.

Place in a cool room and cover with a thin layer of cheesecloth. The pickles will be ready within a week or so and will keep for 2 to 3 months, if kept in a cool place.

To serve, rinse under cold water to remove bran and excess salt, and slice. Chinese cabbage, daikon greens, turnip greens, and mizuna are delicious prepared this way. First remove the leaves from the stem or core, wash, and allow to dry 24 hours. Then layer leaves as above.

Cucumber Pickles

2–3 lbs pickling cucumbers, washed
10–12 cups water
¼–⅓ cup sea salt
3–4 sprigs of fresh or dry dill
1 large onion, halved then each half quartered

Combine the water and salt. Bring to a boil and simmer 2 to 3 minutes until the salt dissolves. Allow to cool. Place cucumbers, dill, and onion slices in a large glass jar or a ceramic crock. Pour the cooled salt-water over the vegetables. Allow to sit uncovered in a dark, cool place for 3 to 4 days. Cover and refrigerate. Let sit 2 to 3 more days. Cucumbers will keep for about 1 month in the refrigerator.

Vegetables such as cauliflower, broccoli, daikon, carrots, red radishes, or watermelon rinds may also be pickled in the same manner.

Sauerkraut

5 lbs cabbage (white kraut cabbage is best), washed
¼–⅓ cup sea salt

Slice the cabbage very thin. Place the cabbage in a wooden keg or ceramic crock and add the sea salt. Mix thoroughly. Place a plate or wooden lid, that is slightly smaller than the crock, on top of the cabbage so that it fits down inside the crock. Place a heavy weight on top of the lid. Cover the top of the crock with a piece of cheese-cloth.

After a day, water should cover the cabbage; if not, apply a heavier weight. Keep in a dark, cool place for about 2 weeks. Check the crock daily. If mold forms on the top, skim and discard. If the mold is not removed, the sauerkraut will develop a moldy taste. The mold is not harmful as it results naturally from the fermentation process. It merely detracts from the taste. To serve, rinse under cold water and place in a serving dish.

Daikon-Sauerkraut Pickles

This pickle is very light and mild tasting. It is especially delicious and refreshing during the hot summer months.

2 large daikon, sliced into ¼-inch rounds
1 cup sauerkraut
½ gallon sauerkraut water

Place the daikon in a glass jar. Cover with the sauerkraut and sauerkraut water. Store the uncovered jar in a cool place for about 3 days. The pickles are now ready to eat.

To store, cover and refrigerate. The pickles will keep for about 1 month.

In warmer seasons the fermentation period may be reduced to 2 days.

The sauerkraut water may be reused several times to make pickles, as long as it is kept refrigerated when not in use. Just add a little fresh sauerkraut water and sauerkraut before each use.

Umeboshi Pickles

Umeboshi plums, paste, or vinegar can be used to prepare either long- or quick-pressed pickles. They have a very nice sour taste that complements most meals. Shiso leaves (beefsteak leaves) that are used to prepare umeboshi plums can be used as well. Shiso leaves give a nice pink or reddish color to vegetables that are pickled with them.

Umeboshi Pickled Red Radish, Daikon, or Turnip

7–8 umeboshi plums
daikon sliced into ¼-inch rounds, small whole red radishes, or sliced turnips
2 quarts water

Place the umeboshi in a large jar and add 2 quarts of water. Shake and let sit for several hours so that the salt from the umeboshi dissolves into the water and the water turns pink. Place sliced vegetables or whole radishes into the water. Keep the uncovered jar in a cool place for about 3 days. To store, cover, and refrigerate.

Quick-pressed Salt Pickles

Quick-pressed pickles are refreshingly light pickles that can be made with many kinds of thinly sliced green vegetables as well as root vegetables. Some vegetables which can be used are: Chinese cabbage; green cabbage; onions; carrots; daikon; cucumber; celery; red radish; white icicle radish; red onions; turnips; daikon or turnip greens; and many others.

When pressing vegetables for quickly made pickles, it is important that they be sliced very thin to help speed up the pickling process.

Brown rice vinegar, sweet rice vinegar, hato mugi vinegar, good quality apple cider vinegar, lemon juice or rind, or tangerine juice or rind may be combined with the salt and vegetables for variations.

Quick pickles are usually prepared in a pickle press and take anywhere from several hours to several days to pickle. The longer the vegetables are pickled, the saltier the taste.

These pickles will usually keep if stored in a cool place for several days to 1 month.

If too salty, rinse them under cold water before serving.

Pressed Quick Red Radish Pickles

2 cups red radish and their greens, sliced thin
1–2 Tbsp umeboshi vinegar

Place the radish, greens, and umeboshi vinegar in a pickle press and mix well. Secure the top on the press and screw down to apply pressure. Let sit for 2 to 3 days. Remove, rinse, and serve.

The following are two delicious pickle recipes I learned from a friend while living in Kyoto, Japan.

Daikon-Lemon Pickles

4 cups daikon, sliced in $\frac{1}{8}$-inch think rounds or rectangles
5–6 matchstick-sized pieces of lemon rind
sea salt

Place daikon and lemon in a ceramic crock or wooden keg. Add a small amount of sea salt to create a mild salt taste. Mix thoroughly. Place a lid or plate on top of the daikon. Place a clean stone or brick on top of the plate to apply pressure. After 4 hours remove the lemon rind and discard.

When the water level reaches the lid or plate, place a lighter weight stone or brick on top. Keep in a cool place for 2 to 3 days.

Rinse and serve.

Turnip-Kombu Pickles

3 medium-sized turnips, washed
1 strip kombu, 8–10 inches long, soaked
sea salt

Slice the turnips in half. Then slice each half into almost paper thin half-moons. Sprinkle several pinches of sea salt on the bottom of a wooden keg or ceramic crock. Place the turnips in the crock, little by little, in layers. After each layer of turnips sprinkle a couple pinches of sea salt. Repeat until turnips are used up.

Place a wooden lid, or a plate small enough to set down inside the crock, on top of the turnips. Place a heavy weight such as a clean stone or brick on top of the lid. When the water level rises to the lid, drain off all the salty water. Remove the turnips.

Slice the kombu into very thin matchsticks and mix the kombu and turnips together and place back in the crock. Replace the disc and stone on top. Keep in a cool place for 1 or 2 days. When pickles are ready to eat, the liquid surrounding the turnips will thicken and become very slippery. This is how they should turn out if correctly made.

They are now ready to eat. Refrigerate to store.

Chapter 12
Whole Grain Breads

When making bread macrobiotically, we usually recommend avoiding the use of yeast. Yeasted bread tends to weaken the digestive system and often causes sinus congestion. Instead, we rely upon the natural fermentation process of grains or grain-based starters as a leavening agent.

Yeasted bread may be eaten periodically on special occasions or when dining out at a restaurant that does not have naturally fermented bread, for those in generally good health.

There are many different ways to make starters for producing naturally light breads. It is not always necessary to add a starter to help bread rise. If bread dough is allowed to sit in a warm place, covered with a damp towel, for 8 to 12 hours, it will rise naturally.

There are many different kinds of bread which can be made simply by combining different flours, whole grains, fruits, nuts, or seeds.

Kneading is very important in making unyeasted bread. The bread is usually kneaded at least 350 times. The more it is kneaded, the better are the chances of creating a bread that rises considerably.

Be patient if bread does not turn out on the first try. There are many factors that influence making good bread. Some of these are how old the flour is, whether the grain used is several days old or freshly made, the weather condition outside, the cycle of the moon, how long the dough is allowed to sit, and others. I have noticed that when I make bread during the full moon, it rises much more. On a rainy day, it does not rise as much as on a warm, sunny day. Occasionally, I have my children help me make bread, which they really enjoy. When they help, they are so happy and really put a lot of happiness into the bread. It has never failed to turn out well whenever I let them help.

I have found that bread that has some type of whole grain such as rice, sweet rice, barley, or millet in it, is much easier to digest than bread made from just flour. Whole grain bread is really a meal in itself.

In the following recipes I have used oil in making the bread. It is not necessary to use oil. In many European countries, oil is not used in bread. The bread will come out a little drier, but is delicious. In any of the recipes given, oil may be used or omitted.

Rice Bread

4 cups whole wheat flour
$\frac{1}{4}$–$\frac{1}{2}$ tsp sea salt
4 cups cooked brown rice
$\frac{1}{4}$ cup sesame oil (optional)
water

Mix the flour and sea salt. Add the rice and sift the flour and rice through both hands until the rice is completely coated with the flour. Add the oil and again sift flour, rice, and oil through the hands until the oil is completely mixed in.

Add enough water to form a ball of dough. Knead about 300 to 350 times (approximately 10 to 15 minutes). While kneading, the dough occasionally becomes moist and sticky. When this happens, sprinkle a small amount of flour on the dough and continue kneading. This may happen 4 or 5 times during the process of kneading.

Oil 2 bread pans with sesame oil. Form the dough into 2 loaves and place in the pans. Press the dough down all along the edges of the pan to create a rounded effect and then make a shallow $\frac{1}{4}$-inch-deep slit down the center of the dough. Place a damp, clean towel over the pans and let sit for 8 to 12 hours in a warm place. Bake at 300°F for 15 to 20 minutes, then at 350°F for about 1 hour and 15 minutes.

If the rice is 2 or 3 days old, the bread will be much sweeter, or if slightly sour it will help the bread to rise.

Raisin-Rice Bread

2 cups raisins
4 cups whole wheat flour
$\frac{1}{4}$–$\frac{1}{2}$ tsp sea salt
4 cups cooked brown rice
$\frac{1}{4}$ cup sesame oil
water

Make the same way as the above rice-bread recipe. Add the raisins after the bread has been kneaded about 250 times, and then knead 50 to 100 times more. Place in bread pans and cover with damp towel. Set in a warm place for 8 to 12 hours, then bake the same as for rice bread.

Amazaké Bread

4 cups whole wheat flour
4 cups homemade amazaké, unblended*
$\frac{1}{4}$–$\frac{1}{2}$ tsp sea salt
$\frac{1}{4}$ cup sesame oil
water

Amazaké bread can be prepared in the same way as plain rice bread. Amazaké bread has a very sweet taste. Also, since the amazaké is fermented, it gives the bread a slightly yeasted flavor without the expansive effects of regular yeast.

Whole Wheat Bread

8 cups whole wheat flour
$\frac{1}{4}$–$\frac{1}{2}$ tsp sea salt
$\frac{1}{4}$ cup sesame oil
water

Mix the flour and sea salt together. Add the oil, and mix thoroughly with the flour by sifting it through both hands. Add enough cold water to form a ball of dough. Knead about 300 to 350 times. Oil two bread pans with sesame oil, form into two loaves, and place in pans. Cover the dough with a damp, clean towel, and let it sit for 8 to 12 hours, in a warm place, to allow it to rise. Bake at 300°F for 15 minutes, then at 350°F for about 1 hour and 15 minutes longer.

Sourdough Starter

A sourdough starter can be made by mixing 2 cups of flour and enough water to make a thick batter. Cover the bowl with a clean damp towel and let it sit in a warm place for 3 to 4 days. As it ferments, it will start to bubble and turn sour. This starter may be added to any of the whole grain bread recipes to make bread rise.

* See dessert section for amazaké recipe.

Simply add 1 to 1½ cups of the starter to bread dough and knead as explained above. Cover with a damp towel and set in a warm place for 8 to 12 hours. Then bake in the same manner as rice bread. This bread will have a slightly sour taste, which is very delicious.

Items such as sour whole grain, sour noodle water, or sour starch water (which results from making seitan and letting the starch water sit in a warm place for 3 to 4 days), can be used as a starter for bread as well.

These starters can also be used in making cakes, waffles, pancakes, and muffins.

Corn Bread

3 cups cornmeal
1 cup pastry flour
¼ tsp sea salt
2 Tbsp corn oil
2–3 cups cold water

Mix the flours and sea salt together. Add the oil and mix thoroughly. Add water and mix. Preheat the oven to 375°F. Oil a bread or cake pan with a small amount of sesame oil and place the empty oiled pan in the oven for 5 minutes, to heat the oil. Remove the pan and place the corn bread batter in it. If the bread is made with 2 cups of water, bake at 375°F for 1 hour and 15 minutes. If 3 cups of water were used in the batter, bake for 1 hour and 45 minutes, at the same temperature.

I usually add 3 cups of water, as it makes the bread softer and sweeter.

As a variation, add 1 cup of cooked brown rice to the batter or 1 cup of cooked millet. The rice will make the bread very light, sweet, and delicious. The millet will make the bread somewhat drier, but also sweet and delicious.

Chapter 13

Desserts

When preparing desserts according to macrobiotic standards or principles, we recommend avoiding the use of dairy, eggs, refined flours, refined sugars, spices, chemical colorings, and leavenings, as these create extreme imbalances in our health and can lead or contribute to serious illnesses.

The best desserts for our health are those made with whole grains; whole grain flours; grain sweeteners such as barley malt, rice syrup, amazaké, or yinnie syrup; fresh or organic unsulfured dried fruit; and good-quality oils such as sesame or corn. Nontropical varieties of fruit juices may also be used in preparing desserts. Occasionally, for those in good health, a small amount of cinnamon may be used, as it is more yang than most spices. Fresh ginger or lemon juice may be used as well. Whole grain milk such as rice, oat, or amazaké can be used, and, very occasionally, so can unsweetened, unflavored, soy milk. Almond milk can be made from cooked and blended almonds. Nut butters such as sesame, tahini, or organic peanut butter may be used on occasion as well for flavoring desserts.

Whenever possible minimize the use of oil in dessert making as oil, flour, sweeteners, and fruit are all yin and the combination is more difficult to digest than other flourless and oilless desserts. This is especially important for children.

It is best to take sweets in the form of natural whole grains, beans, vegetables, and other foods which are very sweet when properly prepared. Cravings for desserts and sweets can be the result of not eating enough naturally sweet grains and other whole foods, an overintake of salt, excessive intake of animal food, or a lack of variety in our diets.

Desserts may be prepared on an average of 2 to 3 times per week, for those in fairly good health.

Basic Dough (*2 crusts*)

4 cups whole wheat pastry flour
¼ tsp sea salt
⅛–¼ cup corn oil
¾–1 cup cold water

Mix the flour and sea salt. Add the oil and sift through both hands, using a rubbing motion, to evenly coat the flour with oil. Add water, gradually, to form a dough. The dough should not be sticky. If it is sticky, add a bit more flour. Knead into a ball. Do not knead very long, since the oil may be absorbed into the skin. Let the dough sit for a few minutes. Sprinkle flour on a board and rolling pin and roll out the dough. The dough can easily be placed in a pie plate by rolling it up on the rolling pin, first and then placing it in the pie plate.

Use about half of the dough for the bottom crust and add desired filling. Then, roll out the remaining half. Wet the edge of the bottom crust with a small amount of water to help seal the pie crusts. Place the second pie crust on top of the filled pie plate. To seal the crusts together, wet a fork and press around the edges, or pinch it together with the thumbs. Make 4 small slits in the top center of the pie crust so it does not crack when baking.

For a pie with only a bottom crust, partially bake the crust in a pie plate for about 10 minutes at 375°F. Make 2 or 3 small slits in the bottom of the crust before baking to avoid bubbling. Then, fill the partially baked crust and bake again until done (approximately 30 minutes).

Apple Pie #1

10–12 medium apples, sliced
(remove skin if nonorganic)

Use the above method for the pie crust. Place the bottom crust in the pie plate. Mix all in-

½ cup rice syrup, yinnie syrup, or barley malt
1–2 Tbsp arrowroot flour
¼–½ tsp cinnamon (optional)
pinch of sea salt

gredients together and fill the pie shell. Add the top crust and seal. Cut 4 small slits in top and bake at 375°F for approximately 30 to 35 minutes or until the crust is golden brown. Test whether apples are done by inserting a chopstick into one of the slits in the crust.

Apple Pie #2

10–12 medium apples, sliced
½ cup raisins, soaked 10 minutes
1–2 Tbsp arrowroot
pinch of sea salt

Mix all ingredients together. Place the bottom crust in the pie plate. Place the filling in the pie plate and place the top crust on. Seal the edges and trim off the excess dough. Make 4 slits in top crust. Bake at 375°F for 30 to 35 minutes, or until golden brown.

Apple-Squash Pie

1 medium buttercup squash, cubed
4–5 medium apples, sliced
pinch of sea salt
water

Place the squash, apples, and salt in a pot with just enough water to lightly cover the bottom. Cook until the squash becomes soft. Purée in a hand food mill. Place the filling in a partially baked pie shell. Bake at 375°F for 25 to 30 minutes or until the crust is golden brown. To make a more attractive and delicious dish, place sliced apples or sprinkle chopped walnuts around the edge of the pie filling before baking.

Unsweetened Squash Pie with Oatmeal Crust

1 large buttercup squash or Hokkaido pumpkin, skin removed and cubed
1 medium onion, diced
pinch of sea salt
¼–½ cup water

Place the cubed squash and diced onions in a pot. Add the sea salt and water. Cover and cook until the squash is soft. Purée in a hand food mill. Then, evenly spread the puréed squash and onions on a partially baked oatmeal crust. Bake at 375°F for approximately 25 to 30 minutes, or until the crust is golden brown.

Oatmeal Crust

3 cups rolled oats
1½ cups whole wheat pastry flour
¼ tsp sea salt

Mix oats, flour, and sea salt. Add the oil and mix. Add water to form a thick batter. Spread the batter evenly on an oiled cookie sheet and bake at 375°F for approximately 10 minutes. Remove

2–3 Tbsp corn oil
2 cups water

from the oven and place desired filling evenly on the crust. Bake again at 375°F for 25 to 30 minutes, or until golden brown.

Squash Pie

1 large buttercup squash or Hokkaido pumpkin, skin removed and cubed
¼ cup water
¼ tsp sea salt
1 cup rice syrup (sometimes called yinnie syrup or *amé*)
¼ tsp cinnamon (optional)
½ cup walnuts, finely chopped

Cook the squash with approximately ¼ cup water and the sea salt until soft. Purée in a hand food mill. The squash purée should be quite thick. If the purée is too thin, cook on a low flame until excess water evaporates. Then, add rice syrup and cinnamon. Cook another 4 to 5 minutes.

Place the crust in a pie plate and cut 2 or 3 small slits in the bottom. Partially bake the crust at 375°F for 10 minutes. Remove from the oven and fill with the squash purée. Sprinkle finely chopped walnuts around the edge of the filling and bake at 375°F for 30 minutes, or until the crust is golden brown.

Oatmeal Raisin Cookies (*24 cookies*)

3 cups rolled oats
1½ cups whole wheat pastry flour
¼ tsp sea salt
3 Tbsp corn oil
2 cups cold water
1 cup raisins

Mix rolled oats, flour, and sea salt together. Add the oil and mix again. Add water to make a thick batter. Mix in the raisins. For a richer, nutty flavor, add ½ cup chopped walnuts. If adding walnuts, slightly more water may need to be added to the batter. Spoon the batter onto an oiled cookie sheet and pat down to form a cookie. Do not make them too thick or they will take longer to bake. Each cookie can be about 2 inches in diameter and about ¼ inch thick. Bake at 375°F for 25 to 30 minutes, or until golden brown.

Kanten

Kanten is a very light, refreshing jelled dessert made from a variety of sea vegetable called agar-agar. Almost any kind of seasonal fruit can be used in making kanten, such as strawberries, blueberries, peaches, pears, nectarines, raspberries, melon, apples, raisins, and others. Agar-agar flakes can be used, along with vegetables and vegetable soup stock, to make an aspic instead of a dessert. Azuki beans and raisins are also very delicious when jelled with agar-agar flakes.

Prepackaged agar-agar flakes are available in most natural food stores. Some packages have different directions printed on them than those used below, so consult these directions before making kanten. The following is more of a winter or fall kanten. Please feel free to use any seasonal fruit.

3 medium apples, sliced thin
1 quart water or ½ water and
½ apple juice
pinch of sea salt
6 Tbsp agar-agar flakes (read directions on package)

Bring the water, sea salt, apples, and agar-agar flakes to a boil. Reduce the flame to low and simmer about 2 to 3 minutes. Stir occasionally. Pour into a dish or mold and refrigerate until jelled (about 45 minutes to 1 hour).

Summer melons and berries do not need to be cooked. Simply pour the hot liquid over the fruit and allow to jell. If using plain water in kanten, ½ cup of raisins may be added to sweeten the kanten. Simply add the raisins at the same time as the apples, and cook as above.

When making a vegetable aspic, use very thin sliced or shaved vegetables and 1 quart of vegetable stock. Cook the vegetables approximately 5 to 10 minutes after they are added to the flakes and vegetable stock.

When making an azuki bean-raisin aspic, cook the azuki beans and raisins until the azuki beans are done (approximately 1½ hours). Then add 1 quart of water, sea salt, and flakes, and cook as above.

Summer Kanten

1 quart apple juice
pinch of sea salt
5–6 Tbsp agar-agar flakes
½ cup strawberries, sliced
½ cup blueberries, washed
½ cup cantaloupe, cubed
½ cup honeydew melon, cubed

Place the apple juice, sea salt, and agar-agar flakes in a pan and bring to a boil. Stir several times to dissolve the flakes. Reduce the flame to low and simmer 2 to 3 minutes.

Place the sliced fruits in a bowl and pour the hot juice over it. Keep in a cool place until jelled (about 1 to 1½ hours).

Baked Apples

Wash baking apples and place in a pan with a small amount of water. Cover and bake approximately 20 minutes at 375°F or until done. For variety, core the apples and fill with a mixture of miso, tahini, and raisins. For this filling use 6 tablespoons tahini, 1 ½ teaspoons barley miso, and ¼ cup raisins. Mix together and spoon into cored apples. Bake as above.

Applesauce

Wash and peel several apples. Slice the apples and place them in a pot with a small amount of water (¼ to ½ cup), just enough water to keep the apples from burning. Add a pinch of sea salt, cover, and simmer for about 10 minutes, or until soft. Purée in a hand food mill and serve.

Apple Crunch (Pear or Peach Crunch)

10–12 sliced apples, pears, or
   peaches (leave skin on if
   organic)
pinch of sea salt
2 Tbsp arrowroot flour
1 cup rolled oats
½ cup walnuts
¼ cup almonds
¼ cup filberts
2 Tbsp rice syrup (yinnie syrup
   or barley malt)

Slice the apples, pears, or peaches. Add sea salt and arrowroot. Mix together and place in a baking dish.

In a dry skillet roast the oats until golden brown on a medium-low flame. Place in a bowl. Roast the walnuts, almonds, and filberts separately, in a dry skillet over a medium-low flame, until they release a fragrant aroma. Remove and chop the nuts. Add the nuts to the rolled oats and mix. Add the yinnie syrup and mix with both hands to coat the oat and nut mixture.

Sprinkle the oat-nut topping evenly over the apples, pears, or peaches. Cover and bake at 375°F for 20 to 25 minutes. Remove cover and bake 5 to 10 minutes more to brown the oat-nut topping.

Raisin Strudel

2 cups raisins
½ cup water
pinch of sea salt
1 cup walnuts, chopped
2 crusts (see Basic Dough
   recipe)

Place the raisins, water, and sea salt in a saucepan and bring to a boil. Reduce the flame to low, cover, and simmer until most of the liquid is cooked away. Allow to cool. Mix the raisins with the walnuts.

Make a pastry dough and roll out as for a pie crust, only slightly thinner. Spread the filling evenly on the crust and roll it up to form a log shape. Seal both ends of the strudel to prevent the juice from flowing out. This is done by folding the ends up slightly and pressing down with a fork.

Place on an oiled cookie sheet and bake at 375°F for approximately 30 minutes or until the crust is golden brown. Remove from oven, cool, and slice the strudel into 1-inch rounds.

A strudel can be made with almost any seasonal fruit and nuts.

Another very delicious strudel filling is to spread evenly a small amount of barley malt or yinnie syrup on a rolled crust. (If the hands are slightly wet, it is easier to spread.) Then sprinkle a small amount of cinnamon ($\frac{1}{4}$ teaspoon per crust) on the yinnie syrup, and spread evenly with the fingers. Sprinkle chopped walnuts on top of the yinnie syrup. Roll up the strudel and bake as for the above recipe. My mother and grandmother used to prepare this with any leftover dough they had when baking pies.

Apple Tart

8 medium apples, sliced
$\frac{1}{2}$ cup raisins
$\frac{1}{4}$ cup walnuts, chopped
pinch of sea salt
1–2 Tbsp arrowroot flour

Mix all filling ingredients together. Roll out a pie crust and place it on an oiled cookie sheet. Place the apple mixture on one half of the crust, and fold the other half over to cover the apples. Turn the edges of the crust up and pinch together to seal or press down with a fork. Bake at 375°F for 30 to 40 minutes, or until golden brown.

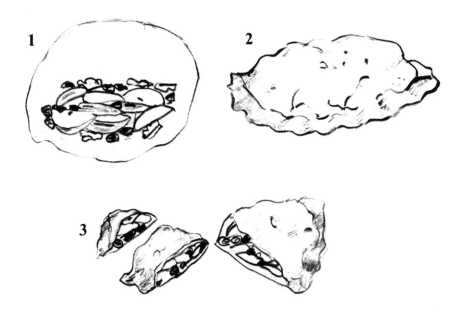

Slice and serve. Individual baking dishes can be purchased to prepare tarts, or cut out small rounds of dough and filling.

Berry Pies

Cook berries with a very small amount of water. Sweeten if necessary with yinnie syrup. Add a pinch of sea salt and thicken with a small amount of diluted kuzu or arrowroot flour to desired thickness. Fill a partially baked pie shell with berry filling. Bake at 375°F until the crust is golden brown (approximately 25 to 30 minutes).

The same recipe can be used with apples, sliced peaches, or nectarines.

Sweet Azuki Beans

Cook 2 to 3 cups of azuki beans for about 20 minutes. Add 1½ cups of raisins and cook until about 80 percent done (1½ hours). Then add ½ teaspoon sea salt and either 1 cup of dried apples or 3 sliced fresh apples. Cook until the beans are soft. When beans are done, turn up the flame and boil off any excess water.

Either eat as is or oil a baking dish and place a layer of approximately 4 cups of mochi (cooked sweet rice as explained in the section on grains) on the bottom of the dish. Spread a thick layer of sweet azuki beans on top of the mochi. Bake at 375°F for about 10 minutes, just enough to heat the mochi and azuki beans. Do not bake much longer, as the mochi will expand and spill over the side of the dish. Serve hot or cool.

Homemade Amazaké

Amazaké is a natural sweetener, dessert, or sweet drink made from fermented sweet rice or regular brown rice. It can be used as a sweetener for cookies, cakes, breads, pancakes, and donuts. Amazaké can also be blended. Serve it hot or cool.

4 cups sweet brown rice, or regular brown rice
8 cups water
1 cup koji
pinch of sea salt

Wash the rice, drain, and soak overnight in 8 cups of water. Place the rice in a pressure cooker. Bring to pressure, reduce the flame to medium-low and simmer for 20 minutes. Turn off the flame and let the rice sit in the pressure cooker for 45 minutes. Allow to cool. When the rice is cool enough to handle by hand, mix the koji in. Place the rice and koji in a glass bowl and keep in a warm place for 4 to 8 hours (no longer than 8 hours). Several times, mix the rice and koji to help the koji melt. Place a pinch of sea salt and the rice in a pot and bring to a boil. As soon as bubbles come to the surface, turn off the flame. Allow to cool. Place the rice in a glass bowl or jar and refrigerate.

To keep for a long time, amazaké can be cooked over a low flame until it becomes slightly brown.

When using as a sweetener either add as is to pastries, or blend to make it smooth.

For a beverage, dilute with a little water and blend until thick and creamy.

Amazaké Pudding (Plain)

1 quart amazaké
4 tsp kuzu, diluted in 5 tsp water
few raisins or chopped roasted nuts for garnish

Place the amazaké and diluted kuzu in a saucepan. Bring to a boil, stirring occasionally to avoid lumping. Reduce the flame to low and simmer 1 to 2 minutes. Remove and pour into individual dishes. Garnish with a few raisins or chopped, roasted nuts.

This amazaké pudding may also be used as a topping for other fruit puddings, custards, or kantens.

For a variation, fruits such as apples and pears may be added at the beginning of cooking. Warmer season fruits such as berries or melon may be added at the end of cooking as they require less time to cook than autumn or winter fruits. Squash purée may also be added or even grain coffee for a chocolate flavor.

Rice Pudding

1 cup cooked brown rice
2 cups water
¼ cup barley malt or rice syrup
2 Tbsp raisins
¼ cup fresh apples, washed, peeled and sliced
1 Tbsp tahini (optional)
pinch of cinnamon (optional)
pinch of sea salt

Place the cooked brown rice and water in a pressure cooker and cook for 25 to 30 minutes. Bring pressure down and remove cover. Add barley malt, raisins, apples, tahini, cinnamon, and sea salt. Mix ingredients together. Place the rice pudding mixture in a baking dish or covered casserole and bake at 375°F for about 35 to 40 minutes. Remove cover and bake slightly longer to brown the top of the pudding. Serve.

Popcorn Balls

Prepare popcorn as usual and season with a small amount of sea salt. Heat a small amount of barley malt or rice syrup or a combination of the 2 sweeteners until it comes to a boil. Reduce the flame to low and simmer 2 to 3 minutes. Remove from flame. Sort out all unpopped kernels and discard. Pour the hot sweetener over the popcorn. Use enough sweetener to evenly but thinly coat all the popcorn.

For variation, mix in a small amount of roasted peanuts or other nuts at this time. Wet both hands slightly with water and form the popcorn mixture into round, firmly packed balls. If the balls are not packed firmly, they will fall apart. (If desired, spread the popcorn mixture evenly on a dry cookie sheet and bake at 350°F for 15 to 20 minutes to make Macro-Jacks instead of popcorn balls.)

Once the balls are firmly packed, do either one of two things:

1) Bake the balls at 350°F for several minutes until the sweetener bubbles slightly and turns dark brown, then remove and cool.
2) Place the firmly packed popcorn balls on a cookie sheet and place them in the freezer to harden.

The first method of baking the balls produces a drier, crispier popcorn ball, whereas the second method produces a less crispy, more moist, and sticky popcorn ball.

Rice Crunchies

2 cups rice crispy cereal
¼ cup barley malt or rice syrup
¼ cup raisins
⅛ cup roasted peanuts or sesame seeds

Place the barley malt in a saucepan and bring to a boil. Reduce the flame to low and simmer 5 minutes or so. Place all other ingredients in a mixing bowl and then pour the hot barley malt over it. Mix the barley malt in with the rice cereal, raisins, and nuts so that it evenly coats the cereal with a thin layer of sweetener. Take a small glass bread dish or baking dish and rinse it with water. Place the rice-crispy mixture in the damp bowl or dish. Wet both hands slightly and pack the rice-crispy mixture down firmly and evenly. Place in the refrigerator or freezer for several minutes until the barley malt hardens. Remove and slice the hardened rice crunchies into rectangular bars.

Sweet Azuki Beans with Chestnuts

½ cup azuki beans, washed and soaked 6–8 hours
1 strip kombu, 2–3 inches long, washed and soaked
¼ cup dried chestnuts, washed, dry-roasted and soaked 10 minutes
⅛ cup raisins
1½ cups water
pinch of sea salt

Place the kombu in the bottom of a pressure-cooker. Add the azuki beans, chestnuts, and raisins. Add water. Cover the cooker and bring to pressure. Reduce the flame to medium-low and place a flame deflector under the cooker. Cook for about 50 minutes. Remove from flame and allow the pressure to come down. Remove cover and add a pinch of sea salt over the apples by using the leftover cooking water in the baking dish which is often very sweet.

Stewed Fruit

Basically, most of the recommended fruits can be used in making this recipe, except perhaps for melons. Some fruits which can be used are: apples, pears, peaches, blueberries, strawberries, apricots, nectarines, dried fruit and raisins, raspberries, plums, and tangerines.

¼ cup raisins or currants
1 quart apple juice or plain water
2 cups apples, sliced (peeled and sliced if waxed)
1 cup pears, sliced
pinch of sea salt
2 Tbsp kuzu, diluted in 3 Tbsp water

Place the raisins or currants in a saucepan. Add the apple juice or water and pinch of sea salt. Bring to a boil. Reduce the flame to low and simmer about 5 minutes. Add the apples and pears. Cover and bring to a boil again. Reduce the flame to low and simmer until the fruit is soft, which is approximately 10 minutes or so. Reduce the flame to low and add the diluted kuzu, stirring constantly to prevent lumping. When the sauce becomes thick and translucent, cook another minute then remove and place in a serving bowl.

Serve either plain or garnish with chopped nuts, granola, or a favorite crunchy topping.

Chestnut Purée ————————————————————————————

Chestnut purée is a nice mildly sweet dessert which our family enjoys very much.

2 cups dried chestnuts
5 cups water
pinch of sea salt

Wash the chestnuts and then dry-roast them in a stainless steel skillet over a medium-low flame for several minutes. Stir constantly to evenly roast and to prevent burning.

Remove the chestnuts and place them in a pressure cooker. Add the water and soak the chestnuts for about 10 to 15 minutes. This will soften them and make them a little sweeter when cooked. Add a pinch of sea salt. Bring up to pressure and reduce the flame to medium-low. Cook for about 40 to 50 minutes. Remove from flame and allow the pressure to come down. Remove cover and place the chestnuts and water in a hand food mill. Purée to a nice smooth consistency. Place in individual serving dishes.

As a variation, cook the chestnuts together with a few raisins and dried apples. Do not purée but simply serve as is after cooking.

Also, another variation for chestnut purée is to wrap a small amount of purée around a tablespoon of freshly made mochi. These are called *ohagi*.

Strawberry Couscous Pie ———————————————————————

1 cup couscous
1 cup apple juice
³⁄₄–1 cup water
pinch of sea salt
Topping:
　1 cup water
　2 cups apple juice
　pinch of sea salt
　5–6 Tbsp agar-agar flakes
　　(first read directions on
　　package for proportions)
　1 cup fresh strawberries,
　　washed, tops removed, and
　　sliced

Wash couscous and then drain. Place couscous, apple juice, water, and a pinch of sea salt in a saucepan. Bring to a boil. Reduce the flame to low, cover, and simmer 5 to 10 minutes until the couscous is fluffy. Remove and place the couscous in a pie plate. Pack the couscous down firmly in the pie plate to form a crust, covering the entire bottom and sides of the plate.

Place water, juice, sea salt, and agar-agar in a saucepan and bring to a boil. Stir the agar-agar flakes in to dissolve them. Reduce the flame to low and simmer 2 to 3 minutes. Allow to sit 5 to 10 minutes to cool off slightly before pouring into the crust. When fairly cool, pour the liquid into the couscous crust. Place strawberries into the liquid. Place in a cool spot or refrigerator to harden. When the agar-agar and juice have hardened, slice the pie into sections and serve.

Other fruits may be used instead of strawberries for variation. If using harder fruits such as apples and pears though, the fruit must be cooked in with the juice and agar-agar.

Chapter 14

Fish and Seafood

Fish and seafood are a source of quick energy and may be enjoyed 1 to 3 times per week by those in good health, if desired.

The white-meat varieties of fish such as scrod, cod, sole, flounder, haddock, and others are less fatty and more yin. White-meat fish is preferable, especially for children and women, than pink or red-meat fish. Examples of pink or red-meat fish are tuna, salmon, mackerel, red snapper, halibut, herring, sardines, smelt, and others.

Among shellfish, the slower moving varieties are preferable such as clams, oysters, octopus, and mussels. These are more yin and also lower in cholesterol than the more active yang shellfish such as lobster, crab, and shrimp.

There are also many varieties of freshwater fish to choose from, such as trout, bass, snapper, catfish, bullhead, carp, and others.

For people living closer to the ocean, shellfish, deep-sea fish, as well as freshwater fish may be eaten. For those living inland or in mountainous areas, freshwater fish and occasionally, seafood, may be eaten, as most ocean fish would otherwise have to be frozen and shipped to their area.

When purchasing fish and shellfish, it is important to choose fresh, unfrozen, unprocessed, unbreaded types. Prepared, breaded fish and shellfish often contain chemical additives, such as MSG (monosodium glutamate). When purchasing whole fish the eyes should be clear. If unfresh, the eyes will be cloudy and the skin may be very slippery. Also, make sure that the fish or shellfish was taken from unpolluted waters.

Usually, we recommend that fish or shellfish be marinated in, or served with, a dip sauce of tamari-water and grated ginger, to balance the strong effects of the animal food as well as protect against unfresh conditions. Grated daikon, wasabi, or lemon may also be served.

When eating fish and shellfish, it is recommended to also eat about 2 to 3 times more vegetables and salads to make balance with the strong yang energy. Animal-quality food in general should be a small proportion of the entire meal.

Steamed Haddock

1½ lb haddock, washed and cut into 4–5 equal-sized pieces
4–5 broccoli, flowerettes
¼ cup carrots, sliced in thick matchsticks or flower shapes
water
3 lemon slices for garnish
1 cup tamari-ginger dip sauce (see p. 112)

Place the fish in a ceramic bowl. Attractively arrange the broccoli and carrots in the bowl with the fish. Set the bowl down inside a pot, with about ½ inch of water in the pot. Cover the pot and bring the water to a boil. Steam for several minutes until the fish is tender and the vegetables are brightly colored and tender. Remove, garnish with lemon slices, and serve with the tamari-ginger dip sauce.

Baked Scrod Almondiene

1½–2 lbs fresh scrod, washed and sliced into 3- or 4-inch pieces
¼ cup tamari soy sauce
⅛ cup mirin
1–2 tsp fresh ginger, grated
½ cup almonds, slivered
1 Tbsp parsley, chopped
grated daikon for garnish

Mix together the tamari, mirin, and ginger. Pour over the fish and marinate for about ½ to 1 hour. Remove the fish and place on a lightly oiled baking pan. Place in a 375°F oven and bake about 15 to 20 minutes (depending on the thickness). Sprinkle the almonds and parsley on the fish and bake another 5 minutes. Remove and place on a serving platter. Serve with 1 to 2 tablespoons of grated daikon for each person.

For a moist fish, bake in a covered dish and remove the cover the last 5 minutes to brown.

Fish may be baked without marinating. Instead simply sprinkle a little fresh lemon juice and tamari on it and bake as above.

Baked Shrimp with Stuffing

10 jumbo shrimp, washed, deveined, and shells removed
1 Tbsp corn oil
1 cup onions, diced

Lightly brush skillet with the corn oil and sauté the onions and celery, until the onions are translucent. Mix together with bread crumbs. Add water and tamari.

½ cup celery and leaves, diced
3 cups whole wheat bread
   crumbs or cubes, dry-roasted
½ cup water
2 tsp tamari soy sauce

Place the shrimp on bottom of baking dish. Spread the bread crumb mixture evenly over the shrimp. Cover the dish and bake at 375°F until almost done, approximately 20 minutes. Do not overcook or the shrimp will become very tough. Remove the cover and bake for another 5 minutes to brown the stuffing.

Stuffed flounder, scrod, or other fish, can also be prepared in a similar manner. Place the fish on top of the stuffing; roll the stuffing inside the fish; or stuff whole fish and bake as above.

Other stuffings may be made with couscous, rice, or wild rice, combined with vegetables.

Broiled Sole

4 fillets of sole, washed
tamari soy sauce
lemon juice and lemon slices
parsley for garnish

Place the sole on a baking sheet. Sprinkle with several drops of tamari and squeeze a little lemon juice on the sole. Broil until done (approximately 5 to 7 minutes). Remove and garnish with parsley. Place on a serving platter and serve with several lemon slices and a sprig of parsley for garnish. Grated daikon may also be served.

Pan-fried Red Snapper

1½–2 lb red snapper fillets,
   washed and sliced into several
   4-inch-wide pieces
½ cup pastry flour
1 cup corn flour or cornmeal
pinch of sea salt
dark sesame oil
lemon slices, parsley sprigs,
   and grated daikon for
   garnish
Marinade:
   ¼ cup tamari soy sauce
   ½ tsp ginger
   ½ cup water

Prepare a marinade by combining the tamari, ginger, and water. Pour marinade over the fish and let sit ½ to 1 hour. Remove.

Mix together the flours and sea salt. Roll the fish pieces in this mixture until evenly coated.

Place enough oil in a skillet to just cover the bottom and heat up. Place the fish in the skillet and fry until golden brown. Turn over and fry the other side until golden brown. Remove and place on a serving platter. Garnish with several slices of lemon, parsley sprigs, and grated daikon.

Freshwater or ocean perch are delicious prepared in this manner. Even whole trout or lake bass may be prepared the same way as above.

For a less salty preparation, eliminate marinating the fish.

Tempura

Cut fish filets into 2- or 3-inch pieces. If using shellfish, remove shells and devein. Deep-fry whole. When making shrimp tempura, make 2 small diagonal slits in the underside of the shrimp to prevent the shrimp from curling up. Roll the fish or shellfish in whole wheat or whole wheat pastry flour, and dip into tempura batter (see Chapter 5 on Vegetable Tempura for batter recipe). Deep-fry until golden brown on one side. Turn over and brown other side. This takes only a few minutes. Drain fish on a paper towel and serve as is with a dip sauce or as a topping for udon and broth.

Fish Soup Stock or Sauce

Boil fish bones, head, or leftovers for several minutes in a pot of water. Remove by straining through cheesecloth, or tie the various parts in a cheesecloth sack and boil the entire sack. Use the water as a stock, or thicken with pastry flour or kuzu to make a fish sauce. Season with tamari soy sauce.

Drippings from broiled or baked fish may also be used to prepare sauces.

Sashimi

Sashimi is raw strips of fish served with tamari soy sauce and wasabi or ginger dip sauce.

The preparation of sashimi requires skill with a very sharp knife along with knowledge of how to properly debone and slice fish. Unless prepared properly with very fresh fish, sashimi may in some cases cause digestive problems.

I suggest that this special delicacy be enjoyed in a good Japanese or macrobiotic restaurant.

Other Uses

There are many other dishes that can be made with fish such as baked stuffed clams, fish patties, croquettes, dumplings, salads, and so on. Please experiment.

Koi-koku

(See Chapter 4 on Soups for recipe.)

Fish Stew

(See Chapter 4 on Soups for recipe.)

Chapter 15
Beverages

The best kind of beverages are those that do not contain artificial dyes, preservatives, sugar, caffeine, or other artificial ingredients. Grain coffee, grain teas, and other high-quality, nonstimulant teas are suitable for regular use. Good-quality beer or saké, which are made from grains, can be used occasionally for enjoyment. Fruit juices may also be enjoyed occasionally.

Bancha

Bancha is probably the best tea for daily use. It is often called *kukicha* or twig tea.

Dry-roast the twigs in a skillet for 2 to 3 minutes, while constantly stirring and shaking the pan, to prevent the twigs from burning. Remove from the skillet, allow to cool, and store in an airtight jar. To prepare bancha, add 2 tablespoons of roasted twigs to 1½ quarts of water and bring to a boil. Reduce the flame to low and simmer for several minutes. For a lighter tea, add only 1 tablespoon of twigs to the same amount of water, bring to a boil, turn off the flame, and let the twigs steep in the water. These twigs can be used several times, adding a little more water or twigs to the pot as necessary. Clean the pot and replenish the twigs about once every 2 days.

Grain Tea

Dry-roast washed grain over a medium flame for about 10 minutes, stirring constantly and shaking the pan occasionally. Brown rice and barley make an especially good tea. Add 2 to 3 tablespoons of roasted grain to 1 ½ quarts of water. Bring to a boil, reduce the flame to low, and simmer 10 to 15 minutes.

For a different flavor tea, mix roasted rice with bancha.

Mugicha

Mugicha is made from unhulled, roasted barley, and can be found in most natural food stores. To prepare homemade mugicha, roast unhulled barley in a dry skillet until very dark brown. Cook as for other grain teas.

Umeboshi Tea

Umeboshi tea has a cooling effect in hot weather, and helps to replace mineral salts which are lost through perspiration.

Remove umeboshi meat from the pits of 2 to 3 umeboshi plums and add to 1 quart of water. Bring to a boil, reduce flame, and simmer about ½ hour.

Grain Coffee

There are many grain coffees available in natural food stores. Try to find a coffee that does not have figs, dates, molasses, or honey added to it. Simply add a teaspoon or so to a cup and pour boiling water over it. Stir and drink.

Mu Tea

Mu tea is made from 16 different herbs. On the whole, it is a more yang beverage, and is good for some stomach problems. It may be used in cold or hot weather. It is sold prepackaged in most natural food stores. Simmer 1 package in a quart of water for about 10 minutes. Mu tea is good as a very occasional supplement to bancha. It may also be diluted with apple juice. We do not recommend using this tea on a daily basis.

188

Mugwort Tea

Mugwort is a more yin beverage that is used mostly for medicinal purposes rather than as a daily beverage. It can be used to relieve overly yang conditions such as jaundice, and has been found to be effective in helping rid the body of intestinal parasites. To prepare, add about 1 tablespoon to 2 cups of water and simmer approximately 5 to 10 minutes. Do not continue use for more than several days as too much of this tea can cause constipation.

Apple Juice or Cider

If one's condition is generally good, an occasional glass of apple cider or juice may be enjoyed. In the summer, juice can be served cool or lightly chilled, but not icy cold, as this has a paralyzing effect on the digestive tract. In cool weather, heat the cider or juice and drink it hot. This can help neutralize an overly yang condition resulting from the intake of too much salt.

Water

The best-quality water for cooking and drinking is deep well water or natural spring water. Sparkling mineral water is not recommended for daily use, but can be enjoyed occasionally by those who are in generally good health.

Green Tea

Green tea is high in caffeine and not recommended for daily use. It can, however, be enjoyed occasionally. It has a nice mild flavor but if steeped too long may become a little bitter.

Vegetable Juice

Especially in hot weather a small amount of fresh raw carrot or carrot-celery juice may be enjoyed. Instead of raw juice, prepare cooked vegetable juice by boiling sweet vegetables such as cabbage, onions, carrots, or squash. Drain the juice from the vegetables and drink hot or room temperature.

Amazaké

(See Chapter 13 on Desserts for recipe and information.)

Chapter 16

Home Care Preparations

The best way to prevent or relieve sickness or imbalance is through our daily food. In some cases, this approach may take more time than symptomatic treatments but it is the only way to relieve the cause of sickness. Whenever an illness appears, reflect on those things that have produced it. Recall what may have been eaten, or what was eaten in the past that may now be discharging.

When people first begin eating macrobiotically, they may occasionally experience various types of adjustments due to their past eating habits. These may manifest as colds, fevers, sore throats, aches and pains, headaches, diarrhea, constipation, or in other ways. Discharges such as these are nothing but the elimination of sugar, animal food, dairy, drugs, medications, and other substances from the body. Since discharges help the body rid itself of past excess, they are actually beneficial, and they serve to keep our condition clean.

I would like to offer several remedies that will help to relieve any discomfort experienced by these adjustments, and to help discharge past foods more comfortably and smoothly.

Ginger Compress (Fomentation) —————————————————

Ginger compresses are recommended for the relief of many types of problems, such as tightness, stagnation, or stiffness. A ginger compress stimulates blood and body fluid circulation. It also relaxes the body. (Do not use for appendicitis, inflammation, or fevers.)

To prepare a ginger compress, grate about 5 to 6 tablespoons of fresh ginger root and place it on a piece of cheesecloth about 6 inches by 6 inches. Tie the cloth around the ginger to form a sack. Bring a gallon of water up to, but not over, the boiling point. Reduce the flame to very low and drop the sack of ginger into the water. (Be careful not to boil the ginger, as this will lessen its effectiveness.)

Keep the water hot but not boiling. When the water turns a milky, yellow color (after about 5 minutes), squeeze the juice out of the sack into the water. Dip the middle portion of a thick cotton towel into the water by holding on to both ends. Squeeze excess water out by wringing the towel. Shake to cool.

Place the hot towel directly on the affected area. If the towel is too hot, shake it a little more to allow some heat to escape. Remember it should be quite hot. Then, place a thick dry cotton towel over the wet towel to hold in the heat. When the towel becomes cool, remove and replace with a fresh hot towel.

Repeat this for about 20 minutes. Try to keep the towel as hot as can be tolerated. This compress stimulates blood circulation, and helps to relieve any type of tension. The skin should become red for the maximum effectiveness.

If a person has cancer, we recommend using this towel for a maximum of 3 to 5 minutes, just to heat up the skin, and only prior to applying a taro or lotus plaster. (Persons with serious illness are advised to consult with a physician and with a qualified macrobiotic teacher beginning the macrobiotic way of life or applying home care.)

Tofu Plaster —————————————————————————

Tofu plasters are very good for reducing fevers, sore throats, or for reducing swelling due to bumps and bruises. Do not use for reducing fevers in cases of chicken pox, or with measles unless the fever becomes *very* high. For measles, use a cabbage leaf on the forehead instead. Change the plaster every 2 to 3 hours. In the case of children, it may be necessary to tie the plaster with a cloth to keep them from taking it off.

Grind fresh tofu in a suribachi and add 10 to 20 percent whole wheat flour. Grate a small amount of ginger and add to tofu. Place on cheesecloth or cotton cloth, and apply to injured or affected area so that the tofu mixture comes in direct contact with the skin.

Dentie—————————————————————————————————

Dentie is a tooth powder made from charred eggplant and sea salt. It can be bought ready-made in most natural food stores, and is black in color. Dentie is good for toothaches and gum problems. Use as a tooth powder occasionally by gargling with dentie and then brushing. I do not recommend brushing teeth every-day with dentie as it is an abrasive powder and will wear down the enamel on teeth.

To make dentie, roast only the top portion of the eggplant closest to the stem in the oven until it turns black. It is then ground together with 20 to 50 percent roasted sea salt, into a fine powder.

Salt Compress

Salt compresses are very good for relieving intestinal cramps, diarrhea, menstrual cramps, or muscle stiffness.

Roast salt in dry skillet for several minutes and place inside a *cotton* pillow case or *cotton* sack. Wrap in a towel and apply to the affected area.

Lotus Root Tea

Lotus root is very helpful in relieving upper respiratory problems, such as colds and coughs, or sinus blockage.

Grate fresh lotus root and squeeze out the juice. Add an equal amount of water to the juice, and a pinch of sea salt. Bring to a boil, reduce the flame to low, and simmer 1 to 2 minutes. Drink hot.

If fresh lotus root cannot be found, substitute prepackaged, powdered lotus root tea, which is sold in most natural food stores. Directions for preparation are listed on the package.

Daikon Tea

Daikon tea is helpful in speeding the discharge of mucus and stored animal fat; for tight kidneys or kidney stones; and for some headaches.

Grate 2 to 3 tablespoons of raw daikon into a cup, and add several drops of tamari soy sauce. Pour hot, weak bancha over it, stir, and drink. If daikon is not available, use turnip or white radish. Take once a day for no more than 3 days at a time.

Ume-Sho-Bancha

This easy to prepare beverage is good for headaches caused by the overconsumption of various types of yin foods; as well as for the relief of digestive disorders.

Place 1 umeboshi plum (remove pit) in a cup and add several drops of tamari soy sauce. Pour hot bancha over the plum, stir, and drink hot.

Ume-Sho-Kuzu Drink

Good for digestive disorders, especially diarrhea; and for weakness or overall lack of vitality.

Dissolve 1 heaping teaspoon of kuzu in a small amount of water and add to 1 cup of water. Add ½ to 1 umeboshi plum. Bring to a boil. Reduce flame and simmer until translucent. Stir constantly to avoid lumping. Add several drops of tamari soy sauce and serve hot. Grated ginger may be added for a more yin preparation.

Sweet Kuzu

Sweet kuzu is very good for overly yang conditions due to excess intake of salt.

Dissolve 1 teaspoon kuzu in 1 cup of water. Place in a saucepan. Add 1 tablespoon of yinnie or rice syrup to the kuzu. Turn the flame to medium and slowly bring almost to a boil. Reduce flame to low and cook for 10 to 15 minutes. Stir constantly to avoid lumping. Serve hot.

Sesame Oil

Dark sesame oil is especially good for burns, and light sesame oil is helpful for ear or eye problems. For eye problems, heat oil in a saucepan. Strain through sterile cheesecloth or a piece of clean cotton cloth. After cooling, keep it in a small jar or container. Apply 1 or 2 drops to the eye with an eyedropper. Strained sesame oil can also be used for ear infections. For earaches, warm, strained oil may be dropped into the ear.

For burns, place the affected area in cool salt water first. Then apply tofu until the pain is gone. Next, apply sesame oil.

Sesame oil is also helpful in cases where constipation has continued for over a week. Drink 1 or 2 tablespoons of raw sesame oil.

Sesame oil can also be used as a hand lotion for chapped, sore, and red skin.

Shiitake Mushroom Tea

Good for helping the body discharge excess yang such as animal food, fish, buckwheat, and salt.

Boil 2 to 3 shiitake in water. Remove shiitake and drink liquid. Do not take for more than 1 day. Wait several days before drinking again. When this drink is taken, drink only 1 small cup as it is very strong.

For a more complete list of medicinal home preparations, please see *Natural Healing through Macrobiotics* and *Macrobiotic Home Remedies* by Michio Kushi, as well as other books listed in the bibliography.

Chapter 17

Leftovers

In most cooking classes I am asked what to do with leftovers. First of all, never throw anything away that is in any way edible, since one of the basic principles of macrobiotics is that we should waste as little as possible. There are practically unlimited ways to use leftovers to create entirely new dishes.

An entire cookbook could be written on just how to prepare leftovers. I would like to explain briefly a few suggestions which may be helpful when using leftovers.

Brown Rice—Add chopped or sliced vegetables to leftover rice and fry the rice. Leftover azuki bean rice is very delicious when fried with a few scallions. Use leftover rice in making rice bread, or add it to corn bread. When rice is added to corn bread, the bread is very sweet and easier to digest. Leftover rice may also be used in making stuffed cabbage. Add diced onions, carrots, or other combinations of vegetables to the rice, roll it up in partially boiled cabbage leaves, and cook as for stuffed cabbage and seitan.

Rice balls may also be made with leftover rice. Old rice balls, or sushi that have become dry and hard, can be deep-fried. Deep-fried rice balls or sushi are very tasty. Another idea is to add diced vegetables like onions, carrots, and celery, along with a little pastry flour, to leftover rice, mold it into small croquettes and bake, pan-fry, or deep-fry it. Save any brown rice on the bottom of the pressure cooker, and place it on a plate or straw mat to dry. When it becomes very hard and dry, it can be deep-fried. This makes a very delicious snack.

A vegetable-rice pie can be made by mixing leftover rice with vegetables and a little water, and baking the mixture in a pie crust in the same way as for a fruit pie.

Leftover rice can also be mixed with seitan and vegetables and used to stuff a hubbard squash. This "squash turkey" is a favorite in our house around Thanksgiving and Christmas. Buttercup squash or Hokkaido pumpkin can also be stuffed.

Leftover rice can be used to make delicious soups such as those outlined under "grain soups." Leftover sweet rice makes a delicious soup when cooked with onions, carrots, and celery.

Make a soft rice for breakfast by adding 3 or 4 cups of water to 1 cup of leftover rice and cooking it on a low flame in a pressure cooker or a pot for 30 minutes.

These are just a few of the many ways leftover brown rice can be used.

Millet—Leftover millet can be used in making millet soup. Dice a little leftover seitan and add it to millet soup. It is very delicious since seitan is a wonderful complement to the millet.

Millet added to corn bread is delicious. Another idea is to add diced onions, celery, and a little flour to millet to make croquettes which can be baked, pan-fried, or deep-fried.

Leftover millet can also be used in making bread.

To make a soft millet breakfast cereal, add 4 cups of water to 1 cup of millet.

Barley—Leftover barley can be used in bread instead of rice. It can also be cooked with lentils, celery, onions, and mushrooms to create a soup. Soft barley can be a nice breakfast item.

Buckwheat—Make a delicious *Kasha Varnitchkes* with leftover buckwheat by sautéing the buckwheat with diced onions and cooked whole wheat elbow macaroni.

Add chopped vegetables to kasha and make stuffed cabbage. Or, make a pastry dough and wrap it around the kasha and vegetables to make *Kasha Knishes*, which can then be baked in the oven until the dough is golden brown.

A kasha soup can also be made by adding diced onions and celery, and seasoning with tamari soy sauce.

Add sliced cabbage, diced onions, sliced carrots, sliced mushrooms and a little water and tamari soy sauce to kasha and bake it in the oven. Baked kasha is especially good when served with a béchamel sauce in cold weather.

Whole or Rolled Oats—Leftover oats can be mixed half-and-half with leftover rice and cooked with 4 parts of water to create a creamy breakfast cereal.

Leftover oats can also be used instead of rice or in combination with rice to make whole grain bread.

A creamy miso soup or cream of vegetable soup can be made with leftover oats.

Noodles—Leftover noodles can be fried with vegetables, or used in combination with grains, beans, or vegetables to make a soup.

To make a delicious noodle casserole, deep-fry vegetables such as onions, mushrooms, and carrots, and layer the vegetable tempura and noodles in a baking dish. Add a little water and tamari soy sauce, cover, and bake.

Make a refreshing noodle salad by adding boiled or raw vegetables to cooked noodles and mixing with a small amount of umeboshi or tahini salad dressing.

Soups—Leftover grain soups are very good when a little miso is added to them. They are also good with leftover seitan. Bean soups such as lentils or kidney bean soups can be completely transformed by adding a few whole wheat elbow macaroni or shells. Barley can be used instead of noodles for this as well. Some soups can be changed simply by adding a few types of vegetables. At the same time, grain soups can be refurbished by adding a few beans.

Sea Vegetables—For leftover arame or hijiki, prepare a pastry dough, roll it out as for a pie crust, spread the sea vegetable evenly on the crust, and roll it up as for strudel. Bake at 375°F for approximately 30 minutes or until golden brown, slice, and serve. Individual tarts or sea vegetable pies can also be made.

The leftover wakame and onion dish can be added to miso, kidney bean, rice, barley, or millet soup.

Leftover kombu can be used several times for soup stock, or made into kombu soup by adding onions, carrots, water, and tamari soy sauce. Cut it into 1-inch pieces and either bake or simmer it with carrots, onions and burdock, or with other vegetables. Leftover kombu can be used to make shio kombu.

Nori can be used as a garnish on soups and noodles, or it can be used to add a different flavor to fried rice.

Vegetables—As long as vegetables have not become sour, they can be used again. Make a vegetable pie, or, for large pieces of vegetables, wrap them in pastry dough and bake until the crust is golden brown, slice, and serve. Leftover vegetables can also be used in soups, or bean, sea vegetable, or noodle dishes. When using leftover vegetables in other dishes, add them toward the end so that they will not become mushy. Leftover sweet corn can be removed from the cob and mixed with corn flour, pastry flour, diced onions, celery, and a little water, and either pan-fried or deep-fried to create corn fritters. If there are not enough vegetables for a soup, simply simmer them in water for several minutes and use the water as a soup stock. Save all vegetable juices for soup stock. Vegetable juices can also be used as a base for making a béchamel or kuzu sauce. Leftover vegetables can also be wrapped in seitan to make croquettes.

Beans—Leftover beans can be used in making soups, or can be baked with onions, carrots, or seitan. Make a bean pie, or fry leftover beans with rice or whole wheat shells or elbow macaroni. Some beans such as kidney, green, or waxed beans can be used in making a bean salad. Azuki beans can be cooked with raisins and agar-agar to make a bean aspic.

Seitan—Leftover seitan can be cooked in soup with grain or noodles, or can be baked with beans. It can also be mixed with rice and vegetables and fried or used to stuff cabbage rolls. Seitan can be used in preparing salads, sandwiches, or vegetable dishes, or can be combined with vegetables to make a seitan-vegetable pie. Sautéed seitan, kale, and carrots create a very wonderful dish, while seitan which is boiled or sautéed with cabbage is very delicious also.

Seitan can be dipped in a batter and deep-fried, and it can also be added to a vegetable sukiyaki. Use the tamari-water left over from cooking seitan as a soup stock. Or, by adding kuzu and diced onions, create a delicious sauce. A different sauce can be made by adding celery and diced onions to the starch water left over from rinsing the seitan. An interesting *chow mein* sauce can be made by adding mung bean sprouts, celery, snow peas, mushrooms, and diced onions to kuzu or starch water sauce. This can be served over deep-fried noodles.

Bread—For bread which is dried out or slightly molded, remove the mold, cube, deep-fry, and use as a garnish for soups or as a stuffing for squash when combined with onions, celery, and seitan. Old bread can also be steamed and it will become fresh again.

Fish—Leftover fish can be used in fish soups, as well as in sauces or soup stock. To make fish croquettes, finely chop the leftover fish, mix with a little flour, diced onions, celery, and add tamari soy sauce. These can be baked, pan-fried or deep-fried. Make sure the fish is stored in the refrigerator to prevent spoiling until used.

These are only a few of the many new dishes that can be created with leftovers. Please use imagination and creativity to develop family favorites. It may seem difficult at first to create something new and delicious from something old, but with practice, one will become very artistic. Try to waste nothing. This will substantially reduce the monthly food bill while at the same time developing one's creativity and imagination.

Appendix A: Breakfast Suggestions

The first meal of the day, breakfast, is usually simple, and foods are light in preparation and seasoning. If heavy or overly salty foods are eaten in the early morning, it may be difficult to get started with the day. When we begin the day with simple, light food, it is easier to become activated and our thinking is clear. The following are a few suggestions of foods to prepare for breakfast:

- **Miso Soup**—Mildly seasoned miso broth soup can be served for breakfast. Miso soup in the Evening can be slightly thicker and saltier if desired. Miso soup can be prepared with wakame, several types of vegetables, and garnished with scallions, parsley, chives, or watercress. For variety, add cubed tofu, fu, natto, noodles, or even pan-fried mochi to the soup.
- **Soft Whole Grain Cereals**—Soft-cooked whole grain cereals such as soft rice, millet, barley, oats, rolled oats, or a combination of these grains may be served for breakfast. Occasionally, buckwheat or corn grits are nice cooked into a soft cereal. These soft-cooked cereals are usually cooked with four to five times more water than grain. They can be prepared plain or occasionally with sweet vegetables such as squash, carrots, onions, or cabbage. These cereals can be served plain with a simple garnish, with condiments, or even on occasion with a few raisins, currants, amazaké, or natural grain sweetener.

    Soft-cooked cereals may be seasoned with sea salt, or occasionally, with umeboshi plum or miso. Miso soft rice, millet, or barley are delicious on cool mornings—providing warmth and vitality.
- **Other Whole Grain Items**—Pan-fried or baked mochi, mochi waffles, noodles, rice balls and, for those in good health, steamed bread, toast, whole grain pancakes or even tofu French toast may be served. Whole grain muffins or corn bread can also be served now and then for those in good health.

    Dry, puffed cereals may also be served on occasion with a little amazaké.
- **Vegetables**—Boiled or steamed greens may be served for breakfast if desired.
- **Pickles**—Pickles that are mildly salted and lightly prepared can be served on a regular basis, if desired. They are an aid to digestion. A small amount, one to two pieces, is sufficient.

These are just a few suggestions to help you get started. For further ideas, information, and recipes please refer to the macrobiotic cookbooks listed in the bibliography.

Appendix B: Menu Guide

	BREAKFAST
Day 1	Soft Brown Rice (Rice Kayu) Basic Miso Soup Boiled Greens Gomashio
Day 2	Soft Barley Daikon Miso Soup Steamed Greens Shiso/Green-Nori-Flake Condiment
Day 3	Soft Millet with Squash Broiled or Pan-fried Tofu Sauerkraut Steamed Greens
Day 4	Rice Balls (Musubi) Steamed Greens Chinese Cabbage Pickles
Day 5	Vegetable Fried Rice Grated Daikon Basic Miso Soup with Tofu Cubes
Day 6	Whole Oats Dulse Condiment Boiled Greens Whole Wheat Toast with Jam
Day 7	Mochi Waffles Stewed Fruit Topping with Kuzu Sauce Vegetable Miso Soup Pan-fried Tempeh and Sauerkraut

- All above meals may include various beverages such as bancha, barley tea, rice tea, grain coffee, and so on.

	LUNCH
Day 1	Fried Udon and Vegetables Turnip/Kombu Pickles Watercress Sushi

Day 2	Millet Croquettes with Vegetable-Kuzu Sauce Boiled Salad with Ume-Sesame Dressing Grated Daikon
Day 3	Fu and Vegetables Sautéed Chinese Cabbage Pickled Red Radish
Day 4	Udon and Broth Boiled Salad Tofu-Umeboshi Dressing Toasted Nori
Day 5	Tempeh Sandwich Dill Pickles Steamed Greens
Day 6	Sushi Fried Seitan and Vegetables Steamed Daikon
Day 7	Scrambled Tofu and Vegetables Whole Wheat Toast Steamed Greens

- All above meals may include various beverages such as bancha, barley tea, rice tea, grain coffee, and so on.

DINNER

Day 1	Pressure-cooked Brown Rice Lentil Soup Pressed Red Radishes Boiled Mustard Greens Arame with Carrots and Onions Fruit Kanten
Day 2	Pressure-cooked Brown Rice with Azuki Beans Clear Broth Soup Boiled Salad with Umeboshi Dressing Kinpira, Burdock and Carrot Nori Condiment Applesauce
Day 3	Pressure-cooked Brown Rice with Hato Mugi French Onion Soup with Croutons Kidney Beans with Miso Steamed Greens Pressed Daikon and Carrot Salad with Rice Vinegar Shio Kombu

Day 4	Sesame and Chestnut Ohagi Puréed Carrot Soup Sautéed Green Beans and Slivered Almonds Nishime Daikon with Kombu and Shiitake Boiled Greens
Day 5	Pressure-cooked Millet with Blanched Almonds Clear Broth Soup with Watercress Tempeh Cabbage Rolls Sea Palm with Carrots and Ginger Chinese Cabbage Pickles Stewed Fruit
Day 6	Pressure-cooked Brown Rice and Sweet Brown Rice Black Turtle Bean Soup Boiled Salad with Tofu-Cream Dressing Kombu Carrot Rolls Scallion/Miso Condiment Baked Apples or Pears
Day 7	Pressure-cooked Brown Rice and Wheat Berries Chick-pea Vegetable Soup Pressed Salad Hijiki with Sesame Seeds and Scallions Steamed Greens Boiled Whole Onions with Parsley and Kuzu Sauce Fruit Kanten Pie

- All above meals may include various beverages such as bancha, barley tea, rice tea, grain coffee, and so on.
- Menus may be altered according to seasonal change

Glossary

Agar-agar—A white gelatin derived from a species of sea vegetable. Used in making kanten and aspics.

Amazaké—A sweetener or refreshing drink made from fermented sweet rice.

Amé—A natural grain sweetener made from either rice, barley, or wheat, or a combination of grains. Frequently called *rice* or *yinnie syrup*.

Aonori—Bright green sea vegetable flakes, derived from a species of nori. Used as a condiment.

Arame—A thin, wiry, black sea vegetable similar to hijiki.

Arepa—A round corn cake made from dried whole corn that has been cooked and ground into a dough called *masa*.

Arrowroot—A starch flour processed from the root of a native American plant. It is used as a thickening agent, similar to cornstarch or kuzu, for making sauces, stews, gravies, or desserts.

Azuki Bean—A small, dark red bean imported from Japan, but also grown in the United States. Especially good for the kidneys.

Bancha Tea—Correctly named *kukicha*, bancha consists of the stems and leaves from tea bushes that are at least three years old. It is grown in Japan. Bancha tea aids in digestion. It contains no chemical dyes or caffeine. Bancha makes an excellent after dinner beverage.

Bonito Flakes—Fish flakes shaved from dried bonito fish. Used in soup stocks or as a condiment.

Brown Rice Miso—Miso made from brown rice, soybeans, and sea salt.

Brown Rice Vinegar—A type of vinegar made from brown rice.

Burdock—A wild, hardy plant that grows throughout most of the United States. The long, dark root is highly valued in macrobiotic cooking for its strengthening qualities. The Japanese name is *gobo*.

Chirimen Iriko—Very small, dried fish. High in iron and calcium.

Chuba—Small, dried sardines, used for seasoning soups, making condiments, or in salads.

Daikon—A long, white radish. It makes a delicious side dish, and is a specific for cutting fat and mucus deposits caused by past animal food intake. Grated daikon aids in the digestion of oily foods.

Dentie—A black tooth powder made from sea salt and charred eggplant.

Dried Daikon—Shredded daikon that has been dried. Used in soups, stews, and vegetable side dishes.

Dried Lotus Root—Fresh lotus root which has been sliced and dried.

Dried Tofu—Sliced tofu which has been frozen and dried repeatedly. It has a spongy texture, light weight, and a creamy beige color.

Dulse—A reddish purple sea vegetable. Used in soups, salads, and vegetable dishes. Very high in iron.

Empanadas—A deep-fried corn tortilla filled with vegetables and beans.

Foley Food Mill—A special steel food mill, which is operated by a hand crank to make purées, sauces, dips, and so on.

Fu—Wheat gluten that is dried into sheets or cakes.

Garbanzo—Chick-peas.

Genmai Miso—Miso made from brown rice, soybeans, and sea salt.

Ginger—A spicy, pungent, golden-colored root used in cooking and for medicinal purposes.

Ginger Compress—Sometimes called a ginger fomentation. A compress made from grated ginger root and water. Applied hot to an affected area of the body, it will stimulate circulation and dissolve stagnation.

Gluten—The sticky substance that remains after the bran has been kneaded and rinsed from flour. Used to make seitan and fu.

Goma-Dulse—A powdered condiment made from roasted sesame seeds and baked dulse.

Gomashio—A condiment made from roasted, ground sesame seeds and sea salt.

Goma-Wakame—A powdered condiment made from roasted sesame seeds and baked wakame.

Gomoku—A rice casserole made from five or more ingredients.

Hatcho Miso—Miso made from soybeans and sea salt and aged at least two years.

Hato Mugi—A variety of barley known for its medicinal properties.

Hijiki—A dark brown sea vegetable which, when dried, turns black. Hijiki is native to Japan but also grows off the coast of Maine.

Hokkaido Pumpkin—A round, dark green or orange squash, which is very sweet. It is harvested in early fall. Originated in New England and introduced to Japan. Named after the island of Hokkaido.

Ito Soba—A very thin type of soba noodle.

Jinenjo—A light brown Japanese mountain potato which grows to be several feet long and two to three inches wide.

Jinenjo Soba—A variety of soba made from a combination of buckwheat flour and jinenjo flour.

Kanpyo—Dried gourd strips used to tie or secure vegetable rolls while cooking.

Kanten—A jelled dessert made from fruit and agar-agar.

Kasha Knishes—Cakes made from buckwheat and vegetables, wrapped in a pastry dough and baked.

Kasha Varnitchkes—Fried buckwheat, noodles, and vegetables.

Kayu—Long-time cooked grain prepared with approximately five times as much water as grain. Kayu is ready when it is very soft and creamy.

Kelp—A large variety of sea vegetable similar to kombu.

Kinpira—A style of sautéing root vegetables that have been cut very thin or shaved and seasoned with tamari soy sauce.

Koi-koku—A thick rich soup made from carp, burdock, bancha tea, barley miso, and ginger.

Koji—Grain that has been inoculated with the same type of bacteria that is used in making such fermented foods and drinks as miso, tamari soy sauce, amazaké and saké.

Kombu—A wide, thick, dark green sea vegetable which grows in deep ocean water. Used in making soup stocks, cooked with vegetables, in soups, condiments, candy, and other dishes.

Kombu Dashi—A soup stock made from kombu and water.

Kome Miso—Miso made from white rice, soybeans, and sea salt.

Kukicha—Usually called *bancha*. Older stems and leaves of a tea bush grown in Japan.

Kuzu—A white starch made from the root of the wild kuzu plant. In this country the plant is called "kudzu." Used in making soups, sauces, gravies, desserts, and for medicinal purposes.

Layering Method—A method of cooking soups, vegetables, beans, and grains, in which ingredients are layered in ascending order in the cooking pot from yin to yang.

Lotus Root—The root of a variety of water lily which is brown-skinned with a hollow, chambered, off-white inside. Especially good for respiratory organs.

Lotus Seeds—Seeds of a variety of water lily.

Masa—Corn dough made from cooked, dried whole corn.

Mekabu—Roots of the wakame plant. Used in making soups and soup stocks. It has a very strong flavor.

Mirin—A sweet cooking saké (wine) made from sweet rice.

Miso—A fermented paste made from soybeans, sea salt, and rice or barley. Used in soups, stews, spreads, baking, and as a seasoning.

Mochi—A rice cake or dumpling made from cooked pounded sweet rice.

Mugicha—A tea made out of roasted, unhulled barley and water.

Mugi Miso—Miso made from barley, soybeans, and sea salt.

Mugwort—A wild plant which can be dried and made into tea, or pounded with sweet rice to make mugwort mochi. Mugwort has medicinal properties.

Musubi—Rice balls covered with toasted nori and stuffed with an umeboshi plum or pickles.

Mu Tea—A tea made from sixteen different herbs. It is very yang and has certain medicinal values.

Nabe—A one-dish meal prepared in a Japanese earthenware casserole dish and served with a dip sauce or broth made from tamari soy sauce or miso.

Natto—Soybeans which have been cooked and mixed with beneficial enzymes and allowed to ferment for twenty-four hours under a controlled temperature.

Nigari—Hard, crystallized salt made from the liquid drippings of dampened sea salt. Used in making tofu.

Nishime—A long, slow method of boiling large chunks of root and ground vegetables or other ingredients.

Nitsuke—A style of boiling vegetables either on a high or low flame. Vegetables may or may not be served in their own juices.

Nori—Thin sheets of dried sea vegetable. Black or dark purple when dried. Roasted over a flame until green. Used as a garnish, wrapped around rice balls, in making sushi, or cooked with tamari soy sauce and used as a condiment.

Nuka—Rice bran used in making pickles.

Oden—A one-dish stew made with either fresh or deep-fried tofu, vegetables, or other ingredients.

Ohagi—A rice cake made from cooked, pounded sweet rice and coated with items such as azuki beans, chestnuts, roasted, ground and chopped nuts, sesame seeds, and soybean flour.

Ohitashi—A quick style of boiling vegetables in a small amount of water from several seconds to a few minutes to remove their raw or bitter flavor and to preserve their bright color.

Ojiya—A dish made from soft cooked rice and often seasoned with miso.

Okara—The coarse soybean pulp left over when making tofu. Cooked with vegetables.

Pearl Barley—A small white variety of barley often called *hato mugi*.

Pearled Barley—A polished variety of barley.

Rice Syrup—A sweetener made from malted brown rice.

Saké—A wine made from either fermented white or brown rice. Traditionally warmed and served in small cups.

Saké Lees—Residue left over from making saké. Used in soups, vegetable dishes, and pickles.

Sashimi—Raw, sliced fish.

Sea Palm—A variety of dark green sea vegetable that has long, thin corregated lines in its strands. It grows in the Pacific Ocean from Canada to central California.

Sea Salt—Salt obtained from the ocean as opposed to land salt. It is either sunbaked or kiln baked. High in trace minerals, it contains no chemicals or sugar.

Seitan—Wheat gluten cooked in tamari soy sauce, kombu, and water.

Shiitake—A mushroom, used fresh or dried, for soups and other dishes, and for medicinal purposes. It is imported from Japan.

Shio Kombu—Pieces of kombu cooked for a long time in tamari soy sauce and used in small amounts as a condiment.

Shio Nori—Nori sea vegetable cooked with water and seasoned with tamari soy sauce to form a slightly salty condiment.

Shish Kebabs—Vegetables and other items served on a bamboo stick or skewer.

Shiso Leaves—Known as beefsteak leaves. Usually pickled with umeboshi plums to give the umeboshi a red color and more sour flavor.

Soba—Noodles made from buckwheat flour or a combination of buckwheat flour with whole wheat flour or jinenjo flour.

Somen—A very thin whole wheat noodle. Used often in warm weather.

Starch Water—Milky white water left over after preparing wheat gluten or seitan. Used as a thickener for stews, vegetable dishes, gravies, and other dishes.

Sudare—A mat made from strips of bamboo tied together with string. Used to make rolled sushi.

Sukiyaki—A one-dish meal prepared in a large cast iron skillet, containing a variety of vegetables, noodles, sea vegetables, seitan, tofu, fish, and so on.

Suribachi—A serrated, earthenware bowl used for grinding and puréeing.

Surikogi—A wooden pestle used to grind or purée foods in a suribachi.

Sushi—Rice rolled with vegetables, fish, or pickles, then wrapped in nori and sliced into rounds.

Sushi Mat—Sudare.

Sweet Rice Vinegar—A type of vinegar made from fermented sweet brown rice.

Tahini—A thick, creamy paste or butter made from ground sesame seeds. Used as a seasoning for dips, sauces, spreads, and other dishes.

Takuan—Daikon which is pickled in rice bran and sea salt.

Taro—A potato which has a thick, hairy skin. Often called *albi*. Used in making taro or albi plasters to draw toxins from the body.

Tamari—Name given to traditional, naturally made soy sauce to distinguish it from the commercial, chemically processed variety.

Tekka—Condiment made from Hatcho miso, sesame oil, burdock, lotus root, carrot, and ginger root. Sautéed on a low flame for several hours.

Tempeh—A traditional Indonesian fermented soybean product. High in protein and vitamin B_{12}. Used in soups, stews, sea-vegetable dishes, sandwiches, salads, dips, and a variety of other dishes.

Tempura—Sliced vegetables, fish, or patties made of such items as grain, vegetables, fish, and tofu, which are dipped into a batter and deep-fried until golden brown.

Tofu—A cake made from soybeans, nigari, and water.

Udon—A thick wheat or whole wheat Japanese noodle.

Umeboshi—A salty, pickled plum.

Umeboshi Vinegar—A salty type of vinegar that is produced when making umeboshi plums. Known as *umezu* and used in soups, vegetable dishes, dips, sauces, spreads, dressings and for making pickles.

Wakame—A long, thin, green sea vegetable used in making soups, salads, vegetable dishes, and so on.

Wasabi—A green Japanese horseradish. Grated, it is served with sashimi or used in making sushi.

Yannoh—A grain coffee made from five different grains and beans which have been roasted and ground into a fine powder.

Yuba—A skin that forms on the surface of soy milk during the tofu making process.

Recommended Reading

Books

Aihara, Cornellia. *The Dō of Cooking.* Chico, Calif.: George Ohsawa Macrobiotic Foundation, 1972.

———. *Macrobiotic Childcare.* Oroville, Calif.: George Ohsawa Macrobiotic Foundation, 1971.

Aihara, Herman. *Basic Macrobiotics.* Tokyo & New York: Japan Publications, Inc., 1985.

Benedict, Dirk. *Confessions of a Kamikaze Cowboy.* Van Nuys, Calif.: Newcastle, 1987.

Brown, Virginia, with Susan Stayman. *Macrobiotic Miracle: How a Vermont Family Overcame Cancer.* Tokyo & New York: Japan Publications, Inc., 1985.

Dietary Goals for the United States. Washington, D. C.: Select Committee on Nutrition and Human Needs, U.S. Senate, 1977.

Diet, Nutrition, and Cancer. Washington, D. C.: National Academy of Sciences, 1982.

Dufty, William. *Sugar Blues.* New York: Warner Books, 1975.

Esko, Edward and Wendy. *Macrobiotic Cooking for Everyone.* Tokyo & New York: Japan Publications, Inc., 1980.

Fukuoka, Masanobu. *The Natural Way of Farming.* Tokyo & New York: Japan Publications, Inc., 1985.

———. *The One-Straw Revolution.* Emmaus, Pa.: Rodale Press, 1978.

Healthy People: The Surgeon General's Report on Health Promotion and Disease Prevention, Washington, D. C.: Government Printing Office, 1979.

Heidenry, Carolyn. *Making the Transition to a Macrobiotic Diet.* Wayne, N.J.: Avery Publishing Group, 1987.

Hippocrates. *Hippocratic Writings.* Edited by G. E. R. Lloyd. Translated by J. Chadwick and W. N. Mann. New York: Penguin Books, 1978.

I Ching or *Book of Changes.* Translated by Richard Wilhelm and Cary F. Baynes. Princeton: Bollingen Foundation, 1950.

Ineson, John. *The Way of Life: Macrobiotics and the Spirit of Christianity.* Tokyo & New York: Japan Publications, Inc., 1986.

Jacobs, Leonard and Barbara. *Cooking with Seitan.* Tokyo & New York: Japan Publications, Inc., 1986.

Jacobson, Michael. *The Changing American Diet.* Washington, D. C.: Center for Science in the Public Interest, 1978.

Kaibara, Ekiken. *Yojokun: Japanese Secrets of Good Health.* Tokyo: Tokuma Shoten, 1974.

Kidder, Ralph D. and Edward F. Kelley. *Choice for Survival: The Baby Boomer's Dilemma.* Tokyo & New York: Japan Publications, Inc., 1987.

Kohler, Jean and Mary Alice. *Healing Miracles from Macrobiotics.* West Nyack, N. Y.: Parker, 1979.

Kotsch, Ronald. *Macrobiotics: Yesterday and Today.* Tokyo & New York: Japan Publications, Inc., 1985.

Kushi, Aveline. *How to Cook with Miso*. Tokyo & New York: Japan Publications, Inc., 1978.

―――. *Lessons of Night and Day*. Wayne, New Jersey: Avery Publishing Group, 1985.

―――. *Macrobiotic Food and Cooking Series: Diabetes and Hypoglycemia; Allergies*. Tokyo & New York: Japan Publications, Inc., 1985.

―――. *Macrobiotic Food and Cooking Series: Obesity, Weight Loss, and Eating Disorders; Infertility and Reproductive Disorders*. Tokyo & New York: Japan Publications, Inc., 1987.

Kushi, Aveline, with Alex Jack. *Aveline Kushi's Complete Guide to Macrobiotic Cooking*. New York: Warner Books, 1985.

Kushi, Aveline and Michio. *Macrobiotic Pregnancy and Care of the Newborn*. Edited by Edward and Wendy Esko. Tokyo & New York: Japan Publications, Inc., 1984.

―――. *Macrobiotic Child Care and Family Health*. Tokyo & New York: Japan Publications, Inc., 1986.

Kushi, Aveline, and Wendy Esko. *Macrobiotic Family Favorites*. Tokyo & New York: Japan Publications, Inc., 1987.

Kushi, Aveline, and Wendy Esko. *The Changing Seasons Macrobiotic Cookbook*. Wayne, N. J.: Avery Publishing Group, 1983.

Kushi, Aveline, with Wendy Esko. *The Macrobiotic Cancer Prevention Cookbook*. Wayne, New Jersey: Avery Publishing Group, 1986.

Kushi, Michio. *The Book of Dō-In: Exercise for Physical and Spiritual Development*. Tokyo & New York: Japan Publications, Inc., 1979.

―――. *The Book of Macrobiotics: The Universal Way of Health, Happiness and Peace*. Tokyo & New York: Japan Publications, Inc., 1986 (Rev. ed.).

―――. *Cancer and Heart Disease: The Macrobiotic Approach to Degenerative Disorders*. Tokyo & New York: Japan Publications, Inc., 1986 (Rev. ed.).

―――. *Crime and Diet: The Macrobiotic Approach*. Tokyo & New York: Japan Publications, Inc., 1987.

―――. *The Era of Humanity*. Brookline, Mass.: East West Journal, 1980.

―――. *How to See Your Health: The Book of Oriental Diagnosis*. Tokyo & New York: Japan Publications, Inc., 1980.

―――. *Macrobiotic Health Education Series: Diabetes and Hypoglycemia; Allergies*. Tokyo & New York: Japan Publications, Inc., 1985.

―――. *Macrobiotic Health Education Series: Obesity, Weight Loss, and Eating Disorders; Infertility and Reproductive Disorders*. Tokyo & New York: Japan Publications, Inc., 1987.

―――. *Natural Healing through Macrobiotics*. Tokyo & New York: Japan Publications, Inc., 1978.

―――. *On the Greater View: Collected Thoughts on Macrobiotics and Humanity*. Wayne, New Jersey: Avery Publishing Group, 1985.

―――. *Your Face Never Lies*. Wayne, N. J.: Avery Publishing Group, 1983.

Kushi, Michio, and Alex Jack. *The Cancer Prevention Diet*. New York: St. Martin's Press, 1983.

―――. *Diet for a Strong Heart*. New York: St. Martin's Press, 1984.

Kushi, Michio, with Alex Jack. *One Peaceful World*. New York: St. Martin's Press, 1987.

Kushi, Michio and Aveline, with Alex Jack. *Macrobiotic Diet*. Tokyo & New York: Japan Publications, Inc., 1985.

Kushi, Michio, and the East West Foundation. *The Macrobiotic Approach to Cancer*. Wayne, N. J.: Avery Publishing Group, 1982.

Kushi, Michio, with Stephen Blauer. *The Macrobiotic Way*. Wayne, New Jersey: Avery Publishing Group, 1985.

Mendelsohn, Robert S., M. D. *Confessions of a Medical Heretic*. Chicago: Contemporary Books, 1979.

———. *Male Practice*. Chicago: Contemporary Books, 1980.

Nussbaum, Elaine. *Recovery: From Cancer to Health through Macrobiotics*. Tokyo & New York: Japan Publications, Inc., 1986.

Nutrition and Mental Health. Washington, D. C.: Select Committee on Nutrition and Human Needs, U.S. Senate, 1977, 1980.

Ohsawa, George, *Cancer and the Philosophy of the Far East*. Oroville, Calif.: George Ohsawa Macrobiotic Foundation, 1971 edition.

———. *You Are All Sanpaku*. Edited by William Dufty, New York: University Books, 1965.

———. *Zen Macrobiotics*. Los Angeles: Ohsawa Foundation, 1965.

Price, Western, A., D. D. S. *Nutrition and Physical Degeneration*. Santa Monica, Calif.: Price-Pottenger Nutritional Foundation, 1945.

Sattilaro, Anthony, M. D., with Tom Monte. *Recalled by Life: The Story of My Recovery from Cancer*. Boston: Houghton-Mifflin, 1982.

Schauss, Alexander. *Diet, Crime, and Delinquency*. Berkeley, Calif.: Parker House, 1980.

Scott, Neil E., with Jean Farmer. *Eating with Angels*. Tokyo & New York: Japan Publications, Inc., 1986.

Tara, William. *A Challenge to Medicine*. Tokyo & New York: Japan Publications, Inc., 1987.

———. *Macrobiotics and Human Behavior*. Tokyo & New York: Japan Publications, Inc., 1985.

Taylor, John F. *The Hyperactive Child and the Family*. New York: Dodd, Mead, and Company, 1980.

Yamamoto, Shizuko. *Barefoot Shiatsu*. Tokyo & New York: Japan Publications, Inc., 1979.

The Yellow Emperor's Classic of Internal Medicine. Translated by Ilza Veith, Berkeley: University of California Press, 1949.

Periodicals

East West Journal. Brookline, Mass.

Macromuse. Washington, D. C.

Nutrition Action. Washington, D. C.

"The People's Doctor" by Robert S. Mendelsohn, M. D. and Marian Tompson, Evanston, Ill.

Macrobiotic Resources

The Kushi Foundation in Boston and related educational centers in the United States, Canada, and around the world offer ongoing classes for the general public in macrobiotic cooking and traditional food preparation and natural processing. They also offer instruction in Oriental medicine, shiatsu massage, pregnancy and natural child care, yoga, meditation, science, culture and the arts, and world peace and world government activities. They also provide way of life guidance services with trained and certified consultants, make referrals to professional health care associates, and cooperate in research and food programs in hospitals, medical schools, prisons, drug rehabilitation clinics, nursing homes, and other institutions. In scores of other cities and communities, there are smaller learning centers, residential centers, and information centers offering some classes and services.

Most of the foods mentioned in this book are available at natural foods stores, selected health food stores, and a growing number of supermarkets around the world. Macrobiotic specialty items are also available by mail order from various distributors and retailers.

Please contact the Kushi Foundation in Boston or other national centers listed below for information on regional and local activities in your area, as well as whole foods outlets and mail order sources.

The Kushi Foundation
17 Station Street
Brookline, Mass. 02147
617–738–0045

Australia
Australian Macrobiotic
  Association
1 Carlton Street, Prahran
Melbourne, 3181, Australia
03–529–1620

Belgium
Oost West Centrum
  Kushi Institute
Consciencestraat 48
Antwerpen, 2000, Belgium
03–230–13–82

Germany
Ost West Zentrum
Eppendorfer Marktplatz
13 D-2000, Hamburg 20
040–47–27–50

Bermuda
Macrobiotic Center of
  Bermuda
In-The-Lee, Deepwood
Drive Fairyland, Pembroke,
Bermuda
809–29–5–2275

Britain
Community Health
  Foundation
188–194 Old Street, London,
ECIV 9BP, England
01–251–4076

Japan
Macrobiotics—Tokyo
20–9 Higashi Mine, Ota-ku
Tokyo 145, Japan
03–753–9216

Canada
861 Queen Street
Toronto, Ontario
M6J IC4, Canada

France
Le Grain Sauvage
  Macrobiotic Association
15 Rue Letellier 75015
Paris, France
33–1–828–4773

United Arab Emirates
Box 4943 SATWA
Dubai, United Arab
Emirates
040440–031
  (national)
97–1–44–4–0031
  (international)

Holland
Oost West Centrum
  Kushi Institute
Achtergraft 17
1017 WL Amsterdam,
Holland
020–240–203

Hong Kong
Conduit RD. 41A,
Rome CT. 8D Hong Kong,
Hong Kong
5–495–268

Israel
24 Amos Street, Tel Aviv,
Israel
442979

Italy
Fondazione Est Ovest
Via de'Serragli 4
50124 Florence, Italy

Lebanon
Mary Naccour
Couvent Street, Elie
Box 323, Antelias
Beirut, Lebanon

Norway
East West Center
Frydenlundsgt 2 0169
Oslo 1, Norway
02–60–47–79

Portugal
Unimave
Rua Mouzinha da
Silveira 25, 1200 Lisbon,
Portugal
1–557–362

Switzerland
Ost West Zentrum
Postfach 2502, Bern,
3001 Switzerland
031–25–65–40

United Nations
United Nations Macrobiotics
  Society
c/o Katsuhide Kitatani
U.N. Development
Programme
1 United Nations Plaza
New York, N.Y. 10017
212–906–5844

United States
Kushi Institute
17 Station Street
Brookline, Mass. 02147
617–738–0045

For those who wish to study further, the Kushi Institute, an educational institution founded in Boston in 1979 with affiliates in London, Amsterdam, Antwerp, and Florence, offers full- and part-time instruction for individuals who wish to become trained and certified macrobiotic cooking instructors, teachers, and counselors. The Kushi Institute publishes a *Worldwide Macrobiotic Directory* every year listing Kushi Institute graduates and macrobiotic centers, friends, and businesses around the world. The Cook Instructor Service is an extension of the Kushi Institute and is comprised of specially qualified graduates of the Kushi Institute's advanced cooking program. These men and women are available to assist individuals and families in learning the basics of macrobiotic food preparation and home care in their home.

Kushi Institute and Cook Instructor Service
17 Station Street
Brookline, Mass. 02146
617–738–0045

Ongoing developments are reported in the Kushi Foundation's periodicals, including the *East West Journal*, a monthly magazine begun in 1971 and now with an international readership of 200,000 The *EWJ* features regular articles on the macrobiotic approach to health and nutrition, as well as ecology, science, psychology, natural child care, and the arts. In each issue there is a macrobiotic cooking column and articles on traditional food cultivation and natural foods processing.

East West Journal
17 Station Street
Brookline, Massachusetts 02146
617–232–1000

Index